टिप्पनीसहितः आख्यातवादः नञ्वादः च

ĀKHYĀTAVĀDA AND NAÑVĀDA ALONG WITH ṬIPPANĪ

Prakashika Series
No. 3

General Editor
DIPTI S. TIPATHI

टिप्पनीसहितः आख्यातवादः नञ्वादः च

प्रथमः भागः

रघुनाथशिरोमणिकृतः आख्यातवादः
भवानन्दसिद्धान्तवागीशकृता आख्यातवादटिप्पनी

द्वितीयः भागः

रघुनाथशिरोमणिकृतः नञ्वादः
भवानन्दसिद्धान्तवागीशकृता नञ्वादटिप्पनी

सम्पादक

सञ्जित कुमार साधुखान

राष्ट्रीय पाण्डुलिपि मिशन
॥ विज्ञानमुपास्व ॥

राष्ट्रीय पाण्डुलिपि मिशन
नई दिल्ली
तथा
देव पब्लिशर्स एण्ड डिस्ट्रीब्यूटर्स

प्रकाशक :

राष्ट्रीय पाण्डुलिपि मिशन

11, मानसिंह रोड,
नई दिल्ली–110 001

दूरभाष: 2338 3894; फैक्स: 2307 3387

e-mail: directornamami@nic.in
website: www.namami.nic.in

सह–प्रकाशक :

देव पब्लिशर्स एण्ड डिस्ट्रीब्यूटर्स

द्वितीय तल, प्रकाशदीप बिल्डिंग,
22, दिल्ली मैडिकल एसोसिएशन रोड
नई दिल्ली–110002

दूरभाष: 4357 2647

e-mail: devbooks@hotmail.com
website: www.devbooks.co.in

ISBN 978-93-80829-02-9 (Series)
ISBN 978-93-80829-13-5 (Vol. III)
प्रथम संस्करण: 2013

मूल्य: ₹ 250.00

ĀKHYĀTAVĀDA AND NAÑVĀDA ALONG WITH ṬIPPANĪ

Part I

Ākhyātavāda of Raghunātha Śiromaṇi

with
ĀKHYĀTAVĀDAṬIPPANĪ
OF
BHAVĀNANDA SIDDHĀNTAVĀGĪŚA

Part II

Nañvāda of Raghunātha Śiromaṇi

with
NAÑVĀDAṬIPPANĪ
OF
BHAVĀNANDA SIDDHĀNTAVĀGĪŚA

Critically edited by
Sanjit Kumar Sadhukhan

राष्ट्रीय पाण्डुलिपि मिशन
॥ विज्ञानमुपास्व ॥
National Mission for Manuscripts
Dev Publishers & Distributors

Published by:
National Mission for Manuscripts
Indira Gandhi National Centre for the Arts
11 Man Singh Road
New Delhi 110 001
Phone: 91 11 2307 3387
e-mail: directornamami@nic.in
website: www.namami.nic.in

and Co-published by:
Dev Publishers & Distributors
2nd Floor, Prakash Deep,
22, Delhi Medical Association Road,
Darya Ganj,
New Delhi-110002
Phone: 91 11 4357 2647
e-mail: devbooks@hotmail.com
website: www.devbooks.co.in

ISBN 978-93-80829-02-9 (Series)
ISBN 978-93-80829-13-5 (Vol. III)
First published 2013

Contents

Key to Transliteration

VOWELS

अ a	आ ā	इ i	ई ī	उ u	ऊ ū
(but)	(palm)	(it)	(beet)	(put)	(pool)
ऋ ṛ	ए e	ऐ ai	ओ o	औ au	
(rhythm)	(play)	(air)	(toe)	(loud)	

CONSONANTS

Guttural	क ka	ख* kha	ग ga	घ gha	ङ ṅa
	(skate)	(blockhead)	(gate)	(ghost)	(sing)
Palatal	च ca	छ cha	ज ja	झ jha	ञ ña
	(chunk)	(catchhim)	(john)	(hedgehog)	(bunch)
Cerebral	ट ṭa	ठ* ṭha	ड/ड़ ḍa	ढ*/ढ़ ḍha	ण* ṇa
	(start)	(anthill)	(dart)	(godhead)	(under)
Dental	त ta	थ tha	द da	ध dha	न na
	(path)	(thunder)	(that)	(breathe)	(numb)
Labial	प pa	फ* pha	ब ba	भ bha	म ma
	(spin)	(philosophy)	(bin)	(abhor)	(much)
Semi-vowels	य ya	र ra	ल la	व va	
	(young)	(drama)	(luck)	(vile)	
Sibilants	श śa	ष ṣa	स sa	ह ha	
	(shove)	(bushel)	(so)	(hum)	
Others	क्ष kṣa	त्र tra	ज्ञ jña	ळ* l	ॠ* ṝ
	(*kṣātriya*)	(*triśūla*)	(*jñānī*)	(play)	

अं *(—)* *ṁ* or *ṃ amusūra* (nasalisation of preceding vowel) like *saṁskṛti/or soṃskṛti*

अः *visarga* = *ḥ* (aspiration of preceding vowel like (*prātaḥ*)

ऽ *Avagraha* consonant #' consonant (like-*imé vasthitā*)

Anusvāra at the end of a line is presented by m (म्) and not *ṁ*

*No exact English equivalents for these letters.

Foreword

The Indian knowledge tradition has accorded great importance to meaning. Therefore, in various disciplines, semantics has been an important topic of discussion and exposition. It is a well acknowledged fact that speculation related to meaning has occupied prime position since the time of *Mahābhāṣya.* It has been the subject matter of exposition in various disciplines but the three main disciplines that have indulged in this exercise are Vyākaraṇa, Mīmāṃsā and Nyāya, especially the Navya Nyāya. This should not come as a surprise because all the three disciplines are closely related to language. Grammar being a discipline of analysis of language is naturally inclined to analyse meaning. Mīmāṃsā being the philosophy of Vedic rituals depends to a great extent on interpretation of Vedic mantras and dictums. Nyāya on the other hand has logic as its firm base and logic can be expressed only through precise statements. The need for precision in language has led to Navya Nyāya dwell in great detail on the meaning of words and sentences.

Bengal is the region where Navya Nyāya originated and flourished to glory. Vāsudeva Sārvabhauma's pupil Raghunātha Śiromaṇi belongs to the rich tradition of Naiyāyikas. His claim to fame lies in his commentary on *Tattvacintāmaṇi* of Gaṅgeśa and *Ātmatattvaviveka* of Udayanācārya. He also wrote some sub-commentaries. He was not only a versatile commentator but also an independent author. He composed works like *Ākhyātavāda*, *Nañvāda* and *Padārthakhaṇḍanaṭīkā.* All the three works belong to the Nyāya Vaiśeṣika school of philosophy. He belonged to a period when India was at the peak of intellectual creativity and there were scholars from different regions who contributed to the growth of knowledge in varied disciplines.

The present volume is in two parts and contains two texts written by Shri Raghunātha Śiromaṇi, namely, *Ākhyātavāda* and *Nañvāda.* There has been a long tradition of engagement and discussion

between the Mīmāṃsakas, Naiyāyikas and Vaiyākaraṇas, regarding verbal import as also import of sentence meaning. The discussion revolves round two areas in the matter of *ākhyāta,* first, the meaning expressed by components of a verb and second, the importance of word category in a sentence. Whereas the grammarians proposed that the verb is the prime component of sentence because there can be no sentence without a verb. The Naiyayikas claimed that the word in the first case ending is the nucleus of sentence import. The Mīmāṃsakas do not agree with either of the propositions and try to establish that action (*bhāva*) *per se* is of prime importance in meaning. As is clear, these different schools of thoughts varied greatly so far as the importance of a component of sentence meaning is concerned, but they all agreed that a verb occupies a very important position in this process. The topic of verbal import has been given due importance by Acharyas dealing with meaning in all the three schools. However, it was Raghunātha Śiromaṇi who chose to write independently on verbal import which is a pointer to the importance, he accorded to it. Vaiyākaraṇas like Bhartṛhari, Nāgeśa Bhaṭṭa and Kauṇḍa Bhaṭṭa, etc. have written extensively on the meaning of verb which forms a part of works like *Vākyapadīya Mañjuṣā* and *Bhūṣaṇasāra.* Similarly, the Mīmāṃsakas have while elaborating on meaning of sentences like *paṭaḥ kṛtaḥ* and *aṅkuraḥ na kṛtaḥ* discussed the meaning of verb. But this is only in the larger context of sentence meaning. This is where Raghunātha Śiromaṇi stands out having written an independent treatise on verbal import by the name of Ākhyātavāda.

The present text contains a commentary on the *Ākhyātavāda* written by Bhavānanda Siddhāntavāgīśa, thus making this unpublished manuscript very useful and interesting to the scholars working in this field.

The second part of this volume contains the *Nañvāda* of Raghunātha Śiromaṇi along with *Nañvādaṭippanī* of Sadānada Yogeśwara.

Negation is a topic of great importance so far as sentence meaning is concerned. There is a multiplicity of meaning of components of a sentence. For example the *ākhyāta* denotes *vyāpāra* (action), *phala* (fruit of action), *vacana* (number) *puruṣa* (person), *kāla* (tense), aspect etc. and the nominal denotes *jāti* (class) *vyakti* (person) *liṅga* (gender) *vacana* (number) and *kāraka* (case). Whereas, it is important to define the meaning expressed by various components of the sentence, it is equally important to clarify what aspects of that meaning are negated through a negation marker. In Sanskrit

a negation marker can be used independently (*na, mā* etc.) and in a compounded form (*a, an* etc.) also. Both the independent and compounded markers have clearly defined roles to play. Whereas the independent marker generally negates the action, the compounded negation markers negate only some aspect of the word which is compounded. Thus defining componential meaning of such negative markers become very important. Raghunātha Śiromaṇi, in his *Nañvāda* has comprehensively dealt with the meaning of *Nañ* in six sections and has treated the meaning of negation markers in the background of what the grammarians and the Mīmāṃsakas have had to propose.

Dr. Sanjit Kumar Sadhukhan has done a tremendous job by critically editing the above two texts. The manuscripts were not easily available and there were not many copies either. His dedication to his work brought to light unknown copies of manuscripts. He has painstakingly edited the text and also provided a detailed introduction. He deserves commendation for these painstaking efforts.

Dr. T.N. Adhikari's coordination of the editing work is equally worthy of acknowledgement for the inputs he has provided.

Dev Publishers and Distributors have done a commendable job by bringing out this edition in a short span of time. I hope, this publication will be of much use to scholars and researchers alike who are working in the field of semantics. It will also prove to be useful for all those who would be interested in knowing the development of semantics in the Navya Nyāya school of thought. The National Mission for Manuscripts would look forward to and gratefully welcome comments from knowledgeable readers.

DIPTI S. TRIPATHI
Director, NMM

Date: 23 August, 2012

a negation marker can be used independently (na, nañ etc.) and in a compounded form (a, an etc.) also. Both the independent and compounded markers have clearly defined roles to play. Whereas the independent marker generally negates the action, the compounded negation markers negate only some aspect of the word which is compounded. Thus defining compositional meaning of such negative markers become very important. Raghunātha Śiromaṇi in his Nañvāda has comprehensively dealt with the meaning of Nañ in six sections and has treated the meaning of negation markers in the background of what the grammarians and the Mīmāṃsakas have had to propose.

Dr. Sanjit Kumar Sadhukhan has done a tremendous job by critically editing the above two texts. The manuscripts were not easily available and there were not many copies either. His dedication to his work brought to light unknown copies of manuscripts. He has painstakingly edited the text and also provided a detailed introduction. He deserves commendation for these painstaking efforts.

[illegible]'s coordination of the editing work is equally worthy of acknowledgement for the inputs he has provided.

The Publishers and Distributors have done a commendable job by bringing out this edition in a short span of time. I hope this publication will be of much use to scholars and researchers who are working in the field of semantics. It will also prove to be useful for all those who would be interested in knowing the development of semantics in the Navya Nyāya school of thought. The National Mission for Manuscripts would look forward to and gratefully welcome comments from knowledgeable readers.

Dipti S. Tripathi
Director, NMM

Date: 23 August, 2012

Preface

It is a matter of fact that after the composition of *Tattvacintāmaṇi* of Gaṅgeśa Upādhyāya (14th century AD), the school of *Navya-Nyāya* was established and numerous works on this neo-logical system were composed. These were in the form of commentary and sub-commentary which were so important due to their contents that they were respected as original works. Out of the hundreds of neologicians, at least two scholars occupy pre-eminent position. They are, Pakṣadhara Miśra of Mithila and Raghunātha Śiromaṇi of Bengal. Out of these two scholars, the tradition of Pakṣadhara Miśra is lost and only Raghunātha's tradition exists, though nowadays, very few scholars can understand his style of language, apart from its contents. Dinesh Chandra Bhattacharya in his book *Bange Navyanyaya Charcha* has done a stupendous job through critical discussion on the true history of' his personal life, birth place, works, shedding aside the myths fabricated around him. (see his book, *ibid.* pp. 79-106).There he has dealt in detail on Raghunātha's works and tradition. Editor Dr. Sanjit Kumar Sadhukhan, besides describing editing methodology, has also written in his Introduction on *Ākhyātavāda and Nañvāda* in philosophical systems along with other works of Raghunātha. He has pointed out the theories of the *Naiyāyikas, Vaiyākaraṇas* and *Mīmāṁsakas,* who chiefly dealt with the coherent substance hidden in these terms. Readers may find it repetitive should I once more reiterate them. I would like to add here that the 'theory of negation' as developed in Indian grammatical tradition and gradually entered into the area of philosophy has a long pre-history. Both negative participles *mā na/nañ* and *ākhyāta* had been dealt with in *Nirukta* of Yāska. Without going to much detail, I would just touch on the issue in order to fill up the gap.

We all know, Yāska's *Nirukta,* one of the six Vedāṅgas, (6th/5th centuries BC), dealt chiefly with Vedic semantics and contextually took up the role of *"na'* and *ākhyāta* (verb) while interpreting Vedic

mantras. Scholars are aware, that to interpret the Vedic language, *Nīruktakāras* followed the *'root theory'*. They held that all words originated from some kind of root depicting action, and for which they are called *Ākhyātavādins.* Their sole emphasis is on *'ākhyāta'*, what later on was termed as *Kriyā.* Yāska in this regard has referred to one *Niruktakāra* 'Śākatāyana' by name, who believed all words originale from verb *(tatra nāmānyākhyatajātānīti śākaṭāyano nairuktasamayaśca*—Nirukta chap. 1.4. Though, all systems of Indian philosophical and grammatical discipline did not agree with it, but we only point out here that the theory of *ākhyāta* was an interesting topic of discussion right from the age of *Vedāṅga* to *Navya-Nyāya.* Again the term *na/nañ,* at least during the Vedic age does not always carry the sense of negation. Yāska in his first chapter on *'Nipāta'* has shown with examples from the Vedic language that the word *na/no* conveys the sense of similarity, even apart from negative on the basis of its position in the sentence structure. *tesām ete catvāra upamārthe bhavanti* (*Nirukta* chap-I.2). Though the concept of negative has undergone changes its terminology in later grammatical and neo-logical philosophical literature, yet it is to be borne in mind that even some 2500 years back, Indian philosophers had started discussion on theory of negation and root theory in language from the standpoint of semantics. This much could be added herewith for information. Otherwise Dr. Sadhukhan has elaborately dealt with these two issues in his Introduction from the view point of both philosophical and grammatical tradition of India. It also reflects the depth of Indian intellectual traditions, which peaked its glory during the period of neo-grammarians and neo-logicians.

Regarding the importance of the text, it could be said that, the language of Raghunātha is not only terse, it is sometimes very sketchy. Without commentaries and notes, the real essences of the text is often elusive. Bhavānanda Sindhāntavāgīśa, a stalwart in this area has done a great job. It is to the credit of the editor, Dr Sadhukhan, that he collected the manuscripts from Sanskrit Sahitya Parisat, Kolkata, and Asiatic Society, Kolkata, and edited them for the academic world. These were supposed to be lost. Dr. Sadhukhan has given a list of works on these two topics to be found in libraries in India or abroad either in printed or in manuscript forms. He sincerely deserves credit for such painstaking effort.

It is of great satisfaction to us that we have been successful to critically edit a Nyāya text named *Akhyātavādaṭippaṇī* of Bhavānānda

Siddhāntaāagīśa, the greatest *Naiyāyika* of Bengal of the 16th century AD on the basis of two unpublished complete manuscripts, It is a ommentary on the *Ākhyātavāda* of Raghunātha Śiromaṇi (15th century AD). The critical text of the commentary has slso been prepared by Dr. Sanjit Kumar Sadhukhan. The text deals with the philosophical semantics of the meaning of the verbal forms like *pacati, gacchati, pacyate, gamyate,* etc. which have been one of the major contending issues in Indian Philosophy, particularly among the *Vyākaraṇa, Mīmāṃsā* and *Nyāya* systems. From the 5th century AD right up to the 17th century AD with the participation of the great scholars like Bhartṛhari, Kumārila Bhaṭṭa, Maṇḍana Miśra, Prabhākara Miśra, Gaṅgeśa Upādhyāya, Raghunātha Śiromaṇi, Kauṇḍa Bhaṭṭa, Nāgeśa, Khaṇḍadeva, Gāgābhaṭṭa, Jagadīśa and their respective commentarors, the issue has assumed a magnificient shape. A good number of research work have already been done in this field. But there are number of important commentaries which are still in manuscript forms and have not come to researchers' use. So the present critical edition of unpublished commentary *Ākhyātavādaṭippanī* will surely be of great help.

We have also been successful to critically edit another *Nyāya* text named *Nañvādaṭippanī* of the same Bhavānanda Siddhāntavagīśa, on the basis of two newly found complete manuscripts and a printed edition of a fragmentary portion of the commentary. *Nañvādaṭippanī* is a commentary on the *Nañvāda* of Raghunātha Śiromaṇi (15th century AD). The meaning of the negative particles had long been a topic of discussion in Indian philosophy. The *Vaiyākaraṇas, Mīmāṃsakas* and the *Naiyāyikas* and sometimes others have contributed so much to the topic that it led Raghunātha to compose a separate treatise entitled *Nañvāda.* The negative particle *nañ* here stands for *na* and *mā* used separately in a sententence and *na, a* and *an* in compounded words. But sometimes the words meaning difference (i.e. mutual absence) or so also come under the purview of *nañ.* Bhavānanda's commentary is obviously a significant one on this topic. The commentary along with the *Nañvāda* was printed in the vol IV part 2 of the *Tattvacintāmaṇi,* edited by Kāmākhyānātha Tarkavāgīsa from the Asiatic Society. But a large portion of the commentary at the end was left out. Now with the help of the manuscripts, the complete commntary is being presented to the scholars. Both the texts are presented within one cover.

I am glad to say now that these texts could not see the light of the day, should the authorities of National Mission for Manuscripts

(NMM) New Delhi not have extended their hands of co-operation. Professor Dipti Tripathi, the Director of NMM in particular, deserves a special mention in this regard as she had readily agreed to our proposal for publication. Publication co-ordinator, Dr. Sanghamitra Basu, also always helped us during the publication process. She deserves thanks for her co-operation. Finally, I must mention, all my colleagues and members of DRS project, Sanskrit, worked hard for years to make it a success. I thank them all. I finish with a line of *Anumānadīdhiti,* the greatest composition of Raghunātha:

> *parajuṣṭanayannivartamānā*
> *mananāsvadyarasasā viśuddhabodhaiḥ/*
> *raghunāthakaverapetadośā kṛtireṣā*
> *viduṣāṃ tanotu modam//* (*Ibid. Śloka* No.3)

Tarak Nath Adhikari
Consultant Editor
Professor of Sanskrit and
Coordinator, DRS (UGC Research Project)
Rabindra Bharati University
Kolkata

Part I

Ākhyātavāda of Raghunātha Śiromaṇi

with
ĀKHYĀTAVĀDAṬIPPANĪ
of
BHAVĀNANDA SIDDHĀNTAVĀGĪŚA

Critically edited by
Sanjit Kumar Sadhukhan

Contents

Introduction

This critical edition has a little history behind its making. It all began with the present editor's delving into the pages of Dinesh Chandra Bhattacharya's pioneering work, *Vaṅge Navya-nyāya Carcā*, which for valid reasons has come to be regarded as an authoritative source to glean scholarly information about the Nyāya-Vaiśeṣika manuscripts. The editor was, in particular, looking for some lead on the works of Bhavānanda Siddhāntavāgīśa; and the search was not in vain–with a reference catching the eye that a rare manuscript of *Ākhyātavādaṭippanī* of Bhavānanda is preserved in the library of Sanskrit Sahitya Parishat at Kolkata. Providence seemed to be smiling upon the editor's cause, since the said library was quite easily accessible, being located close tohis residence. So a number of visits were made to search through the hand-written catalogue available in that repository of Sanskrit scholarship and finally, one fine evening in the month of September 2007, gold, or what looked like gold, was struck. Then followed the phase of due diligence: verification of the manuscript with the description given by Bhattacharya and making a copy thereof. The manuscript was rather small, containing only 16 folios, copying of which took only a few days.

But alas, all that glitters is not gold.There seemed to be too many mistakes, in particular those tell-tale omissions of single letters, which were indicative of inexpert and unreliable scribal work. So things were back to square one, and a fresh search was launched for other manuscripts, if any. The effort led to a fragmentary folio of the same commentary contained in the manuscript of *Nañvādaṭippanī* of Bhavānanda Siddhāntavāgīśa. But with this fragment, one could only make a limited verification of the corresponding concluding portion of the commentary appearing in the other manuscript, leaving the editing of the remaining sections to the rather unsatisfactory device of making some conjectural corrections in the readings. Given all these constraints, it was decided to bring out an

edition with as many corrections as could thus be incorporated. But then fortune smiled again, in the shape of discovery of another manuscript of *Ākhyātavādaṭippanī* named *Ākhyātavādasāramañjarī.* This happened to be the very manuscript that was described by Bhattacharya as the best one; and indeed, it was totally free from scribal errors.The first part of the editorial mission was thus accomplished.

In a parallel effort, the editor had also collected a fine edition of the main *Ākhyātavāda* and its commentary by Rāmabhadra Sārvabhauma, done by Prabal Kumar Sen. Drawing immense help from the said edition, and putting in a few months of rigorous application of mind to the editorial work, it was at last possible to present this critical edition of the *Ākhyātavāda* of Raghunātha Śiromaṇi and its commentary by Bhavānanda Siddhāntavāgīśa before the scholars. And finally there was the stage of finishing the edition with more critical polish. Completion of editing of the commentary was followed by verification of the already printed mūla with two other manuscripts of *ākhyātavāda* of Raghunātha Śiromaṇi. One may reasonably expect therefore, that the text reading in the present edition has now become more authentic.

A few words on the editing technique adopted in this edition in respect of the texts of the *mūla* and the commentary may also be in place. It has been observed that both the texts have profusely variant readings in the manuscripts. These have been annotated, leaving out only some minor and palpably scribal errors, in the notes sections. Moreover, as the following 'Notes and References' portion annexed to this Introduction itself will bear out, the present edition also contains a number of very relevant add-ons, such as: short notes on Raghunātha and Bhavānanda and their works; a short resume of the *ākhyāta* theory and its place in Indian philosophy; quotations in the texts; relevant bibliography etc.

Given the earnest efforts put in, it is hoped that this edition sensitises worthier scholars to bring out editions of other unpublished commentaries on the *Ākhyātavāda* to enrich the literature on the subject. That by itself would be the present editor's vindication.

Introductory Notes and References

a. Raghunātha Śiromaṇi (1455-1500 AD)

The pre-eminent exponent of the Navya-nyāya school in Bengal

is none else but Vāsudeva Sārvabhauma's pupil, Raghunātha Śiromaṇi, who belonged to the second half of the fifteenth century AD. His extraordinary talent led him to blaze a new trail of revolutionary views to confront and supplement the traditional ones. The sheer logical force of his razor-sharp arguments made such a telling impact on the then Naiyayikas, that with him as the preceptor, a new Navya-nyāya line was established in Bengal. He attained great prominence as a commentator of Gaṅgeśa's *Tattvacintāmaṇi.* His commentary on the *Ātmatattvaviveka* of Udayanācārya also won critical acclaim. In addition, the following sub-commentaries were composed by him:

(1) Relating to the commentary *śloka* by Jayadeva Miśra of Mithila, on Gaṅgeśa's *Tattvacintāmaṇi*;
(2) Relating to the commentary *Prakāśa* by Vardhamāna Upādhyāya, on Udayanācārya's *Kiraṇāvalī*;
(3) Relating to the commentary *Prakāśa* by Vardhamāna Upādhyāya, on Vallabhācārya's *Nyāyalīlāvatī.*

Raghunātha's phenomenal talent is also writ large in several independent treatises composed by him. These are: *ākhyātavāda*, *Nañvāda* and *Padārthakhaṇḍana* on the Nyāya-Vaiśeṣika, and *Malimlucaviveka* on Dharmaśāstra.

D.C. Bhattacharya, in his *Vaṅge Navya-nyāya Carcā* (p. 83), observes that the *Ākhyātavāda* of Raghunātha Śiromaṇi had become so popular and extended such widespread influence that study of *ākhyātavāda* of Gaṅgeśa had practically stopped in the academic circle of Navadvipa, Commentaries on Raghunātha's *Ākhyātavāda* started being composed in large numbers. As a result, even the commentary of Mathurānātha on the *Ākhyātavāda* of Gaṅgeśa had disappeared in course of time. The factor that lay at the root of Śiromaṇi's grand success was his extraordinary power to state things in a nutshell. Another plausible contributing factor was that the then Naiyayikas of Bengal were all so absorbed in expanding the subject matter of the Anumāna section, that they liked brevity in the treatment of other matters. So compared to the long-winded *ākhyātavāda* of Gaṅgeśa, the concise treatment of Raghunātha Śiromaṇi earned more favour from them.

Lastly, it is to be noted that although a number of minor works are attributed to Raghunātha in different books, but D.C. Bhattacharya has outright rejected those as his works (*Vaṅge Navya-nyāya Carcā*, p. 87).

b. Bhavānanda Siddhāntavāgīśa (Career span: 1550-1575 AD)

Bhavānanda Siddhāntavāgīśa was the greatest Naiyāyika of Bengal in the 16th century AD. There is a verse about four great Naiyāyikas of Bengal:

guṇopari guṇānandī bhavānandī ca dīdhitau/
sarvatra mathurānāthī jāgadīsī kvacit kvacit//

Quite in tune with the spirit of this verse, Bhavānanda was given the seat of honour among the commentators on *Anumāna-dīdhiti*.There was a time when the works of this Naiyāyika were studied all over India, but unfortunately now his name is almost forgotten even in Bengal,his own birthplace.

The most creative phase of Bhavānanda: Jagadīśa composed his commentaries before 1600 AD,surely not later; and at that time Bhavānanda had either settled in Kashi, or had perhaps expired. A copy of Bhavānanda's *Kārakacakra* at Guptipara, records the date of copying as 1594 A.D. (1516 Śaka 30 Bhādra). In its colophon, the word 'śrī' is absent. On the other hand,career-wise, Bhavānanda was a close predecessor of Mathurānātha and a proximate successorto Mathurānātha's father ŚrīrāmaTarkālaṅkāra. So the period of Bhavānanda's career of composing major works should be assessed as not later than 1550-75 AD.

Bhavānanda's Works: Bhavānanda composed superb commentaries on all the eight works of Raghunātha Śiromaṇi. A brief outline of the commentaries which have been discovered till now is furnished below:

(1) *Pratyakṣadīdhitiṭīkā*: In the printed catalogue of Calcutta Sanskrit College, only one fragmentary copy of this commentary has been mentioned. (Description under 404 in Philosophy section; vide p. 243 of printed catalogue). But there is another copy of this commentary, mentioned in an unpublished catalogue of manuscripts at the Sanskrit College itself. This manuscript, however, is incomplete at the beginning itself. The number of folios is 94, but one folio bore no. 105,which means that the available portion also is not a complete text. The commentary extends from Utpattivāda upto Anyathākhyāti of *Dīdhiti*.

(2) *Anumānadīdhitimīkā*: This is by far the best work of Bhavānanda, and is the very basis of his India-wide fame. Copies of this commentary are easily available in the manuscript libraries of Kashmir, Pune, Madras, Tanjore, and several other places, besides Bengal. Its initial portion (up to Vyāptigrahopāya prakaraṇa) has been printed under the editorship of Late MM Gurucaran

Tarkadarsanatirtha. From the beginning of the eighteenth century,with gradual acceptance by scholars of the commentaries of the two subsequent Naiyāyikas: Jagadīśa and Gadādhara,the study of these outstanding commentaries of Bhavānanda practically ceased at Navadvīpa. The followers of Bhavānanda still continued to influence readers up to the lifetime of Bhavānanda's grandson Rudra Tarkavāgīśa. The style of commenting of the three greatest commentators on *Dīdhiti* – Kṛṣṇadāsa Sārvabhauma, Bhavānanda Siddhāntavāgīśa and Rudra Tarkavāgīśa – was unique, and though there were differences of opinion, many striking similarities are also found in the works of these masters.

Outside Bengal,the greatest centre for the study of Navya-nyāya has been at Kashi. When the study of Bhavānanda's works ceased in Bengal, specifically Navadvīpa, it was still pursued, with great devotion and care, by non-Bengali scholars of Kashi for a long time. In fact,outside Bengal, Bhavānanda's name is more famous than Jagadīśa's and Gadādhara's. A Maharashtrian poet named Dhuṇirāja composed a small word-book type treatise named *Girvāṇavāṅmañjarī* (Baroda Oriental Research Institute, No. 21 of 1919-24, 20 fols). The author composed it probably in 1708-10 during the lifetime of the minister Asad Khan and his son Julfikar Khan. In that book (fol. no. 10), Bhavānanda's commentary finds mention in a conversation between one Daṇḍin and Purandara Bhaṭṭācārya–'*are tava pitā vārāṇasīṁ tyaktvā gauḍadeśe bahuvarṣaparyantam kimarthaṁ sthitaḥ? vidyābhyāsārthaṁ sthitaḥ. Tarhi kāśyām adhyāpanam na bhavati kim? na bhavati kutaḥ, bhavati, parantu tatra tarke adhītam. Kiṁkim abhyastam tvayā? mayādau pañcaprakaraṇānyadhītāni, tataḥ cintāmaṇir adhītaḥ, paścāt Śiromaṇirabhyastaḥ. Tadanu mathurānāthī adhītā, tataḥ* ***bhavānandī*** *paṭhitā, tataḥ miśrāntā api granthāḥ dṛṣṭāḥ.*'

It is important to note that even at that time, Jagadīśa-Gadādhara could not overshadow Bhavānanda. Mahādeva Bhaṭṭa, the well-known Naiyāyika of Kashi, who authored *Nyāyakaustubha,* composed a voluminous commentary named *Bhavānandīprakāśa* on Bhavānanda's *Anumānadīdhitiṭīkā* in the last quarter of the seventeenth century AD, and a small commentary named *Sarvopakāriṇī* on the same *ṭīkā*. Copies of these two works are available at many places in India. Besides, Mahādeva's son Dinakara Bhaṭṭa, Gurupaṇḍita, Viśveśvara (the manuscript of his works are available in the Asiatic Society), Viśvanātha's son Vireśvara (Baroda List, I, No. 359) and also Kṛṣṇamitrācārya, who wrote commentaries on several treatises at the end of the eighteenth century AD, also composed sub-commentaries on Bhavānanda. All of these

commentators are of non-Bengali origin. The number of folios of a copy of *Bhavānandīpradīpa* by Kṛṣṇamitra is 914 (Oudh Cat. Fasc. X, 1878, pp. 16-7). Bhavānanda's work was studied in Kashi area in the nineteenth century also.

(3) *ākhyātavādaṭīkā:* This is a commentary on *ākhyātavāda* of Raghunātha Śiromaṇi. The manuscript of this commentary is very rare. Dinesh Chandra Bhattacharya had seen a complete manuscript of this rare work (number of folios. 16, date of copying 1658 Śaka) in Sanskrit Sahitya Parishat. Another 'incomplete in the beginning' mutilated copy of this work was claimed by Bhattacharya to be had with him. We have noted our own findings about the manuscripts of this work in the discussion 'Commentaries on the *ākhyātavāda* of Raghunātha Śiromaṇi' in this very Introduction a little later.

(4) *Nañvādaṭīkā*: Śiromaṇi's *Nañvāda* with two commentaries has been published along with the Śabda section of *Māthurī* under the editorship of Paṇḍita Kāmākhyānātha Tarkavāgīśa. But the second commentary where the commentator's name is missing, is surely composed by Bhavānanda, because another copy of that commentary (Madras, D. 4256) records the name of the commentator:

śrībhavānandasiddhāntavāgīśena vinirmmitaḥ/
nañvādārthapradīpoyaṅ nihantuṁ sudhiyāṁ tamaḥ//

The above are findings of Bhattacharya. However, the present editor has found after verification that in the printed *Nañvādaṭīkā* of Bhavānanda, a large portion has been left out at the end; another edition of this commentary is therefore a desideratum.

(5) *Guṇadīdhitiṭīkā*: There is a copy of this rare work (105 fols, complete), in Navadvīpa. The abbreviation of the title runs on every page – guṇa śi si ṭī. The name of the owner of the manuscript – *śrīśrīharisārvvabhaumasya pustakam idam.Guṇaśiromaṇi* i.e. *Guṇakiraṇāvalīprakāśadīdhiti* was extensively studied in Navadvīpa, with the help of many other commentaries, even at the end of the 17th century. Of the commentaries, the ones by Kṛṣṇadāsa Sārvabhauma, Guṇānanda and Bhavānanda were current in Navadvīpa. Jagadīśa or Gadādhara did not comment upon the *Guṇaśiromaṇi*, and study of the commentary of Rāmakṛṣṇa and others had not then commenced. But the commentary of Bhavānanda does bear allusions to other earlier commentators (e.g. *anye, kecit, navyāḥ, mānyāḥ*).

(6) *Līlāvatī Śiromaṇiṭīkā*: This also is quite rare. A copy of this

work has been traced in the India Office Library, London (India Office Catalogue I, p. 668, 58 fols, Incomplete). At the end of a Pune manuscript (ms no 178 of 1895-98 fol. no. 41b) the author's name is mentioned: '*iti śrībhavānandasārvabhaumaviracitam evakāraṭippanam.*' The initial portion of *Līlāvatī Śiromaṇi* actually deals with Evakāravāda. Though it is designated as *Evakāraṭippana*, but in the incomplete manuscript of Pune, the text also deals with denotative power of the word *mātra* and the theory of Nirdhāraṇa–both being topics subsequent to Evakāra.

Padārthakhaṇḍanaṭīkā and *Bauddhādhikāra Śiromaṇiṭīkā* of Bhavānanda are still undiscovered. Bhavānanda's commentary on *āloka* of Pakṣadhara Miśra has, however, been discovered.

(7) *Pratyakśālokasāramañjarī:* There are a number of manuscripts of this text in the Asiatic Society, Kolkata. But most of them are incomplete. It is not rare elsewhere either. A complete copy (315fols) of this, preserved in the temple of Raghunathji in Jammu, is worth mentioning (Stein: Jammu Catalogue, 1894, pp. 145, 332-3).

(8) *Anumānālokasāramañjarī:* A single copy of this work is preserved in the Kashi Sarasvati Bhavana. Number of folios is only 53.

(9) *Śabdālokasāramañjarī*: The work has been mentioned many times in *Anumānadīdhitiṭīkā* (Bibliotheca Indica Edition, pp. 56, 248, 575). An incomplete manuscript of it has been discovered (India Office Catalogue, II. 561).

(10) *Śabdamaṇisāramañjarī*: Bhavānanda has mentioned this rare work in the Satpratipakśa prakaraṇa in his *Anumānadīdhitiṭīkā*: '*etenaśābdabodhādikamapivyākhyātam. Adhikaṁ ca śabdamaṇisāra (ma)ñjaryyām vivecitam asmābhiḥ* (fol 251b in the manuscript kept with Bhattacharya). Bhattacharya had an incomplete manuscript of this *Mañjari* (fols 1-35, 43-92) with him. The starting verses there run as follows:

śrīgobindapadāmbhojanakhacandramarīcayaḥ/
niguḍaṁ gāhamānasya mama santvavalambanam//
namaskṛtya guruṁ śabdamaṇau sāraṁ prayatnataḥ/
śrībhavānandasiddhāntavāgīśena prakāśyate//

At one place (fol 7a), Bhavānanda writes: '*sārvabhaumamatam apāstam*', and at another (fol 65b): '*ityasmadguravaḥ*'. Perhaps Bhavānanda composed commentaries on the Pratyakṣa and

Anumāna sections of the *Tattvacintāmaṇi*, but neither any manuscripts of these has been discovered, nor any reference to them is found elsewhere.

(11) *Śabdārthasāramañjarī:* It is an original treatise of Bhavānanda, and its different sections are available separately. The sections discovered so far are enumerated below:

(a) Kārakacakra: This well-known Prakaraṇa has saved Bhavānanda's name from fading into oblivion till now; everywhere in Bengal it was respectfully studied and is still being studied. On this, several commentaries and notes have been composed. Some of those are discussed here. The *Raudrī* commentary by Bhavānanda's grandson Rudra(deva) Tarkavāgīśa, has been printed a number of times. In a number of copies, the name of the commentator is clearly mentioned in the colophon: *"iti mahāmahopadhyāya-śrīrudradevatarkavāgīśabhaṭṭācāryyaviracitā pitāmahakṛta-kārakārthanirṇayaraudrī samāptā* (the reading in the manuscript with Bhattacharya). Many paṇḍitas starting from Puruṣottama Deva composed '*Kārakacakra*'. For example: Rudra Nyāyavacāspati composed*Kārakapariccheda* (Tanjore Catalogue, p. 4488); Jayarāma Nyāyapancānana did *Kārakavāda* (published); and Ramānātha Bhaṭṭācārya composed *Kārakacakra* (vide *Samāsaṭippanī* of Abhirāma Vidyālaṅkāra, p. 55). So it was necessary for Raudrīkāra to mention the *Kārakacakra* as composed by his grandfather. The second commentary on Bhavānanda's *Kārakacakra,* named *Mādhavī,* was also printed many times. Its composer was the famous chief Naiyayika of Navadvīpa— Mādhavacandra Tarkasiddhānta (not Mādhava Tarkālaṅkāra). Two more unpublished commentaries on the *Kārakacakra* had come to Bhattacharya's notice. One commentary is available in Navadvīpa area. The name of the commentator is unknown. This commentary is older than the commentary by Mādhavacandra Tarkasiddhānta and has been utilized by Mādhavacandra. Mādhavacandra Tarkasiddhānta himself said that this commentary is composed by Jayakṛṣṇa who composed *Sāramañjarī.* At the margin of the copy kept in Mādhavacandra's house the following benedictory verse is recorded :

praṇamya śirasā kṛṣṇaṁ jayakṛṣṇena dhīmatā/
kārakādyarthavivṛtervivṛtistanyate mudā//

Bhattacharya notes that he had not come across this verse in

three-four other copies which he had examined. He had a complete manuscript of a commentary, and there is the marginal title Gobinda kā ca ṭī. It appeared to him that some unknown commentator named Gobinda had composed it. A new commentary on *Kārakacakra* copied in 1720 Śaka has been found in Vikrampur area. It begins:

praṇamya paramātmānaṁ vāgīśāṅśca gurūn naman/
bhāvaṁ kārakacakrasya vivṛṇomi satāṁ mude//

The colophon on the last folio (41b) runs thus:

vinirmmitā kārakacakragupta-bhāva-prakāśā varavarṇamālā/
kaṇṭhe vilagnā navakāmiṇīva mudaṁ satāmāvahatu prakāmam//
itiśrītarkavācaspatibhaṭṭācāryyaviracitā kārakacakrabhāvaprakāśā samāptā.

Two paragraphs at the end have been printed in the Bengal edition of *Kārakacakra (ekovṛkṣaḥ pañca naukā bhavati* etc.). These have not been commented upon by the commentators, possibly implying that the portion is not genuine in the *Kārakacakra* text. But the portion is surely the composition of Bhavānanda. Because, the author himself writes at the end:*prapañcitam idam evakārārthavicāre asmābhiḥ.*

(b) *Daśalakāravivecanam:* It has also been printed. (Ref. *Lakārārthanirṇaya* edited by Sriyuta Taranatha Tarkatirtha, 1324, 32 pages). Bhattacharya had a manuscript of it with him. The work is not popular like *Kārakacakra* and is not easily available.

(c) *Ākhyātavicāra*: It is a small prakaraṇa of two folios only. The starting line is: *Ākhyātasya vācyaṁ nirūpyate* etc. Śiromaṇi's view has been discussed in it. No doubt it is a part of the *śabdārthasāramañjaī.*

(d) *Ṣaṭsamāsavivecanam*: Bhattacharya possessed a copy of this prakaraṇa. It starts thus: *nāmnāṁ samāso yuktārtha iti vaiyākaraṇāḥ. Nāmnāmityatra bahutvamavivakṣitam, nāmatvaṁ supaḥ prakṛtitvaṁ* . . . . The ending line runs thus: *yathāprayogamanyatrāpyūhyam. Madhyavarttivibhaktilope samāsottaravarttivibhakterapi lopaḥ, Samāsasya pratyekapadānyatvālliṅgasañjñāyāṁ Kārakavibhaktyādikamupadyate. Iti śrīmanmahāmahopādhyāyaśrībhavānandasiddhāntavāgīśvarabhaṭṭācāryyaviracitaṁ ṣaṭsamāsavivecanaṁ samāptam*(fol 7a).

Like *śaṭkārakavivecana* i.e. *Kārakacakra,* it is also a part of the *śabdārthasāramañjarī.*

Bhattacharya comments that besides these, a few small available

prakaraṇas like *Ktvā-vicāra, Upasarga-vicāra* etc., which do not contain the name of their author, may also be of Bhavānanda.

(12) Kāraṇatāvicāra: The manuscript of this Vāda-type work has been discovered. Bhattacharya examined a copy of it in Pune (Bhandarkar Oriental Research Institute, No. 159 of 1899-1915, 12 fols). It starts with, '*atha kiṁ kāraṇatvam*', and ends with, '*nimittakāraṇateti saṁkṣepaḥ. iti bhavānandabhaṭṭācāryyaviracite kā(raṇa)tāvicāraḥ samāptaḥ.*' He conjectures that Bhavānanda might have composed more of such Vāda works, but the spread of Vāda works of Harirāma Tarkavāgīśa had been the cause of disappearance of this genre of works of Bhavānanda and others.

Bhavānanda's preceptor: Some Naiyāyikas of Navadvīpa thought Bhavānanda was a student of Mathurānātha Tarkavāgīśa (Vide *Navadvīpa Mahimā*, 1st edition, p. 69). But that is not true. Mathurānātha was the pupil of Rāmabhadra Sārvabhauma and came a little later than Bhavānanda. Again some try to prove Bhavānanda as a direct pupil of Raghunātha Śiromaṇi (Sarasvati Bhavana Studies, V. p. 137). This also is not supported by evidence. Bhavānanda was much later than Śiromaṇi, and the chronology is evident from the former's language at some particular places in the text. A statement in Pūrvapakṣa prakaraṇa of Vyāptivāda in the commentary of Bhavānanda runs thus (Society edition, p. 293): '*tasmāt vastuta ityādipāṭhaḥ kālpanikaḥ. ataeva prācīnapustake uttolita eva tiṣṭhati iti bahavaḥ.*' (The text reading in the manuscript, kept with Bhattacharya, runs thus: '*prācīnapustake tanna tiṣṭhati iti bahavaḥ*". Fol. No. 59a). This type of explanation is impossible for a direct student of Śiromaṇi. In fact Bhavānanda's preceptor was Kṛṣṇadāsa Sārvabhauma, and the latter too came much later than Śiromaṇi.

Bhavānanda's pupil: According to the Naiyayikas of Navadvīpa, Jagadīśa was Bhavānanda's pupil. But it is contrary to evidence. In the society of paṇḍitas of Kashi, there runs a traditional belief that Mahādeva Bhaṭṭa who wrote a commentary on Bhavānanda's works was a direct pupil of Bhavānanda. But that also is not true. Mahādeva actually lived 100 years later than Bhavānanda. The names of Bhavānanda's two pupils have been discovered: (i) Rāghavendra Śatāvadhāna Bhaṭṭācārya of Guptipārā, and (ii) Devidāsa Vidyābhūṣaṇa of Pāmali. Bhattacharya wrote at length about this Śatāvadhāna Bhaṭṭācārya in a journal called *Pravāsī* (issued in Bengali era, Pauca 1354, pp. 244-45; Kārttika 1355, pp. 66-69). Devidāsa

was the great great grandfather (*vṛddha-prapitāmaha*) of Kṛṣṇakānta Vidyāvāgīśa, who was a resident of Navadvīpa and was the famous commentator on Nyāya and Smṛti.

Kṛṣṇakānta in the beginning of his *Tarkāmṛtataraṅgiṇī* commentary recorded his ancestral lineage:

sarvānujo'bhut kila tatra devīdāsāhvayaḥ sarvaguṇākaraḥ saḥ/
adhītya śāstraṅ sakalaṅ krameṇa pituḥ sakāśe 'tha samāgato 'yam//
nyāyādiśāstraṅ paṭhituṅ prayatnāt siddhāntavāgīśaguroḥ samīpe//
tam ālapya śāstrārthavādena tuṣṭo bhavānandasiddhāntavāgīśae caḥ/
bhavān mahīyān bhavitātra śāstre ūce mahādhīrakulātidhīraḥ/
adhītya tarkaśāstrāṇi tasmāt sarvāṇi sarvaśaḥ/
āhūya pitarau nāṅṅ samānīya prayatnataḥ//
vārāṇasīmāśritavān vidyābhūṣaṇanāmakaḥ/
adhyāpayāmāsa ciraṅ sarvaśāstraṅ ca tatra vai//
(Nyāya Ms. No. 785 in the collection of Kashi Saraswati Bhavana)

Later Devīdāsa came to Pāmali village for the purpose of his son's marriage and settled there. He got high recognition among the contemporary paṇḍitas. Kṛṣṇakānta recorded a very important 'old verse' about this incident. The verse is reproduced below:

jayadevo navadvīpe rudranā(thaḥ) tathāparaḥ/
pūrvasthalyāṅ ramānāthaḥ pāṭalyāṅ bhūṣanadvayam//
tā ḍiterāmarāmaśca sarvvaśāstraviśāradaḥ/
pṛthīvyāṅsārabhūtāśca ca
ete śāstradiggajāḥ// (fol. no. 1b)

There is no way to know about the other five personalities besides Devīdāsa. It appears from the words of Kṛṣṇakānta that Devīdāsa had studied under Bhavānanda,quite surely in Kashi, and that his period of tutelage would have been in between 1575-1600 AD.

The above account of Bhavānanda is taken from *Vaṅge Navya-nyāya Carcā* (pp. 133-44) of D.C. Bhattacharya, except for some additional comments on the *ākhyātavāda* and *Nañvāda*, because the manuscripts of these commentaries have been independently examined during the present editing process.

c. Ākhyātavāda

In the philosophical semantics, meaning of the verbal forms like *pacati, gacchati, pacyate, gamyate,* etc. has been one of the major contentious issues in Indian Philosophy, particularly between the

Vyākaraṇa, Mīmāṅsā and the Nyāya schools. From the fifth century right up to the seventeenth century AD, debate on the issue has had been phenomenally enriched with the participation of the great VaiyākaraṇaBhartṛhari, Kumārila Bhaṭṭa, Maṇḍana Miśra, Prabhākara Miśra, Gaṅgeśa Upādhyāya, Raghunātha Śiromaṇi, Kauṇḍa Bhaṭṭa, Nāgeśa, Khaṇḍadeva, Gāgābhaṭṭa, Jagadīśa and also their relevant commentators. A good number of research work has already been done in this field. But there are a number of important commentary texts which are still in manuscript form and have not been used by researchers. So the edition of unpublished Sanskrit Ākhyātavāda works will surely be of help in that context.

The verbal form is composed of two parts, *dhātu* i.e. the verbal stem, and *ākhyāta* i.e. the verbal suffix *tiṅ*. In the verbal forms like *pacati, pacyate* etc., *pac* etc. are the verbal stems and *ti, te,* etc. the verbal suffixes. Now when somebody utters sentences like *caitraḥ pacati* (Caitra is cooking), *taṇḍulaḥ pacyate* (Rice is being cooked), the comprehension of verbal forms may involve the meaning like locus (*āśraya*), effort (*kṛti*), operation (*vyāpāra*), result (*phala*), time (*kāla*), nominative (*kartṛ*), accusative (*karman*), etc. according to different philosophers. As the philosophers admit separate meanings for stem as well as for suffix, the question arises as to what particular meaning is denoted or implied by them. The discussion on the meaning of *dhātu,* i.e. the verbal stem, has been the subject matter of *dhātuvāda* and the same regarding the meaning of the *ākhyāta,* i.e. the verbal suffix, has been the subject matter of *ākhyātavāda.* The present work of Raghunātha Śiromaṇi involves the second one.

Raghunātha's *Ākhyātavāda* at its outset deals with the old Naiyāyikas' view regarding the meaning of the verbal suffix. The view being inconclusive has been supplemented by the view of the Navya-naiyāyika school that Raghunātha belongs to. The work then proceeds to deal with the views of the Vaiyākaraṇas, Bhāṭṭa Mīmāṃsakas, and lastly of Prābhākara Mīmāṃsakas, incorporating also the expected, but relevant, refutation of those views by the author. A brief summary of the different views is furnished below:

1. According to the old Naiyāyikas, the verbal suffix denotes effort. In Sanskrit terminology, effort is called *kṛti, yatna* or sometimes *prayatna* in some other Nyāya works. The effort is not the actual action, but rather the readiness of the mind, coupled with an attempt towards performing that action, such as when a dying person makes an effort to speak, but cannot do so owing to a failure

of his power of speech. Now why has the effort been a factor in the verbal comprehension? Pradip Kumar Mazumdar in his 'Philosophy of Language' (p. 38) has given an authoritative analysis in this regard: 'The necessity of inserting this psychological factor has been explained by Kṛṣṇamitra, the author of *Kuñcikā* commentary on Nāgeśa's *Laghumañjuṣā.* A person may decide not to cook even after enkindling fire in the oven. The fuel is left burning and the water is left boiling without any other effort on the part of the cook. We then say that the cook does not cook. The burning of fuel and boiling of water undoubtedly belong to the operational process of cooking. Yet it is said that the cook does not cook, because of his lack of efforts or exertion. Again a person struck down by paralysis makes efforts to rise but cannot rise. We say he does not rise despite efforts.'

The Naiyāyikas argue that the meaning of the verbal suffix can be known by paraphrasing (*vivaraṇa* or *vivṛti*), which is an accepted way of apprehending the denotative power of a certain word. The verbal form *pacati* (is cooking) may be paraphrased by *pākaṅ karoti.* Here *pākaṅ* clearly stands for the verb *pac* and *karoti* for *ti.* In this way all the verbal suffixes can be paraphrased by the verb *kṛ.* Now as *kṛti,* i.e. effort, is the denotative meaning of the verb *kṛ,* the expression *caitraḥ pacati* denotes 'Caitra is endowed with the effort conducive to cooking'. Here we see Caitra is an animate being. But when an inanimate entity is associated with expressions like *pacati, gacchati,* etc., the verbal suffix cannot denote effort there, as the latter (i.e. effort) cannot exist in an inanimate being. So in expressions like *rathaḥ gacchati* (chariot is moving), the verbal suffix *ti,* having no denotative power, only implies the operation conducive to a certain result.

But the above-mentioned view of the old Naiyāyikas is not conclusive. It cannot satisfactorily explain the meaning of the verbal suffix in many other cases. When a person pushes a chariot to move, there is in the person 'the soundless conjunction' (i.e. *nodana,* a type of operation) conducive to the movement of the chariot; still we refrain from saying that the person himself is moving because the movement exists in another entity. Furthermore, in the expressions like *caitraḥ jānāti* (Caitra is having a knowledge), etc. we do not signify Caitra as a locus of any effort conducive to some action, because there is no effort at all in Caitra. We feel no readiness of mind before having knowledge of a pot remaining on the ground. Or in the expressions like *ghaṭaḥ vidyate,* etc. we do not apprehend the pot as a locus of any operation conducive to

some action, because there is no operation at all in pot. So the verbal suffix in these cases means locus-hood only, as a well-established implication (*nirūḍa-lakṣaṇā*). Again, in expressions like *ghaṭaḥ naśyati* etc. we do apprehend the pot as only a counterpositive category (*pratiyogi*). So the verbal suffix *ti* here means counterpositiveness (*pratiyogitva*). In this case also the Naiyāyika admits as well-established an implication as above.

In case anybody asks, how do you come to the conclusion that the verb *kṛ* denotes *kṛti* (effort) and not *kriyā* (action), Raghunātha now proceeds to answer. The Mimāṁsakas themselves express:*paṭaḥ kṛtaḥ* (cloth is done i.e. woven) and *aṅkuraḥ na kṛtaḥ* (sprout is not done i.e. not come into being). If the verb *kṛ* here would denote action there could have been no verbal expression *na kṛtaḥ*, because by the verbal expression *kṛtaḥ* the action is already admitted to exist, and what exists cannot be denied. So the verb *kṛ* must denote nothing but effort. Where there is effort, *kṛta* is used as in the cases of *paṭa* etc.; and where there is no effort (relevantly god's effort to bring out sprout),*na kṛta* is used as in the cases of *aṅkura* etc. Raghunātha now puts forward another argument to prove effort as the denotative meaning of the verb *kṛ*. The *tṛc* suffix in the word *jñātṛ* means locus. So the same suffix in the word *kartṛ* must mean locus. And then the word *kartṛ* would justifiably denote the locus of effort. If the meaning of the verb *kṛ* is action, or operation conducive to action, the word *kartṛ* would denote the locus of action, or simply denote a performer (*kāraka*) because the operation conducive to action is related to the pot, wood, rice, etc.

2. According to the Vaiyākaraṇas, the verbal suffix (*lakāra*) denotes agent and object in *kartṛvācya* (active voice) and *karmavācya* (passive voice), respectively; for example, *ti* in *caitraḥ pacati,* and *te* in *taṇḍulaḥ pacyate* etc. If the agent or object were not denoted (*abhihita*) by the verbal suffix, the nominative *caitra* would take third case-ending and the accusative taṇḍula, second case-ending according to the grammatical rule of *anabhihita.* The denotation of effort is not a factor at all here, because in both the cases the effort exists. Both *ti* and *te* denote effort. And if it is so, taṇḍula would not take second case-ending in *taṇḍulaṅ pacati* or *caitra,* third case-ending in *caitreṇa pacyate.* But both the expressions are grammatically correct. So it cannot be admitted that the verbal suffix denotes effort. In this context, it is relevant to mention that *te* in *karmavācya* denotes effort according to the old Naiyāyikas.

The opponent Naiyāyikas contend that the verbal suffix *tiṅ* denotes number in case of *abhihita* and the rule of taking or not-

taking the first case-ending in *kartṛ* and *karman* depends on the denotation or non-denotation of their number by the verbal suffix *tiṅ*; i.e. if the number of *kartṛ* and *karman* is denoted by the verbal suffix, *kartṛ* and *karman* take the first case-ending. If it is not denoted, then *kartṛ* takes the third case-ending and *karman* takes the second case-ending. But in expressions like *caitreṇa dṛṣṭaḥ ghaṭaḥ* the deviation of the rule may be seen. There is no *tiṅ*, yet the number is denoted. So how can it be said that the *tiṅ* denotes number? Here the Naiyāyikas say that though in the above-mentioned expression the number is apprehended even without a *tiṅ*, yet one should not think that as the number is possible to be denoted from the *sup* in the word *dṛṣṭaḥ*, it is illogical to admit *tiṅ* as a denotator of number. In the expression *caitraḥ maitraḥ ca gacchataḥ*, we apprehend duality, even though there is no case-ending in dual number. If it is argued that for the sake of logical parsimony (*lāghava*), singleness etc. are denoted by single number etc., the explanation is not acceptable to the Vaiyākaraṇas, because the *kṛt* suffix does not denote number. So in *caitreṇa dṛṣṭaḥ ghṭaḥ*, etc. *ghaṭa* would take the second case-ending and not the first one; or in *caitraḥ paktā* Caitra would take the third case-ending and not the first one. So the denotation and non-denotation of number by this suffix are not the regulating factors for a first case-ending or a third case-ending to be applied. The regulating factors are the denotation and non-denotation of agent and object only.

The opponents may argue that the verbal suffixes denote number, and *kṛt* suffixes denote agent and object, and without any harm, the taking or non-taking of a particular case-ending will depend on their (i.e. of number, agent and object) denotation and non-denotation. But this position is not acceptable to the Vaiyākaraṇas. Even the Naiyāyikas aver that in the case of comprehension of number, there is no rule that sometimes the number will connect with the agent or sometimes with the object. We comprehend any particular number with agent or object according to our expectancy etc. So it is admitted that the number is denoted by the verbal suffixes, but it cannot connect with agent or object without any regulating factor. Therefore, according to the Vaiyākaraṇas, when the verbal suffix denotes the agent, the number denoted by the same suffix is connected with the agent only; and when the verbal suffix denotes the object, the number denoted by the same suffix is connected with the object only.

Raghunātha contradicts the Vaiyākaraṇa view; the view to the effect that the meaning of the verbal suffix is *kartṛ*, i.e. the agent in

general suffers from the fault of logical prolixity (*gaurava*). When the Vaiyākaraṇas say that the meaning of the verbal suffix is *kartṛ*, they actually mean that the meaning is *kṛtimān*, because *kartṛ* is that which possesses *kṛti*. In that case, the *śakyatāvacchedaka* (i.e. limiting factor regarding the character of a denoted thing) should be *kṛtimattva*, i.e. the character of having a *kṛti*. But this limiting factor, 'character of having a *kṛti*', is evidently a heavier property than *kṛtitva* i.e. the character of *kṛti*. Between *kṛtitva* and *kṛtimattva*, the latter property is heavier because it is not a universal but only a logical construction, while the former is a universal one. If, on the other hand, the Vaiyākaraṇas say that when the meaning of the verbal suffix is *kṛtimān*, then let *śakyatāvacchedaka* be *kṛti* itself and one need not go upto *kṛtimattva*, still the theory does not escape the fault of prolixity. *Kṛti* as a particular differs from person to person, while *kṛtitva* as a universal is the same in all possible *kṛti*s belonging to all possible persons. Hence *kṛti* as a *śakyatāvacchedaka* cannot be a universal property. When it is possible to have a universal property as the *śakyatāvacchedaka*, one should not accept the prolixity of imagining innumerable particular *kṛti*s as innumerable particular *śakyatāvacchedaka*s corresponding to innumerable actions of innumerable persons.

Regarding the connection of number, the Naiyāyikas do not agree with the Vaiyākaraṇas. The Naiyāyikas do not admit agent or object as the denotative meaning of the verbal suffix, like the opponents. They admit *bhāvanā* being effort, operation, locushood or counterpositiveness, as the denotative or other meaning as the case may be, of the verbal suffix. So the number is connected with it. And as the number is comprehended from the same suffix, it is logical to have its connection with the same qualified (*dharmin*) only.

3. According to the followers of Maṇḍana Miśra, a noted Bhāṭṭa Mīmāṁsaka, the meaning of the verbal stem is result, and the same of the verbal suffix is operation conducive to a certain result, or only operation in some cases. But when there is only operation and the result is yet to come, how is it known that the operation is conducive to the result being the meaning of the verbal stem? Here the Bhāṭṭa Mīmāṁsaka says that the produced-producer relation between the result being the meaning of the verbal stem and operation being the meaning of the verbal suffix, is apprehended through expectancy (*saṁsargamaryādā*). Furthermore, we see that the present time etc. which are the meaning of *laṭ* etc. and the character of a performer of some desired thing (*iṣṭasādhanatva*),

etc. which are the meaning of *liṅ* etc., are also apprehended by the same verbal suffix. So those meanings must be connected with operation, i.e. the meaning of the verbal suffix, as the case may be. And the verbal suffixes in *bhāvavācya* -ghañ etc. mean only the operation conducive to a certain result. In *bhāvavācya,* the suffixes *ghañ* etc. denote the meaning of the verb itself. As a result, the meaning of the suffixes being merged with the meaning of the principal verb would stand without its own meaning. For this reason, the Bhāṭṭa Mīmāṁsaka admits operation conducive to a certain result as to be the meaning of *ghañ* etc. Based on this position alone the expression *pākaḥ bhaviṣyati* (cooking will be done) is justified. It means that there is operation but the result, which is the meaning of the verbal stem, is yet to come. If *ghañ* would not mean operation,then the very meaning of the verbal stem 'result' would only be connected with future time. Then where there is operation and the result is awaited, there *pākaḥ bhaviṣyati* cannot be used. Only where there is no operation, but result is expected in future, the use would be justified. But such a position is contrary to our experience.

Maṇḍana followers admit that the verbal suffix used in *kartṛvācya,* as well as the third case-ending in the word meaning accusative used in case of the verbal suffix in *karmavācya,* is fit to mean operation. The verbal suffix used in *karmavācya* means the character of substratum (*adhikaraṇatva).* The *kṛt* suffix used in *karmavācya* means locus of result while the same used in *kartṛvācya* means the locus of operation.

The view of the opponents is not acceptable to Raghunātha. There is a basic difference in the two views. According to Maṇḍana followers, the limiting factor (*śakyatāvacchedaka*) of the verbal suffix is the character of operation, but according to the Naiyāyikas it is the character of effort. As such, according to Maṇḍana followers, there would be no comprehension of effort at all. Furthermore, according to them the verbal suffix means operation conducive to a certain result. But it is not logically sound. If the opponent's view is to be accepted, a person having fortune conducive to softening of rice would be called 'he is cooking (*pacati*)'. Or, a motionless bird having prior connection conducive to the disjunction would be called 'it is leaving (*tyajati*)'. But it is contrary to our experience. So the Maṇḍana followers have been disregarded by the Naiyāyikas.

4. According to the Prābhākara Mīmāṁsakas, the verbal stem (*dhātu*) means operation conducive to a certain result. The agent (*kartṛ*), without any exception, means locus of the meaning of the

verbal stem. And the verbal suffix (*ākhyāta*) means number (*saṅkhyā*), time (*kāla*) and sometimes counterpostiveness (*pratiyogitva*). For example, in the verbal form *gacchati, pacati* etc. the verbal stem means operations like quivering (*spanda*), enkindling fuel, etc. conducive to a certain result like conjunction, softening of rice, etc. The agent and verbal suffix are easily understandable. The verbal suffix sometimes means the locus also.

The view is not acceptable to Raghunātha. He argues, if the view is accepted the usages like *caitraḥ pacati* would not take place, because Caitra cannot be a locus of the operation conducive to a certain result, at all. The result here is the softening of rice and the operation conducive to it is conjunction between pot and fire, etc. Caitra, in fact, cannot have this operation. Furthermore, according to the Prābhākara view, there is no scope of direct knowledge of the effort with time, etc. from the verbal suffix. While the locus is the primary meaning of the verbal suffix, the effort which exists in the locus can be known only secondarily. But according to the Naiyāyikas, the effort is an established category to be known primarily from the verbal suffix. Therefore, the Prābhākara view, which stands contradictory to the Nyāya view, has been rejected by Raghunātha.

The Navya Naiyāyika Gaṅgeśa Upādhyāya composed two chapters, viz. 1) *Dhātuvāda,* dealing with the meaning of the verbal stem, and 2) *ākhyātavāda,* dealing with the meaning of the verbal suffix, in the fourth Section (i.e. Section on the verbal testimony) in his *Tattvacintāmaṇi. ākhyātavāda* of Raghunātha Śiromaṇi, though an independent treatise by itself, covers almost the same ground of the latter chapter; but compared to that of Gaṅgeśa, Raghunātha's treatment of the subject matter is very concise. Till now, we get three printed commentaries on the *ākhyātavāda* of Raghunātha Śiromaṇi: 1) By Rāmabhadra Sārvabhauma, 2) By Mathurānātha Tarkavāgīśa, and 3) By Rāmacandra Nyāyavāgīśa. Now, with the present edition, the commentary by Bhavānanda Siddhāntavāgīśa is expected to join them. Compared to the commentaries by Mathurānātha and Rāmacandra, the commentary by Bhavānanda is smaller in volume; however the latter i.e. the commentary by Bhavānanda appears to be bigger than that by Rāmabhadra, as the editor of the latter commentary mentions its length as of 430 Ślokas whereas the length of the commentary by Bhavānanda is 550 Ślokas approximately. Though it appears from a rough verification that the Mathurānātha commentary contains a good number of explanations of the earlier commentators, still the early

commentaries are no less necessary in order to get fuller explanations as provided by the concerned commentators on certain topics, and also to verify whether the later commentators have quoted or presented the earlier ones faithfully. So the commentary of Bhavānanda will help the scholars to gather more specific knowledge on *ākhyātavāda.*

d. Commentaries on the Ākhyātavāda of Raghunātha Śiromaṇi

1. *Ākhyātadīdhitiprasariṇī* by Kṛcṇadāsa Sārvabhauma (c. 1500 – 1550 AD), preceptor of Bhavānanda Siddhāntavāgīśa. Manuscript available in Sarasvati Mahal Library at Tanjore; 14 folios. No benedictory verse. The text starts with the explanation of the catchword *bādhakaṁ vineti,* which is the first line of Śiromaṇi's *ākhyātavāda.* The colophon states *kṛṣṇadāsasārva-bhaumanirmitā.* (Vide VNNC, p. 115).

2. *Ākhyātavādavyākhyā* of Rāmabhadra Sārvabhauma (first half of the sixteenth century). Printed from the *codex unicus* i.e. a single manuscript. Edited by Prabal Kumar Sen. Kolkata, 1979.

3. *Ākhyātavādaṭippanī* of Bhavānanda Siddhāntavāgīśa (fl. 1550–75 AD). Manuscripts available in the library of Sanskrit Sahitya Parishat, Kolkata. A complete manuscript of this rare commentary (16 folios, date of copying: 1658 Śaka, i.e. 1736 AD) was noticed by Bhattacharya in the library of Sanskrit Sahitya Parishat. During present editing, a complete manuscript of 16 folios (assigned as A) could be traced in the same library. But the date of copying of this manuscript is 1607 Śaka (i.e. 1685 AD). It could be the same copy of the commentary which was mentioned by Bhattacharya as copied in 1658 āaka, which would mean conjecturing some mistake on the part of Bhattacharya. Anyway, Bhattacharya mentioned another copy of the commentary fragmented in the beginning, which was in his possession. With reference to the post-colophonic statement in that copy, Bhattacharya thinks that 'Rudra' mentioned there (*malākhye śrāvaṇe māsi rudraḥ kṣudramatiḥ punaḥ/lilekha grantham enaṁ tu jvarasantāpasaṁyutaḥ//*) is most probably Bhavānanda's grandson Rudra himself. Quite fortunately, during present editing, a manuscript of the commentary (assigned as C) could be found in the Sanskrit Sahitya Parishat, which totally tallies with the description given by Bhattacharya.It therefore appears likely that the manuscript which was in his possession was somehow collected in the library of the Parishat. Besides these two manuscripts, the present search also led to discovery of another stray folio of the commentary (assigned as B), which was utilised in comparing the corresponding

portion of the commentary.

4. *Ākhyātavādarahasya* of Mathurānatha Tarkavāgīśa (1550 – 90 AD). Printed in the *Tattvacintāmaṇi* (vol. IV, Part 2), pp. 867 – 909.

5. *Ākhyātavādasadvyākhyā* of Rāmakṛṣṇa Bhammācārya Cakravartin (1st half of the sixteenth century AD). Manuscript available in Tanjore Sarasvati Mahal Library (Catalogue p. 4795). The text starts with: *mukundacaraṇadvandvam ādāya hṛdayāmbuje/ ākhyātavāda-sadvyākhyā rāmakṛṣṇena tanyate//*

6. *Ākhyātavādatippanī* of Rāmacandra Nyāyavāgīśa (1600–76 AD). Printed in the *Tattvacintāmaṇi* (vol. IV, Part 2), pp. 867-1009.

7. Commentary on the *Ākhyātavāda* by Rūpanārāyaṇa (? Date). Manuscript available in the library of the Asiatic Society (ms no. 4346).

8. *Ākhyātavādavyākhyāna* by Rudra Nyāyavācaspti (fl. 1590 AD). Manuscript available in Pune (No. 99 of A. 1879-80, 26 fols). Last verse runs thus: *vidyānivāsaputrasya nyāyavācaspateridam/ ākhyātavādavyākhyānam ānandayatu kovidān//*

9. *Ākhyātavādamīkā* by Viśvanātha Siddhāntapañcānana (*c.* 1550 AD). Manuscripts available in Pune (No. 407 of 1886-92, 2-37 fols). Colophon runs as under:

vidyānivāsasunoḥ kṛtireṣā viśvanāthasya/
viduṣām atisūkṣmadhiyā amatsarāṇāṁ mude bhavitā//
kaṭhine nirmāṇe'smin kauṭilyenāpi sukṣmatarabuddhyā/
datto doṣo'pi mude kuce iva vihito nakhāghātaḥ//

Viśvanātha refutes the explanation of his elder brother Rudra.

10. *Ākhyātavādaṭikā* of Raghudeva Nyāyalaṅkāra (fl. *c.* 1657 AD). Manuscript available at Tanjore (Cat, p. 4787).

11. *Āhyātavādavyākhyā* by Jayarāma Nyāyapañcānana (fl. *c.* 1657 AD). Manuscript at Pune (Catalogue, p. 4786), and also at the Asiatic Society (Indian Museum collection, No. 452, fols 2-58, Incomplete, Government Collection, No. 65, Sl. No. 7823).

New Catalogus Catalogorum mentions a few more commentaries on the *ākhyātavāda* of Raghunātha Śiromaṇi, but verification is needed as to their contents. Only two of them are being mentioned here:

12. *Ākhyātavādadīpikā* of Tolāppārya. Travancore University 9481 A.

13. *Granthivimukti* of Rāghavabhaṭṭa. India Office Library, 2048.

e. About the manuscripts of Raghunātha

There are a large number of manuscripts of *ākhyātavāda* of Raghunātha in different libraries. As there are two standard printed editions of the text, those have been primarily utilised in drawing up the present edition.Additionally, two manuscripts of this work preserved in the library of Sanskrit Sahitya Parishat were utilised for vindication of the text reading and recording the variants therein. The descriptions of those manuscripts are as follows:

1. Ākhyātavāda. Ms. No. 8150. Handmade paper. A small square-shaped blank space is left at the centre of every page, but there is no actual perforation. Incomplete. Assigned as AVM_1 in the present edition.

Size: 38x7 cm
No. of folios: 6
Lines per page: 6
Letters per line: 60 approx.
Script: Bengali

2. Ākhyātavāda. Ms. No. 8191. Handmade paper. A small square-shaped blank space is left at the centre of every page but there is no actual perforation. Running title: *ākhyāta Śi* at the verso. All rectos record *śrīḥ* at the left margin. Complete. Assigned as AVM_2 in the present edition.

Size: 33x7.5 cm
No. of folios: 6
Line per page: 7/6
Letter per line: 65 approx
Script: Bengali.

f. About the manuscripts of the ākhyātavādaṭippanī of Bhavānanda Siddhāntavāgīśa

The manuscripts traced in the library of the Sanskrit Sahitya Parishat are described below:

1. Ākhyātavādaṭippanī. Ms No. 12895. Handmade paper with actual perforation at the centre. Assigned as **A** in the present edition.

Size: 42×7 cm.
No. of folios: 16
Lines per page: 8

Letters per line: 83 (approx.)
Script: Bengali
Foliation: 1-16
Double foliation: 114-129

2. Ākhyātavādaṭippanī. A single folio (fol 16a1-16b2) in the Ms. No. 7764. Handmade paper with actual perforation at the centre. Assigned as **B** in the present edition.
Size: 38×7 cm.
Script: Bengali

3. Ākhyātavādasāramañjarī. Ms. No. 11377. Handmade paper with actual perforation at the centre. First folio is missing. Second and third folios are mutilated at the right side, causing the loss of approximately 8 letters per line. Assigned as **C** in the present edition.
Size: 39 × 7 cm.
No. Of folios: 15
Line per page: 7
Letter per line: 84 (approx.)
Script: Bengali
Foliation: 114-28

Signs and Abbreviations

....	: Text inbetween
xxxxx	: Omission due to damage to the manuscript.
[ ]	: Emendation
?	: Doubtful reading or appropriateness of the word in the context
o	: put at the left of a word or a segment of a word indicates text at the left side, put at the right of a word or a segment of a word indicates text at the right side.
A	: Manuscript of *Ākhyātavadaṭippanī* of Bhavānanda Siddhāntavāgīśa. Ms. No. 12895. Preserved in the library of Sanskrit Sahitya Parishat.
AV	: *Ākhyātavāda*
AV(K)	: *Ākhyātavāda* of Raghunātha Śiromaṇi. Edited by Pt. Kamakhyanath Tarkavagisa. Vide TCM (vol IV), part 210 pp. 867–09
AVM_1	: Manuscript of *Ākhyātavāda*. Ms. No. 8150. Preserved in the library of Sanskrit Sahitya Parishat.
AVM_2	: Manuscript of *Ākhyātavāda*. Ms. No. 8191. Preserved in the library of Sanskrit Sahitya Parishat.
AV(P)	: *Ākhyātavāda* of Raghunātha Śiromaṇi. Edited by Prabal Kumar Sen
AVR	: *Ākhyātavādarahasya* of Mathurānātha Tarkavāgīśa. Edited by Pt. Kamakhyanatha Tarkavagisa. Vide TCM (vol IV, part 2), pp. 867–1009
AVT(B)	: *Ākhyātavādaṭippanī* of Bhavānanda Siddhāntavāgīśa

AVT(R)	: *Ākhyātavādaṭippanī* of Rāmacandra Nyāyavāgīśa. Edited by Pt. Kamakhyanatha Tarkavagisa. Vide TCM (vol IV, part 2), pp. 867–1009
AVV	: *Ākhyātavādavyākhyā* of Rāmabhadra Sārvabhauma. Edited by Prabal Kumar Sen.
B	: A fragmentary leaf (no. 16) containing a few concluding lines of *Ākhyātavādaṭippanī* of Bhavānanda Siddhāntavāgīśa. Ms. No. 7764. Preserved in the library of Sanskrit Sahitya Parishat.
BP	: *Bhāṣāpariccheda* ascribed to Viśvanātha Siddhāntapañcānana.
C	: Manuscript of *Ākhyātavādasāramañjarī* of Bhavānanda Siddhāntavāgīśa. Ms. No. 11377. Preserved in the library of Sanskrit Sahitya Parishat.
fol	: Folio/s
Ms	: Manuscript
TCM	: *Tattvacintāmṇi* of Gaṅgeśa Upādhyāya (volume IV, p]art 2). Edited by Pt. Kamakhyanatha Tarkavagisa.
VNNC	: *Vaṅge Navya-nyāya Carcā* (i.e. The culture of neo-logic in Bengal) by Dinesh Chandra Bhattacharya.

रघुनाथशिरोमणिकृतः
आख्यातवादः

१. आख्यातस्य[1] यत्नो वाच्यः[2], पचति पाकं करोतीत्यादियत्नार्थककरोतिना[3] सर्वाख्यातविवरणात्। व्यवहारादिव बाधकं विना विवरणादपि व्युत्पत्तेः, किं करोतीत्यादि[4] यत्नप्रश्ने पचतीत्याद्युत्तरस्य[5] यत्नार्थकत्वं विना अनुपपत्तेश्च[6]। अचेतने रथो गच्छतीत्यादौ च[7] अनुकूलव्यापारे लक्षणा।।

२. अन्यदीयगमनानुकूलनोदनादिमति गच्छतीत्यप्रयोगात्[8], जानातीच्छति-यतते-द्वेष्टि-विद्यते-निद्रातीत्यादौ च[9] क्रियानुकूलकृतिव्यापारयोरप्रतीतेः गत्यादिमत्त्वमात्रप्रतीतेश्चाश्रयत्वे[10] नश्यतीत्यादौ प्रतियोगित्वे निरूढलक्षणा। चैत्रः पचति तण्डुलः[11] मैत्रः[12] पच्यते तण्डुलः इत्यादावन्वयाबोधात्[13] धात्वर्थ-प्रातिपदिकार्थयोर्भेदेन साक्षादन्वयस्याव्युत्पन्नतया सम्बन्धमर्यादया तद्भानस्या-सम्भवादिति तु <u>नव्याः</u>।।

३. कृञश्च यत्नाभिधायकत्वम्, क्रियाजन्यत्वप्रतिसन्धानाविशेषेऽपि यत्नजन्यत्वाजन्यत्वप्रतिसन्धानात् पटाङ्कुरयोः कृताकृतव्यवहारात्, ज्ञात्रादिवदाश्रयपरतृजन्तकर्तृपदस्य यत्नाश्रयबोधकत्वाच्च[14]। क्रियाया-स्तदनुकूलव्यापारस्य वा कृञर्थत्वे[15] तदाश्रयः कारकमात्रं वा[16] कर्तृपदार्थः स्यात्। अथ रथो गच्छति गमनं करोति, वीजादिना अङ्कुरादिः कृतः इति[17] विनाऽपि[18] यत्नं कृञः प्रयोगान्न तस्य यत्नवाचकत्वम्, कर्तृपदे च कृञो यत्ने निरूढलक्षणा यदि क्रियाद्याश्रयमात्रे न[19] तत्प्रयोगः, एवंचाचेतनेऽपि पचतीत्यादिप्रयोगात्[20] क्रियानुकूलव्यापारप्रतीतेर्बाधकं विना गौणत्वायोगात् जनकव्यापार एवाख्यातार्थः, तण्डुलक्रयणादेश्च[21] न पाकादिजनकत्वमिति नातिप्रसङ्गः।।

४. कथं तर्हि पचतीत्यादौ पाकजनकयत्नानुभव इति चेत्, यत्नाविनाभूतपाकादिना क्रियाविशेषकारणस्य[22] यत्नस्यानुमानात्।[23] पचति पाकविषयकयत्नवान्[24] इति[25] तात्पर्यविवरणम्। अन्यथा धर्मिणोऽपि[26] वाच्यतापत्तेः। अथैवं यत्नस्य[27] वर्तमानत्वं[28] न प्रतीयेत[29] तस्यापदार्थत्वात्, अन्यत्र धात्वर्थक्रियायां स्वार्थव्यापारे वा लडादेर्वर्तमानत्वाद्यनुभावकत्वव्युत्पन्नत्वाच्च[30]। न च पाकजनकवर्तमान-

यत्नानुमानम्[31]। यत्नविगमेऽपि व्यापारानुवृत्तेः[32]। धर्मिविशेषनिष्ठता च यत्नस्य न स्यात्[33], तद्व्यधिकरणव्यापारस्यापि पाकजनकत्वात्। चैतन्याविनाभूतचैत्रत्वादिविशेषितेन तेन यत्नानुमानमिति चेत्, सत्यम्[34], चैत्रत्वाद्यप्रतीतावपि[35] शोभनः पचतीत्यादौ शोभनादेः पाकयत्नवत्त्वप्रतीतेः[35], तत्राख्यातस्य[37] जनकयत्ने लाक्षणिकत्वात्।।

५. मैवम्, जनकव्यापारमपेक्ष्य[38] लाघवेन[39] जनकयत्नस्यैव शक्यत्वात्। यत्नं विहाय जनकत्वमात्रे[40] शक्तिरस्तु लाघवात्, तथाचाचेतनेऽपि प्रयोगो मुख्य एवेति चेन्न, अपचत्यपि[41] पाकजनकादृष्टवति पचतीति प्रयोगापत्तेः। पाकजनकादृष्टजनककृतेश्च[42] न पाकजनकत्वं मानाभावात्। अतएव क्षित्यादेः कृत्यादिजन्यत्वे साध्ये तज्जनकादृष्टजनककृत्यादिना अर्थान्तरप्रसङ्गोऽपि प्रत्युक्तः[43]। भावे वा तादृशकृतिनिराकरणाय[44] अदृष्टाद्वारकजनकतायास्त्वयापि[45] वाच्यत्वात्। यत्नमात्रं शक्यं विषयित्वं[46] जनकत्वं वा सम्बन्धमर्यादया भासत इति तु <u>नव्याः</u>।।

६. कर्तृकर्मणी लकारवाच्ये[47], चैत्रः पचति पच्यते तण्डुलः इत्यादौ[48] सामानाधिकरण्यानुरोधात्[49]। अन्यथा पचतीत्यादावपि[50] कर्तरि[51] तृतीया, पच्यते इत्यत्र[52] कर्मणि द्वितीया स्यात्, तयोरनभिहिताधिकारीयत्वात्, कृत्यभिधानस्याविशिष्टत्वात्[53]। कर्तृकर्मसंख्याभिधानानभिधानाभ्यां नियमः, न चैवं[54] चैत्रेण दृष्टो घटः इत्यादौ विनापि तिङं[55] संख्याप्रतीतेः क्लृप्तशक्तेः सुप एव संख्योपस्थितिसम्भवे तिङो[56] न तदभिधायकत्वमिति वाच्यम्, चैत्रो मैत्रश्च गच्छतः इत्यादौ विनापि तादृशसुपं[57] द्वित्वादिप्रत्ययात्, लाघवादेकवचनत्वादिनैव एकत्वादौ शक्तत्वाच्चइत्येतदपि[58] नास्ति, कृता संख्यानभिधानात्। किंच एकत्वादिसंख्याभिधाने[59] न नियमः, पदार्थतावच्छेदकावच्छिन्नस्याकाङ्क्षादिवशात् कर्तृकर्मसाधारण्येनान्वयबोधस्य दुर्वारत्वात्। कर्त्रेकत्वत्वादिनाऽभिधानेऽपि[60] कर्त्रादेरप्यभिधेयत्वम्[61], शक्तौ शक्ततावच्छेदकशक्यतावच्छेदकयोः[62] गौरवमधिकम्। तस्मादाख्यातत्वेन कर्तरि कर्मणि च आत्मनेपदत्वेन, एकवचनत्वादिना तत्तद्रूपेण वा एकाख्यातस्य च[63] एकत्वादौ शक्तिः। एकपदोपात्तत्वाच्च[64] संख्याया वाच्यगामित्वम्, कर्तृकर्मबोधकत्वं च[65] एकदाऽव्युत्पन्नम्, अतएव[66] चैत्रः[67] पक्ष्यते[68] तण्डुलः इत्यादयो न प्रयोगाः। कर्तरि यकोऽसाधुत्वाच्च पच्यते चैत्रः इत्यादयोऽपि कर्तरि[69] नेति <u>वैयाकरणाः</u>।।

७. अत्र वदन्ति-भावनाविशेष्ये[70] संख्यान्वयः[71] समानपदोपात्तत्वेनैकान्वयित्वस्योचितत्वात्[72]। भावनायाश्च विशेष्यत्वेनान्वययोग्यः प्रथमान्तपदोपस्थाप्यः कर्मत्वाद्यनवरुद्धः[73]। चैत्रः[74] पचति, पच्यते तण्डुलः[75] इत्यादौ कर्तृकर्मणी

प्रथमान्तपदोपस्थाप्यतया[76] भावनाविशेष्ये इति[77] तत्रैव संख्यान्वयः तथैवाकाङ्क्षितत्वात्[78]। चैत्रेण[79] सुप्यते गगनेन स्थीयते इत्यादौ प्रथमान्तपदाभावात् धात्वर्थस्य भावनाया[80] विशेषणतयैवान्वयस्य व्युत्पन्नत्वात् भावनाया बाधितत्वाच्च भावनाविशेष्यविरहादनन्वितैव संख्या, एकवचनं तु[81] साधुत्वार्थम्[82]। अतएव स्वापस्य द्वित्वबहुत्वेऽप्यौत्सर्गिकमेकवचनमेव[83]। एवं च भावतिङा[84] यथायथं[85] वर्तमानत्वादीष्टसा नत्वादिकमर्थः। तच्च धात्वर्थ एवान्वेति, तथैव प्रत्ययात्। तदबोधकानां तु घञादीनां[86] प्रयोगसाधुत्वमात्रम्[87]। भावनायाश्च कर्तर्याश्रयत्वेन[88] कर्मणि पुनरन्यथाऽन्वयः, तव कर्तृकर्माभिधायित्ववत्[89] अस्माकमपि तथाऽन्वयबोधकत्वम्। अतो मैत्रेण पचति तण्डुलः, तण्डुलं पच्यते मैत्रः, मैत्रः पक्ष्यते[90] तण्डुलः इत्यादयो[91] न प्रयोगाः। भावना च व्यापारमात्रोपलक्षिका[92], अचेतनानुरोधात्। भिन्नाभ्यां रूपाभ्यामेकधर्मिबोध-कत्वलक्षणं[93] सामानाधिकरण्यमसिद्धं[94] सम्भवदन्यादृशं न[95] वार्यते।।

८. अथ तण्डुलं पचति मैत्र[96] इत्यत्राश्रयतया मैत्रो[97] भावनाविशेष्यः, मैत्रेण[98] पच्यते तण्डुल इत्यत्र तण्डुलस्तु कथम्? विषयतयेति चेत्, रथेन गम्यते ग्रामः इत्यादौ सविषयव्यापारानभिधाने[99] का गतिः? अत्र <u>प्राञ्चः</u> मैत्रेण पच्यते तण्डुलः इत्यत्र मैत्रनिष्ठपाकभावनाविषयः मैत्रनिष्ठभावनाविषय-पाकजन्यफलशाली वा तण्डुलः प्रतीयते इति साक्षात् परम्परया वा भावनाविशेष्यस्तण्डुलः[100]। रथेन गम्यते ग्रामः इत्यत्र तु[101] रथनिष्ठग-मनानुकूलव्यापारजन्यफलशाली ग्रामः प्रतीयते[102] इति व्यापारविशेष्यो ग्रामः इति।।

९. <u>नव्यास्</u>तु—भावनादेराख्यातलभ्यत्वात् आधेयत्वमात्रं[103] तृतीयार्थोऽस्तु[104] संख्यामात्रं वा, सम्बन्धस्तु पचतीत्यादाविव[105] वाक्यार्थः[106]। अस्तु च फलकर्मणोरपि सम्बन्धस्तथा, फलं[107] तु कस्यार्थः? न च तदपि तथा, प्रकारीभूय भासमानत्वात्। फलावच्छिन्नक्रियाया धात्वर्थत्वेऽपि क्रियाजन्यफलालाभात्, विशेषण-विशेष्यभावविपर्ययस्याशक्यत्वात्[108]। तस्मात् फलमात्मनेपदार्थः। इत्थं चाख्यातोपस्थापिताया[109] भावनायाः क्रियाविषयिण्याः फलेऽन्वये फलस्य क्रियाजन्यत्वं न लभ्येत[110], भावनाविषयक्रियायाः[111] फलेऽन्वये तिङुपस्थापित-भावनायाः[112] क्रियाविशेषणत्वेनान्यत्र[113] अन्वयो क्लृप्तः[114] भज्येत। तस्मात् कृत्यनभिधायकभावकर्मकृद्योगे क्लृप्तशक्तेः सुपो लब्धया भावनया विशिष्टायाः क्रियायाः फलेऽन्वयः, सुबर्थकृतेर्विक्लित्यां[115] विशेषणत्वेनैवान्वयस्य व्युत्पन्नत्वात्[116]। कर्तृकर्मवच्च कृतिफलयोरप्यभिधाने नियमान्नातिप्रसङ्गः। न वा पक्ष्यते तण्डुलो मैत्रः इत्यादयः[117] प्रयोगाः। तिङुपस्थाप्यायाः[118] संख्याया भावनाया इव[119] प्रथमान्तपदोपस्थाप्येनैवान्वयो[120] व्युत्पन्नः[121]।।

चैत्रो[122] गन्ता गतो ग्रामो मित्रा पक्त्री गतं पुरम्[123]।
भोक्ता तृप्यति पक्वानि भुङ्क्ते पक्ताऽपसार्यताम्[124]॥

[ ]

इत्यादौ[125] सामानाधिकरण्याद्यन्यथाऽनुपपत्त्या कर्तृकर्मणी कृद्वाच्ये। चैत्रस्य नप्ता[126] मैत्रादन्यो[127] घटात् पृथक् परोऽपरो वेत्यादाविव पदार्थतावच्छेदकेनैव कृत्यादिना धात्वर्थेऽन्वयः[128], तथैव साकाङ्क्षत्वात्। अस्तु वा कृत्यादिघटित एव[129] कर्त्रादिना सममन्वयः[130]। मुख्यभाक्तसाधारणस्य फलादिलक्षणकर्मत्वस्य कृत्यादिलक्षणकर्तृत्वस्य चानभिधाने द्वितीयादयः[131]। कृता विशिष्टाभिधाने विशेषणस्याप्यभिधानात्॥

१०. यत्तु–धातूत्तरप्रत्ययत्वेनैव[132] कृतौ शक्तिः, पाचकादिपदे[133] तु सामानाधिकरण्यानुरोधात् कृतिविशिष्टे लक्षणा इति, तन्न, भावकृतोऽपि कृतिवाचकतापत्तेः[134], धातुत्वादिघटितत्वात्, तस्मादाख्यातत्वस्यैव लघुत्वाच्च॥

११. यदपि कर्तृकृतोऽपि कृतौ शक्तिः, कृतिविशिष्टे तु[135] लक्षणैवेति[136], तदप्यसत्। यतो विनाऽवच्छेदकरूपं[137] शक्यत्वासम्भवात्। गोत्वत्वादिना शक्तौ चातिगौरवादस्तु[138] गवादिपदानां गोत्वादिविशिष्टं[139] शक्यम्, विशिष्टान्तराणां तु[140] शक्यत्वं विलीयेत, केवले च विशेषणे[141] स्वारसिकप्रयोगविरहस्तुल्य एवेति॥

१२. एवं च–गतो ग्रामो[142] गम्यते इत्यादौ फलस्य कृदात्मनेपदाभ्यामेव[143] लाभात् लाघवाद् धातोरनन्यलभ्यव्यापारविशेषमात्रवाचकत्वस्थितौ[144] ग्रामं गच्छति, ग्रामस्य गन्ता इत्यादौ द्वितीयादेः फलजनकत्वलक्षणं[145] कर्मत्वमर्थः[146], फले च प्रातिपदिकार्थोऽधिकरणत्वेनान्वेति, फलमात्रं वाऽर्थः जनकत्वं तु संसर्गमर्यादया लभ्यमित्यपि केचित्[147]। तदसत्[148] ग्रामं गच्छति त्यजतीत्यादौ द्वितीयादितः[149] फलसामान्यलाभेऽपि नियतसंयोगविभागाद्यलाभात्[150] फलविशेषावच्छिन्नव्यापारस्यैव धात्वर्थत्वात्, इतरथा त्यजि–गमि–प्रभृतीनां पर्यायतापत्तेः[151]॥

१३. तवापि[152] गम्यते ग्रामः इत्यादौ ग्रामादेः संयोगादिफलशालित्वं[153] कुतः[154] प्रतीयत इति चेत्, तदवच्छिन्नव्यापारवाचिधातुसमभिव्याहारादेव, यथा इष्टसाधनत्ववाचकाद् विधेरेव स्वर्गकामादिपदसमभिव्याहारात् स्वर्गजनकत्वम्[155]। प्रतीतिस्त्विष्टफलयोरिष्टफलत्वाभ्यां[156] स्वर्गत्वसंयोगत्वाभ्यां[157] वेत्यन्यदेतत्॥

१४. अस्तु वा बुद्धिविषयवाचकतदादेरिव[158] व्युत्पत्तिवशादेव प्रकृत्यर्थतावच्छेदकफलतच्छालिवाचकाख्यातकृतोरपि विशेषरूपेण बोधकत्वम्॥

१५. अपि च धात्वर्थतावच्छेदकफलशालित्वं कर्मत्वम्, न तु[159] धात्वर्थजन्यफलशालितामात्रम्,[160] गमिपत्योः कर्मत्वस्य पूर्वस्मिन् देशे, त्यजेश्चोत्तरस्मिन्[161] देशे[162], स्पन्देः[163] पूर्वापरदेशयो[164] प्रसङ्गात्॥

१६. फलावच्छिन्नव्यापारबोधकत्वादेव च धातूनां सकर्मकत्वव्यवहारः, भाक्तस्तु जानातीत्यादेः[165], तादृशधातुप्रयोग[166] एव च कर्मप्रत्ययाः[167]। तत्र च[168] द्वितीययाऽऽधेयत्वमभिधीयते, तच्चाकाङ्क्षावैचित्र्याद्[169] धात्वर्थतावच्छेदकफलेऽन्वेति[170], अतएव चास्याः[171] पदार्थान्विताधेयत्वबोधिकायाः सप्तम्या भेदः[172]।

१७. अस्तु वा कर्माख्यातस्येव द्वितीयाया अपि[173] फलमर्थः। स्तां[174] वा फलव्यापारौ पृथगेव धात्वर्थौ[175], विशिष्टस्त्वन्वयबललभ्यः[176]। भूमिं प्रयाति विहगो विजहाति[177] महीरुहं न त स्वात्मानम्[178] इत्याद्यनुरोधात्[179] क्रियान्वयिपरसमवेतत्वमपि कर्मप्रत्ययार्थः।।

१८. ईयांस्तु विशेषः यत्[180]-परत्वं सुपा प्रकृत्यर्थाद्यपेक्षिकं[181] तिङादिना च स्वार्थफलाश्रयापेक्षिकं प्रत्याय्यते[182]। घटं जानातीच्छति कुरुते चैत्रः, मैत्रेण[183] ज्ञायते इष्यते क्रियते घटः इत्यादौ सविषयपदार्थाभिधायिधातुयोगे[184] कर्मप्रत्ययेन यथायथं विषयित्वं विषयत्वं च, कर्तृतिङा स्वाश्रयत्वम्[185], तृतीयया चाधेयत्वं बोध्यते। अन्वयबोधे त्वयं विशेषः यदेकत्र[186] कर्तर्याश्रयत्वम्, तत्र क्रिया, तत्र[187] विषयित्वम्[188], तत्र कर्मविशेषणम्। अन्यत्र कर्मणि विषयता[189], तत्र क्रिया, तत्राधेयत्वम्[190], तत्र च[191] कर्तेति[192]। ज्ञातो ज्ञाता[193] नष्ट इत्यादौ[194] कर्तृकर्मकृतां[195] विषयाश्रयप्रतियोगिबोधकत्वम्। यतते इत्यादौ[196] यत्यादिनोपस्थिते[197] यत्ने विषयित्वेन[198] नान्वयः किन्तूद्देश्यत्वेन[199], पदस्वाभाव्यात्[200]। अतएवाभुञ्जानेऽपि भोजनाय यतते इत्यादयः प्रयोगाः।।

१९. धातोरर्थः[201] फलम्, अनुकूलव्यापारो[202] व्यापारमात्रं वा, आख्यातस्य जन्यजनकभावः संसर्गमर्यादया[203] लभ्यः। लडादिलिङाद्यर्थो वर्तमानत्वादीष्टसाधनत्वादिकमेकपदोपात्तत्वप्रत्यासत्त्या[204] तत्रैवान्वेति, भावप्रत्ययस्य घञादेरनुकूलव्यापार एवार्थः। तेन व्यापारसत्त्वे फलानुत्पाददशायां पाको[205] भविष्यतीति न प्रयोगः, न वा व्यापारविगमे फलसत्त्वे[206] पाको विद्यते इति। नापि घटभूतलयोर्मिथः संयोगः इतिवत्[207] मिथोगमनमित्यादि[208] प्रत्ययोपनीतपरसमवेतव्यापारजन्य-धात्वर्थफलशालित्वं च कर्मत्वम्, फलनिष्ठाधेयत्वं[209] द्वितीयादिना, व्यापारनिष्ठं[210] च तृतीयादिनाऽभिधीयते। एवं च तण्डुलं पचति चैत्रः[211] इत्यस्य तण्डुलवृत्तिफलविशेषजनकव्यापारवांश्चैत्रः[212], मैत्रेण[213] पच्यते तण्डुलः इत्यस्य[214] मैत्रनिष्ठव्यापारजन्यफलविशेषशाली[215] तण्डुल इत्यर्थः। फलव्यापारयोर्विशेषणविशेष्यभावभेदादेव[216] कर्तृकर्मप्रत्ययव्यवहारः[217]।।

२०. वस्तुतस्त्वाख्यातस्येव तृतीयाया अपि व्यापार एवार्थः[218], कर्माख्यातस्य च[219] धात्वर्थफलनिरूपितम् अधिकरणत्वम्, कर्मकृतफलस्य[220] आश्रयः,

कर्तृकृतश्च व्यापाराश्रय:, कमकर्तृसामानाधिकरण्यानुरोधात्। जानातीत्यादिप्रयोगे तु पूर्वोक्तैव रीतिरनुसर्तव्या। चैत्रेण पच्यते पक्व: इत्यादौ[221] सुबर्थ एव व्यापारे वर्तमानत्वाद्यन्वय:, पचमान:, पक्ववान्, इत्यादौ पुनरनायत्या पदार्थतावच्छेदक एव व्यापारे तदन्वय:। स्तां वा[222] व्यापाराश्रयौ शक्यौ, विशिष्टमन्वयबललभ्यम्, एवकारस्येवान्ययोगव्यवच्छेदादौ[223] अन्ययोग-प्रतियोगिकव्यवच्छेदस्यातिप्रसक्तत्वात्[224] अन्ययोगत्वावच्छिन्न प्रतियोगिक-व्यवच्छेदस्य[225] शक्यत्वे शक्याप्रसिद्धि[226] बाधितत्वं[227] च, पार्थ एवेत्यादौ पार्थान्ययोगत्वावच्छिन्नव्यवच्छेदस्याप्रतीतिप्रसङ्ग:[228], तस्य ततोऽन्यत्वात्।।

२१. स्वान्ययोगव्यवच्छेदेन[229] शक्यत्वे[230] च स्वत्वस्याननुगमाच्छक्त्यानन्त्यम्[231], नीलो घटो नास्तीत्यादौ नीलघटत्वाद्यवच्छिन्नस्येव[232] पार्थ एवेत्यादावपि पार्थान्ययोगत्वावच्छिन्नस्याभावप्रतीति:[233], समानं चेदं कृतौ कालान्वयवादिनाम्। धात्वर्थानुकूलव्यापारविरहिण्यपि महीरुहादौ संयुज्यते[234] इत्यादिव्यवहारात् संयोगत्वमात्रप्रतीते:[235], न तु[236] तत्र प्रत्ययस्य व्यापारवाचितेति न सकर्मकत्वम्[237] संयोग: इत्यादौ धात्वर्थमात्रप्रतीतेर्घञादे: प्रयोगसाधुतामात्रमिति[238], मण्डनमतानुयायिन:[239]। तन्न, पचतीत्यादौ पाकानुकूलवर्तमानयत्नान-नुभवप्रसङ्गात्[240], फलानुकूलादृष्टवत्यपि पचतीत्यादेर्विभागाद्यनुकूलपूर्व-संयोगादिमति निश्चलादावपि विहगे[241] त्यजतीत्यादे: प्रयोगस्य प्रसङ्गाच्च।।

२२. तत्र तत्र तत्तत्फलानुकूलतत्तदव्यापारविशेष एव धात्वर्थ:, सर्वत्र धात्वर्थाश्रय-त्वमेव कर्तृत्वम्, संख्यावर्तमानत्वादिकं क्वचिदाश्रयत्वादिकमपि वा[242] आख्यातार्थ इति[243] गुरुमतमपि तत्र तत्र[244] तादृशयत्नाननुभवप्रसङ्गादनु-पादेयम्।।[245]

।इति महामहोपाध्यायश्रीरघुनाथशिरोमणिभट्टाचार्यविरचित: आख्यातवाद: समाप्त:[246]।।

सन्दर्भसंकेतः

1. AVM_1 starts with the salutation to Gaṇeśa: ओं नमो गणेशाय
   AVM_2 starts with the salutation to Durgā : ओं नमो दुर्गायै
2. AV(K): यत्नवाचकत्वम् for चलो बाच्यः
3. AVM_1 and AVM_2 omit आदि.
4. AVM_1 and AVM_2 omit आदि. Reading without आदि appears to be correct according to AVT (B).
5. AVM_1 and AVM_2 omit आदि.
6. AVM_1 omits च.
7. AVM_1 omits the word.
8. AVM_1 omit प्र.
9. AVM_1 omits the word.
10. ? ज्ञान for प्रतीति according to AVT(B).
11. AVM_2 : तण्डुलं
12. AVM_2: मैत्रेण
13. AVM_2 : ०न्वयानुरोधात्
14. AVM_1 and AVM_2 omit च.
15. AVM_1: कृञ्धात्वर्थत्वे
16. AVM_2 च
17. AVM_1 omits the word.
18. AVM_2 omits अपि
19. AVM_2 : क्रियाश्रयमात्रेण for क्रिया . . . न
20. AVM_1 omits आदि.
21. AVM_2 : तण्डुलक्रियादेः
22. AVM_2 : क्रियाविशेषेण कारणस्य
23. AVM_1 omits यत्नस्य
24. AVM_1 and AVM_2 omit विषयक.
25. AVM_1 adds तु after इति.
26. AVM_2 omits इति.
27. AVM_2 : तस्य for यत्नस्य
28. AV(K) : वर्तमानत्वं यत्नस्य
29. AVM_2 : प्रतीयते
30. AVM_1 and AVM_2 : ०भावकत्वस्य व्युत्पन्न०
31. AVM_1 adds पाकजनकवर्तमानव्यापारेण before this word. AVM_2 : पाकजनकव्यावर्तमानव्यापारेण पाकजनकवर्तनानयत्नानुभवमानम्
32. AVM_1 : पाकानुकूलव्यापारा०
33. AVM_1 : प्रतीयते, AVM_2 : प्रतीयेत
34. AVM_1 and AVM_2 omit the word.
35. AVM_1 and AVM_2 omit आदि०
36. AVM_1 and AVM_2 : पाकजनकयत्नवत्त्वप्रतीतेः इति चेत्, सत्यं for the word.
37. AVM_2 omits स्य.
38. AV (K) :? अविनाभावमपेक्ष्य
39. AVM_2 : लाघवे
40. AVM_1 and AVM_2 and : जनकमात्रे

41. AVM_2 : अपचयत्यपि
42. AVM_2 omits च.
43. AVM_1 : निरस्तः
44. AV(K) and AV (P) : निवारणाय for निराकरणाय, AVM_2 : वाराणाय for निराकरणाय
45. AV(K) : अदृष्टाद्वारकजनक, AV(P) : अदृष्टद्वारकजनक, AVM_2: अदृष्टद्वारकत्वेन जनक
46. AVM_1 and AVM_2 and : विषयत्वं
47. AVM_2 : दशलकारवाच्ये
48. AVM_1 and AVM_2 omit आदौ.
49. AVM_2 : ०करण्यान्वयबोधात्
50. AVM_1 and AVM_2 : पचतीत्यत्रापि
51. AVM_1 : कर्तृ for कर्तरि
52. AVM_1 and AVM_2 add अपि after इत्यत्र.
53. AVM_2 : कृत्यभिधानस्य चाविशिष्टत्वात्
54. AVM_1 and AVM_2 omit एवं.
55. AVM_2 : तिङा
56. AVM_2 : तिङा
57. AVM_2 : ०सुपा
58. AVM_1, AVM_2 and AV(K) omit एतत्.
59. AVM_1 : एकत्वत्वादिना संख्याभिधाने, AVM_2 : एकत्वादिना संख्यानभिधाने
60. AVM_1 : तु for अपि, AVM_2 :कर्त्रेकत्वादिनाऽभिधाने
61. AVM_1 omits अपि.
62. AVM_1 : ०वच्छेदकयोश्च, AVM_2 : शक्तता (? शक्यता) शक्ततावच्छेदकयोश्च
63. AVM_1 and AVM_2 omit एकाख्यातस्य च.
64. AV(K) omit : एकपदोपात्तत्वाच्च.
65. AVM_2 : ०बोधकत्वाच्च
66. AVM_1 omits the word. AVM_2 : अतो
67. AVM_1 and AVM_2 : मैत्रः
68. AV(K) : पच्यते
69. AVM_1 and AVM_2 omit the word.
70. AVM_1 : भावनाया विशेष्ये
71. AVM_2 : संख्याया अन्वयः
72. AV(P) and AVM_2 : औचित्यात् for अचितत्वात्
73. AV(K), AVM_1 and AVM_2 : कर्मत्वाद्यनवरुद्धः प्रथमान्तपदोपस्थाप्यः, Changed the order according to AVT (B).
74. AVM_1 adds तथैव साकांक्षत्वात्। तथाच before the word. AVM_2 adds तथैव साकांक्षत्वात् before the word.
75. AVM_1 : चैत्रः पचति तण्डुलं, चैत्रेण पच्यते तण्डुलः for चैत्रः ० तण्डुलः
76. AVM_2: प्रथमान्तोपस्थाप्यतया
77. AVM_1 omits the word.
78. AVM_1 and AVM_1 omit तथै · · · त्वात्०
79. AVM_1 : मैत्रेण
80. AVM_2: भावनायां
81. AVM_1 omits the word.
82. AVM_2: साध्वर्थं
83. AVM_1 and AVM_2 : द्विबहुत्वे०
84. AVM_1 and AV(P) : भावतिङामपि, AVM_2 omits: भावतिङां.

85. AVM_2 adds भावतिङा after the word.
86. AVM_1 adds तु before this word.
87. AVM_1 and AVM_2 : ०साधुतामात्रम्
88. AVM_2 : कर्तर्याश्रयत्वे
89. AVM_1 and AVM_2 : ०धायित्ववच्च
90. AVM_2 : पक्ष्यते मैत्रः
91. AVM_1 adds अपि after this word.
92. AV(K) and AVM_2 : व्यापारमात्रोपलक्षिता, AVM_1 : व्यापारोपलक्षिका
93. AVM_1 : रूपाभ्यामेकार्थबोधकत्वलक्षणं, AVM_2 : ०बोधकत्वं लक्षणं
94. AV(K), AVM_1 and AVM_2 : अप्रसिद्धं for असिद्धं
95. AVM_1 and AVM_2 add तु before न०
96. AVM_1 : चैत्रः
97. AVM_1 : चैत्रोऽस्तु, AVM_2 : मैत्रस्तु
98. AVM_1 and AVM_2 : चैत्रेण
99. AV(K) : सविषयकव्यापारा०
100. AVM_2 : विषय for विशेष्य
101. AVM_1 and AVM_2 omit the word.
102. AVM_2 : प्रतीत
103. AVM_1 omits the word.
104. AVM_1 : तृतीयार्थस्तु निष्ठत्वं, AVM_2 : तृतीयार्थः। ऽस्तु
105. AVM_1 : इच्छतीत्या०
106. AVM_2 : वाच्यार्थः
107. AVM_1 : जन्यं फलं
108. AVM_1 and AVM_2 : विपर्यास for विपर्यय
109. AVM_2 : ०पस्थाप्य
110. AVM_1 : लभ्यते
111. AVM_1 : भावनाविषयस्य च क्रियायाः
112. AV(K) and AVM_1 : ०भावनायां
113. AVM_1 : क्रियाया विशेषण.
114. AVM_1 and AVM_2 : क्लृप्तान्वयो for अन्वयो क्लृप्तः
115. AVM_1 : क्रियायां for विक्लित्त्यां, AVM_2 : कृत्यभिधायकभावकर्मकृद्योगे क्लृप्तशक्तिः सुपे लब्ध भावनायाः विशिष्टायाः क्रियायाः फलेऽन्वयः, सुबर्थकृतेश्च क्रियायां for कृत्य ० क्लित्यां
116. AVM_1 : व्युत्पन्नत्वाच्च, AVM_2 : अव्युत्पन्नत्वात्
117. AVM_1 : इत्यादयोऽपि
118. AV(K) and AVM_1 : तिङुपस्थापितायाः, AVM_2 : तिङोपस्था०
119. AVM_2 : भाव
120. AVM_1 omits एव
121. AVM_2 : व्युत्पन्नत्वात्
122. AVM_1 and AVM_2 : मैत्रो
123. AVM_2 : कुलं (?corrupt)
124. AVM_2 : ०सार्यत
125. AV(P): इत्यत्र
126. AVM_2 omits चैत्रस्य नप्ता
127. AVM_1 : चैत्रादन्यो, AVM_2 : मैत्रादन्यश्चैत्रस्य नप्ता
128. AVM_1 and AVM_2 : धात्वर्थान्वयः
129. AVM_2 omits the word.

130. AVM_2 : सहान्वय:
131. AVM_1 : तृतीयादय:
132. AVM_1 and AVM_2 omit एव.
133. AVM_2 adds कृतौ before the word.
134. AVM_1 : ०वाचकत्वापत्ते:
135. AVM_1 omits the word.
136. AVM_1 and AVM_2 omit एव
137. AVM_1 and AVM_2 : विनाऽवच्छेदकं रूपं
138. AVM_1 and AVM_2 add वा after this word.
139. AV(K): गोत्वविशिष्टं
140. AVM_1 omits the word. AVM_1 : शक्यम्, तथात्वे विशिष्टा.
141. AVM_2 : केवलविशेषण
142. AVM_1 and AVM_1 omit the word.
143. AVM_2 : कृतात्मने.
144. AVM_1 : ०विशेषमात्रोपस्थापकत्वस्थितौ
145. AVM_2 : ०जनकत्वं लक्षणं
146. AVM_1 : ०लक्षणकर्मत्वमर्थ:
147. AVM_2 : लभ्यमिति कश्चित्
148. AVM_2 : तन्न
149. AVM_1 : द्वितीयादे:
150. AV(K) and AVM_1 : ०द्यलाभेन. Changed according to AVT(B). AVM_2 : नियतसंयोगाद्यलाभात्
151. AV(K) : पर्यायित्वापत्ते:, AVM_2: पर्यायितापातात्
152. AVM_1 : तथापि
153. AVM_1 omits फल. AVM_2 : संयोगशालित्वं
154. AVM_1 : adds तवापि before कुत:
155. AV(K) : स्वर्गादिजनकत्वं
156. AV(P) : ०रिष्टत्वफलत्वाभ्यां
157. AVM_1 : संयोगत्वस्वर्गत्वाभ्यां
158. AV(P) : बुद्धिविषयतावाचकतदादेरिव
159. AVM_1 omits the word.
160. AVM_1 : ०फलशालित्वं, AVM_2 : ०फलशालित्वं मात्रम्
161. AVM_2 : त्यजे: कर्मत्वस्य उत्तरस्मिन्
162. AVM_1 omits the word.
163. AVM_1 : स्पन्देश्च, AVM_2 : स्पन्दे च कर्मत्वस्य
164. AVM_1 omits देश.
165. AV(K) : जानात्यादे:
166. AVM_1 and AVM_2 : तादृशधातुयोग, AV(K) : तादृशप्रयोग
167. AVM_2 : कर्मप्रत्यय:
168. AVM_2 : न
169. AVM_1 : ०काङ्क्षादिवैचित्र्याद्
170. AVM_1 : धात्वर्थावच्छेदकेऽन्वेति, AVM_2 : धात्वर्थावच्छेदके फलेऽन्वेति
171. AVM_2 : इत एव अस्या:
172. AVM_1 : ०धेयत्वबोधकसप्तमीतो भेद:, AVM_2 : ०बोधिकाया: सप्तमीतो भेद:
173. AVM_2 : omits the word.
174. AVM_2 : आस्तां
175. AVM_1 : धातोरर्थौ, AVM_2 : अपृथगेव धातोरर्थो for पृथगेव धात्वर्थौ

176. AVM_2 omits बल०
177. AVM_2 : जहाति
178. AVM_1 : आत्मानम्
179. AVM_1 omits आदि० AVM_2 : इत्यन्वयबोधात्
180. AV(K) : यत् यत्
181. AVM_1 and AVM_2 : प्रकृत्यर्थापेक्षिकं, AV(K) : सविषयकपदार्था०
182. AVM_2 : प्रयुज्यते
183. AVM_2: चैत्रेण
184. AV(K): सविषयकपदा०
185. AVM_1 and AVM_2 : आश्रयत्वम्
186. AVM_2 : यदैकत्र
187. AVM_2 : क्रियते for क्रिया तत्र
188. AVM_1 : विषयिता
189. AVM_2 : विषयिता
190. AVM_2 : क्रियते for क्रिया तत्र
191. AVM_1 omits the word.
192. AVM_1 omits इति.
193. AVM_2 omits the word.
194. AVM_2 adds च after the word.
195. AVM_2 : कर्मकर्तृकृति
196. AVM_1 and AVM_2 : इत्यादौ च
197. AVM_1 and AVM_2: ०नोपस्थापिते
198. AVM_2 : विषयित्वे
199. AVM_1 and AVM_2 : अपि तु for किन्तु
200. AVM_1 : पदस्वभावात्
201. AVM_2: धात्वर्थ:
202. AVM_2: तदनुकू०
203. AVM_1 and AVM_2 : सम्बन्धमर्यादया
204. AVM_2: ०साधनत्वादिकपदोपात्तत्वात् प्रत्यासत्त्या
205. AVM_1 omit the word.
206. AVM_2 : फलसत्त्वेऽपि
207. AVM_1 : इव तस्मिन्
208. AVM_1 : ०मित्यादि:।
209. AVM_1 and AVM_2 : फलनिष्ठं चाधेयत्वं
210. AVM_1 : व्यापारनिष्ठत्वं
211. AVM_1 : मैत्र:
212. AVM_1 : मैत्र: for चैत्र:, AVM_2 : ०व्यापारविशेषवांश्चैत्र:
213. AVM_2 : चैत्रेण
214. AVM_2 : इत्यस्य च
215. AVM_2 : चैत्र for मैत्र
216. AVM_1 : विशेष्यविशेषण for विशेषणविशेष्य
217. AVM_2 : ०प्रत्ययस्य व्यवहार:
218. AVM_2 : व्यापारार्थ: for व्यापार एवार्थ:
219. AVM_1 omits the word.
220. AV (K), AV(P) and AVM_1 omit the word.
221. AVM_1 : इत्यादौ च, AVM_2 adds तण्डुल: before पक्व:.

222. AVM_2 omits स्तां वा.
223. AVM_1 ends at ०योगव्यव. AVM_2 : व्यवच्छेदौ
224. AVM_2 : अन्यथा अन्ययोग . . . . च्छेदकमात्रस्या.
225. AVM_2 : ०वच्छिन्नत्वप्रतियोगिक.
226. AVM_2 : शक्यासिद्धिः
227. AVM_2 : बाधितं
228. AVM_2 : ०व्यवच्छेदकप्रत्ययप्रसङ्गाच्च
229. AVM_2 : व्यवच्छेद्यत्वेन
230. AVM_2 : शक्यत्वेन
231. AV(K) and AVM_2 : ०च्छक्यानन्त्यं, AV(P) : शक्त्यानन्त्यम्, Changed according to AVT(B). AVM_2: स्वत्वस्य च for च स्वत्वस्य
232. AVM_2 omits आदि.
233. AVM_2 : अभावस्य प्रतीतिः
234. AVM_2 adds संयुक्त after संयुज्यते.
235. AVM_2 : संयोगमात्रप्रतोतेश्च
236. AVM_2 omits the word.
237. AVM_2 : सकर्मत्वम्
238. AVM_2 : घञादिप्रयोगः साधुत्वार्थमात्रम्
239. AVM_2 : ०मतानुसारिणः
240. AVM_2 : ०यत्लानुभव.
241. AVM_2 omits the word.
242. AVM_2 omits क्वचिदाश्रयत्वादिकम् and वा.
243. AVM_2 adds क्वचित् before इति
244. AVM_2 omits the word.
245. AVM_2 : ०यत्लानुभव.
246. AVM_2 : इति श्रीतार्किकशिरोमणिभट्टाचार्यकृत आख्यातवादः समाप्तः।। श्रीकालिकायै जगन्मात्रे नमो नमः।।

भवानन्दसिद्धान्तवागीशकृता आख्यातवादटिप्पनी

।।ओं दुर्गायै नमः।।

१. **आख्यातस्ये**ति। आख्यातत्वं च लकारत्वं दशलकारसाधारणं तदज्ञानदशायां च शाब्दबोधस्तिप्त्वादिना शक्तिभ्रमादेवेति ध्येयम्।[1] **यत्नो** यत्नत्वविशिष्टः। इदं च जीवनयोनियत्ननिवृत्त्याख्ययत्नयोरनभ्युपगमे तदभ्युपगमे तद्व्यावृत्त-प्रवृत्तित्वमेव शक्यतावच्छेदकम्[2], तच्चेश्वरयत्नयाधारणं तेन ''ईश्वरो वेदं वक्ति'' इत्यादौ नानुपपत्तिः। **सर्वाख्याते**ति। सर्वजातीयाख्यातेत्यर्थः[3]। पक्ष्यति पाकं करिष्यति अपचत् पाकम् अकरोत् इत्यादिक्रमेण दशलकाराणामेव विवरणादित्यर्थः। **विवरणाद्** अर्थकथनात्।[4] ननु विवरणं शक्तिग्राहकं न, शब्दविषयाः शक्तेः पदार्थत्ववाक्यार्थत्वयोरभावादत आह–**व्यवहारादिवे**ति। तथा चानुमानविधयेति भावः। तच्च आख्यातं यत्नबोधकं बाधकाभावे सत्यभियुक्तैर्यत्नार्थकधातुना प्रतिपाद्यमानार्थकत्वात् इति क्रमेण बोध्यम्। **बाधकं विने**ति। तेन पचति पाकयत्नवानिति विवरणे धर्मिणो न वाच्यत्वम्। तत्रान्यलभ्यत्वस्यैव बाधकत्वात्। **व्युत्पत्तेः** शक्तिग्रहात्। ननु धर्मिण इव यत्नस्याप्यन्यलभ्यत्वमेव बाधकं पाकादिना क्रियाविशेषेण यत्नानुमानस्य वक्ष्यमाणत्वात् अत आह–**किं करोती**ति। किम्विषयकयत्नवानित्यर्थके प्रश्ने पाकविषयकयत्नार्थकत्वं विनानुपपत्तेरित्यर्थः। यद्रूपविशिष्टजिज्ञासितस्य सम्बन्धः प्रश्नवाक्येन प्रतिपद्यते तद्रूपविशिष्टे विशिष्टतत्सम्बन्धबोधेनैव प्रश्ननिवृत्तेः। आम्रस्य को रस इति प्रश्ने मधुर इत्यस्यापि रसपदावृत्त्या तादृशबोधजनकत्वादिति भावः। **अचेतने** सचेतनबोधकपदसमभिव्याहृते।।

२. एतन्मतं दूषयति–**अन्यदीये**ति। रथगमनानुकूलनोदनाभिघातसंयोगवति निश्चलेऽपि पुरुष इत्यर्थः। ननु गमनोपहितव्यापारस्य[5] लक्षणया बोधनेनैव नैष दोष इत्यतो **जानाती**त्यादि **द्वेष्टी**त्यन्तेन क्रियानुकूलकृतेर्बाधात् अप्रतीतेश्च[6]। तत्र ज्ञानाद्युपहितात्ममनोयोगादिबोधनेऽनतिप्रसङ्गादाह–**विद्यत** इत्यादि। अत्र च सत्ता विद्यमानकालसम्बन्धतः तदनुकूलव्यापाराभावस्तु[7] घटत्वादावतिस्फुट

एव। **निद्राती**ति। निद्रा च मेध्यान्तःकरणसंयोगः[8] तदनुकूलव्यापाराभावश्चात्मनि स्फुट एव, तदाश्रयत्वं च तादृशपरम्परया बोध्यम्। तेन मनो निद्रातीत्यादेर्न प्रसङ्गः। यद्यपि सुषुप्तिदशायां मेध्यान्तः-करणसंयोगाभावात्[9] निद्रातीति प्रयोगानुपपत्तिः तथापि मेध्यान्तरावच्छिन्नमनः-संयोग[10] एव निद्रा, तदानीमपि तदवच्छिन्नगगनादिसंयोगोऽस्तीति भावः। नन्वेतावता तादृशकृतौ व्यापारे वा मास्तु शक्तिः आश्रयत्वशक्तिस्तु कुत इत्यत आह–**गत्यादिमत्त्वे**ति। **मात्र**पदं तु व्यापारादिव्यवच्छेदकानुवादकमेव। **ज्ञाना**दिपदं आश्रयत्वं समवायेना-वच्छेदकतया बोध्यम्। तेनात्मनि चैत्रशरीरे च जानातीत्यादेर्नानुपपत्तिः। **नश्यती**त्यादि। अत्र नाशप्रतियोगिनो घटादेर्नाशाश्रयत्वासम्भवात् तदाश्रय-कपालादौ तदानीं नश्यतीत्यप्रयोगाच्च प्रतियोगित्वे लक्षणेत्यर्थः[11]। **निरूढे**ति। अनादिप्रयोगानुसारिणी लक्षणेत्यर्थः। तत्रानादिप्रयोगेऽपि यत्नत्वापेक्षया गौरवान्न[12] शक्तिः। यथा गुणवाचकशुक्लादिपदानां गुणिनीत्यर्थः। ननु चैत्रो जानातीत्यादौ आश्रयत्वादिसम्बन्धेन साक्षादन्वयोऽस्तु[13], अतएव[14] मणिकृतोऽपि[15] तथैव वर्णयन्ति इत्यत आह–**चैत्र** इत्यादि[16]। यदि धात्वर्थप्रातिपदिकार्थयोर्भेदेन साक्षादन्वयबोधस्तदा तण्डुलपाकयोः कर्मत्व-स्य संसर्गविधया[17] भानात् तण्डुलीयपाकानुकूलकृतिमानित्याद्यः[18], चैत्रपाकयोः[19] कर्तृत्वस्य संसर्गविधया भानात् चैत्रीयपाकानुकूलव्यापारजन्यफलशाली[20] तण्डुल इति द्वितीयो[21] बोधः स्यादित्यर्थः। स्तोकं पचति इत्यादौ स्तोकपाकयोः साक्षादन्व- यबोधा**द्भेदेने**ति, तण्डुल[22] पचतीत्यादौ विभक्त्यर्थद्वारा[23] पाकादेरन्वयबोधात् **साक्षादि**ति[24]। **तद्भानस्य** आश्रयत्वादिभानस्य। अत्र अभेदातिरिक्तसम्बन्धेन[25] तण्डुल-पदजन्यतण्डुलप्रकारकबोधं प्रति विभक्तिजन्या प्रत्ययजन्या वा[26] उपस्थितिः[27] कारणम्[28], समानविशेष्यकत्वं[29] प्रत्यासत्तिः। तेन पाकादेर्विभक्तिजन्यो-पस्थित्यभावात् तण्डुलः पचतीत्यादौ नान्वयबोधः। यद् वा तादृशसम्बन्धेन[30] तण्डुलपदजन्यकर्मताविशेष्यकतण्डुलप्रकारकशाब्दबोधं[31] प्रति तण्डुलपदोत्तर-विभक्तिजन्यकर्मोपस्थितिः[32] कारणम्। एवं कारणत्वादौ विभक्त्यर्थे ऊह्यः।[33] तण्डुलः पचतीत्यादौ तथाविधफलाभावात् न[34] कार्यकारणभावान्तरं कल्प्यते[35]। यद् वा तण्डुलपदजन्यतण्डुलप्रकारकपाकविशेष्यकबोधं[36] प्रति विभक्तिजन्य-पाकोपस्थितिः कारणम्, तादृशोपस्थितिस्तु लक्षणयैव सुलभा, तण्डुलः पचतीत्यादौ तादृशोपस्थित्यभावान्नान्वयबोधः। एवं धातुजन्यधात्वर्थप्रकारान्वय-बोधं[37] प्रति विभक्तिजन्योपस्थितिः समानविशेष्यकत्वप्रत्यासत्त्या कारणं बोध्यम्[38]। तेन धात्वर्थस्यापि नामार्थे साक्षाद्विशेषणतया[39] न भानमिति मणिकृतां पुनराशयः[40]। तण्डुलः पचतीत्यादौ[41] तादृशबोधापत्तिभयेन[42] नामार्थस्य[43] धात्वर्थे साक्षादन्वयबोधबाधकः[44] पूर्वकार्यकारणभावोऽस्तु[45], चैत्रो जानातीत्यादौ

धात्वर्थस्य साक्षान्नामार्थे[46] भानेऽतिप्रसङ्गाभावादुत्तर:[47] कार्यकारणभाव: किमर्थं[48] कल्पनीय:? न च चैत्रो[49] जानातीत्यादौ धात्वर्थस्य क्वचिदेवान्वयबोध[50] इति नियमोपपादनाय अवश्यं तदादर इति वाच्यम्। तत्र धातुजन्यज्ञानादि-प्रकारकबोधं प्रति[51] प्रथमान्तपदोपस्थितेरेव[52] नियामकताया आवश्यकत्वात्। अन्यथा आश्रयत्वलक्षणावादिनामपि[53] आश्रयत्वस्य तथाविधनियमोपपादनाय तन्नियामकताया अवश्याभ्युपेयत्वादिति युक्त: पन्था:[54]। न च चैत्र: पचति तण्डुल: इत्यादावाख्यातेन कर्मत्वानभिधानात्[55] द्वितीयायाश्चैत्र: पच्यते इत्यादावपि कर्तृत्वस्यानभिधानात् तृतीयाया एवासाधुत्वज्ञानादेव[56] नैतादृशप्रयोगादन्वयबोध[57] इति वाच्यम्। एवमप्यसाधुत्वज्ञानाभावदशायां तथान्वयबोधस्य दुर्वारत्वात्। वस्तुतस्तु अनभिहिते कर्मत्वे तत्प्रकारक-बोधे[58] एव द्वितीया साधु:। अत: कर्मत्वादिसंसर्गबोधे[59] द्वितीयादेर्न प्रसक्तिरिति[60]।।

३. आख्यातस्य यत्नवाचकत्वम्[61], करोतेर्यत्नार्थकत्वे स्यात्, तदेव तु[62] कुत इत्यत आह–**कृञश्चे**ति। कृञो यत्नार्थकत्वे

कृताकृतविभागेन कर्तृरूपव्यवस्थया[63] [ ]

इत्याचार्ययुक्तिं दर्शयति–**क्रिये**त्यादिना। क्रिया संयोगादिरूपा, अङ्कुरस्यापि ईश्वरयत्नजन्यत्वात् तत्प्रतिसन्धानेन कृतव्यवहाराच्च[64] प्रतिसन्धान-पर्यन्तानुसरणम्[65]। कर्तृरूपव्यवस्थामाह–**ज्ञात्रादी**ति। अन्यथा कर्तरि कृत:[66] कृत्याश्रयबोधकत्वे कृञो यत्नार्थबोधकत्वे[67] च कृतिकर्ता इत्यन्वयबोध: स्यादिति भाव:। **आश्रयपरे**ति। सविषयकधातूत्तरकर्तृकृतामाश्रया[68] एव निरूढलक्षणया[69] ज्ञात्रादिस्थलेऽपि[70] क्लृप्तत्वात् कृञो यत्नार्थकत्वे तृजश्चाश्रयकत्वे[71] कृत्याश्रयकर्तृपदार्थ:[72] स्यादित्यर्थ:। **क्रियाया** इत्यादि। प्रथमे **तदाश्रय:** क्रियाश्रय:[73], द्वितीये **कारकमात्रं कर्तृपदार्थ: स्यात्,** क्रियानुकूलव्यापारस्य सर्वकारकसाधारण्यादित्यर्थ:। अङ्कुर:[74] कृत इत्युक्ते ईश्वरयत्नकत्वमादाय[75] उपपत्ते: सम्भवात्[76] **बीजादिने**ति। **तस्य** कृञ:। **यदी**ति[77]। वस्तुतोऽचेतनेऽपि[78] रथादौ कारकमात्रे च कर्तृपदप्रयोग इति। तदुक्तम्–

स्वव्यापारे च कर्तृत्वं सर्वत्रैवास्ति कारके [ ]

इत्यादि[79]। **तत्प्रयोग:** कर्तृपदप्रयोग:। आख्यातस्यानुकूलव्यापारार्थकत्वे युक्तिमाह[80]**–एवं चे**त्यादिना। एवं कृञो यत्नार्थकत्वसिद्धौ[81] अचेतने काष्ठादौ रथो गच्छतीत्यादौ गत्यादिमत्त्वप्रतीतेराश्रयत्वलक्षणाया[82] एव उभयसम्मत-

त्वादुपेक्षितम्[83]। **जनकव्यापार** इति। व्यापारत्वं[84] संयोग- यत्नस्पन्दादिसाधारणं जन्यभावत्वं[85] ईश्वरकर्तृकेऽपि कार्ये ईश्वरस्यापि संयोगलक्षणव्यापार-वत्त्वान्नातिप्रसङ्गः[86]। तण्डुलक्रयणादेरपि पाकजनकव्यापारवत्त्वात्[87] तदानीमपि पचतीत्यादिप्रयोगापत्तिं[88] वारयति-**तण्डुलक्रयणादेश्चे**ति।।

४. **तर्ही**ति। आख्यातस्य यत्नबोधकत्वे[89] इत्यर्थः। **पाकादिने**ति। तादात्म्येनेति[90] हेतुत्वाभिप्रायेण[91]। इत्यरथा तु[92] पाको यत्नजन्यः तादृशपाकत्वादिति क्रमेण बोध्यम्। ननु करोतिना विवरणादाख्यातस्य यत्नवाचकत्वं[93] वास्तु[94] पचति पाकजनकयत्नवानिति विवरणात् तथा स्यादत आह-**पचती**ति। **तात्पर्ये**ति। अनुमानलभ्यत्वादिति[95] भावः। **एवं यत्नस्या**नुमानिकत्वेन[96]। **तस्य** यत्नस्य। नन्वध्याहृतयत्नपदार्थे[97] वर्तमानत्वान्वयो[98] भविष्यतीत्याशङ्क्य निरस्यति-**अन्यत्रे**ति[99]। **अन्यत्र** चैत्रः पचतीत्यादेरन्यत्र **धात्वर्थक्रियायां** जानातीत्यादौ, **स्वार्थव्यापारे** काष्ठं पचतीत्यादौ। तथाचाध्याहृतपदार्थे[100] यत्नेन लडर्थवर्तमानत्वान्वयधीः।

आश्रयत्वबोधकाख्यातपदजन्यवर्तमानत्वप्रकारान्वयबोधे[101] प्रकृतीभूत-धातुजन्योपस्थिते-र्व्यापार-बोधकाख्यात-जन्य-वर्तमानत्व-प्रकारान्वय-बोधे[102] आख्यात-जन्यव्यापारोपस्थितेः समानविशेष्यकतया हेतुत्वकल्पनात्[103]। पूर्वोक्तरीत्या तस्यापि[104] निष्कर्षो बोध्यः। ननु[105] पाकजनकवर्तमान-यत्नतथाविधव्यापारयोश्च कालिकी व्याप्तिः[106], तथाचाख्यातेन तादृशव्यापारे बोधिते[107] अयं कालः पाकजनकवर्तमानयत्नवान् तथाविधव्यापारवत्त्वादित्यनुमानं भविष्यतीत्याशङ्क्य निषेधति-**न चे**त्यादिना। **यत्नविगमेऽपी**ति। तथाच न कालिकी व्याप्तिरिति भावः[108]। व्यापारस्य संयोगादिलक्षणस्यानुवृत्तेर्न तादृशव्याप्तिरिति भावः। ननु स्थूलकालमादाय तथा व्याप्तिर्भविष्यति इत्यतो[109] दोषान्तरमाह[110]-**धर्मिविशेषे**ति[111]। **तद्व्यधिकरणे**ति[112]। **तद्व्यधिकरणस्य**[113] यत्नव्यधिकरणस्य[114] काष्ठादिव्यापारस्य। तथाच दैशिकव्याप्त्यापि[115] न[116] तथोपपत्तिरिति भावः। चैत्रः पाकजनकवर्तमानयत्नवान्[117] चैत्रत्वे सति पाकजनकवर्तमानव्यापारवत्त्वादिति[118] दैशिकव्याप्तिमूलकमनुमानमाशङ्क्य[119] निषेधति-**चैतन्ये**त्यादिना।[120] **तेन** पाकजनकवर्तमानव्यापारेण। **चैत्रत्वाद्य-प्रतीताविति**[121] शब्दात् तत्प्रतीतिर्नास्त्येव[122] उपायान्तरात् तत्प्रतीतिस्तु न सावत्रिकी, तादृशयत्नवत्त्वप्रतीतिस्तु सर्वत्रैवेति तदर्थं तत्र शक्तिः स्वीकार्येति भावः। **शोभन** इति। शोभनत्वस्य स्थाल्यादि-साधारणत्वात् शोभनत्वे सति तारृशव्यापारवत्त्वं न यत्नानुमापकमिति भावः[123]। **लाक्षणिकत्वादि**ति। तादृशयत्नबोधस्य प्रकारान्तरेणानुपपत्तेर्लक्षणायां वर्तमानत्वान्वयेऽपि[124] तत्र सुघट एवेति[125] भावः।।

५. व्यापारे शक्तावपि न सर्वत्र शक्त्या प्रयोगोपपत्तिः[126], तथाच लाघवं किमित्यतो न कृतमित्याशयेनाह[127]—**मैवमि**त्यादि[128]। **लाघवेने**ति। व्यापारत्वस्य जन्यत्वात्मकतया[129] यत्नत्वस्य[130] जातित्वाल्लाघवमिति भावः। शङ्कते—**यत्नमि**ति। **लाघवात्** जनकयत्नत्वापेक्षया जनकत्वस्य[131] लघुत्वात्[132]। **अचेतनेऽपी**ति। स्थाल्यादावपि, पाकजनकसंयोगादेः सत्त्वादिति भावः। यत्नशक्तावपि[133] अदृष्टजनककृतिकाले[134] पचतीतिप्रयोगापत्तिं[135] वारयति—**पाकजनके**त्यादिना।[136] अतएवादृष्टजनककृतेस्तदहष्टजन्यकार्यं प्रति अजनकत्वादेव। **तज्जनके**ति। क्षित्यादिजनकेत्यर्थः। ननु कृतीष्टसाधनतावादिमते तादृशकृतेः[137] क्षित्यादिजनकत्वस्य वेदेनैव[138] बोधनात् कथं नार्थान्तरम् अत आह—**भावे वे**ति। **त्वयापि**[139] जनकशक्तिवादिना[140] अपि। स्वमतमाह—**यत्नमात्रमि**ति। **विषयित्वम्**[141] अजनकेऽपीत्यतो **जनकत्वमि**ति। तस्य स्वरूपसम्बन्धविशेषोऽन्यथा वास्तु[142] उभयथापि सम्बन्धविधया तस्य भानं[143] न विरुद्धमिति भावः। जनकत्वं च चेष्टादिद्वारा विलक्षणमेव[144] संसर्गतया भासते। अतएवास्मदादिकर्तृके ईश्वरः पचतीत्यादेर्न प्रसङ्गः[145]।

६. **सामानाधिकरण्ये**ति[146]। नामाख्यातयोर्भिन्नप्रवृत्तिनिमित्तयोरेकस्मिन्नर्थे वृत्तिः सामानाधिकरण्यम्। आख्यातस्य यत्नाद्याश्रयबोधकत्वं विना अनुपपन्नमिति भावः। **अन्यथा** कर्तृकर्मणोरनभिधाने। **तयोः** तृतीयाद्वितीययोः[147] **अनभिहिताधिकारीयत्वात्** कर्तृकर्मणोरनभिधान एवानुशिष्टत्वात्[148]। ननु कृत्यनभिधान एव तृतीयेति न तदनुरोधेन[149] कर्तरि शक्तिसिद्धिरत[150] आह—**कृत्यभिधानस्य**[151] इति। **अविशिष्टत्वात्** कर्तृकर्माख्यातसाधारणत्वात्[152]। तथाच तत्रापि तृतीया न स्यादिति भावः। इदं च प्राचां मते। स्वमते तु[153] तृतीययैव कृत्यभिधानात्[154]। **नियमः** अभिहितानभिहितनियमः। तथाचाख्यातेनानभिहितत्वात्[155] कर्तृसंख्यायां तृतीया कर्मसंख्यायां च द्वितीयेति भावः। "सर्वं हि वाक्यं क्रियया परिसमाप्यते" इति न्यायेन चैत्रः सुन्दर इत्यादि[156] वाक्ये अस्तीत्यादिपदाध्याहारे[157] तिङर्थसंख्याया एव बोध इति कदाचित् भ्रमात् अतस्तदुपेक्ष्य सक्रियमेव वाक्यमुदाहरति—**चैत्रेण दृष्टो घट** इति। **न तदभिधायकत्वं** न संख्याभिधायकत्वम्। तथाच चैत्रः पचतीत्यादावपि तृतीया स्यादिति भावः। **तादृशसुपं** द्वित्वबोधकसुपम्। न चैकवचनस्य[158] द्वित्वे लक्षणा, सुब्विभक्तौ लक्षणाया असाधुत्वात्[159]। अतएव

द्व्येकयोर्द्विवचनैकवचने [पा. सू. 1-4-22]

इति सूत्रं[160] नियमपरतया[161] व्याख्यातं शाब्दिकैः। एवं चैत्रपदोत्तरसुपस्तथा

लक्षणायां चैत्रद्वयं मैत्रपदोत्तरसुपश्च लक्षणायां मैत्रद्वयमित्यादिकं[162] प्रतीयेत। न च[163] चैत्रमैत्रोभयम्, सुब्विभक्तेः प्रकृत्यर्थमात्रगतत्वार्थबोधकत्वनियमात्। न चैकवचनेन एकत्वरूपेणोपस्थापिते चैत्रमैत्रे[164] कथं तिबुपस्थापित-विरुद्धद्वित्वान्वय[165] इति वाच्यम्। एकत्वस्य तत्राविवक्षिततत्वात्। विवक्षिततत्वेन वा एको[166] मैत्र एकश्चैत्रः उभौ गमनानुकूलकृतिमन्तौ इत्यन्वयबोधे बाधकाभावादिति भावः[167]। नन्वेकवचनेषु[168] तिबादिषु[169] एकत्वे शक्तिर्न[170] सिध्यति अत[171] आह-**लाघवादि**ति। सुत्वेन[172] अम्त्वेन टात्वादिना च[173] नानाशक्तिकल्पनामपेक्ष्य एकवचनत्वेन एकत्वे शक्तिकल्पने लाघवात्। तिबेकवचनस्यापि[174] सामान्यतः शक्तिसिद्धिरिति[175] भावः। एकवचनत्वं च एकवचनत्वेनाभियुक्तैः परिभाषितत्वम्–

तान्येकवचनद्विवचनबहुवचनानि [पा.सू. 1-4-102]

इति सूत्रे। तिबेकवचनद्विवचनबहुवचनानां[176] तथा परिभाषितत्वात् तद्ग्रहे[177] शक्तिभ्रमादेव व्यवहारः। एतेन एकवचनत्वं नैकत्वशक्तत्वं आत्माश्रयात्, नैकत्वबोधकत्वम्[178], पदमात्रस्यैव लक्षणादिना[179] एकत्वबोधकत्वादिति[180] दूषणमनवकाशम्। वस्तुतः पचतीत्युक्ते शक्त्या लक्षणया वा उपस्थिते कर्तरि[181] एकत्वस्यैव नियमतः प्रतीतेः एकत्वे सुप्त्वादिनैव[182] शक्तिः। न च न्यायमते[183] एकत्वविशिष्टकर्तर्येव लक्षणेति वाच्यम्, नियमतः प्रतीयमानेऽपि लक्षणायां यत्नेन[184] तथात्वस्य सुवचत्वात्। स्वस्तिष्ठतीत्यादावव्ययोत्तरं सुबनुसन्धानं विनापि एकत्वप्रतीतेरिति[185] स्थितम्। एकत्वे शक्तिरित्यप्याहुः[186]। **कर्तृसंख्या**[187] इत्यारभ्य **एतदपि**[188] **नास्ति** इत्यन्तमेकं मतम्। **कृते**ति। तदुत्तरसुप एव संख्योपस्थितिसम्भवे कृतः संख्यायां न[189] शक्तिरिति। तथाच[190] चैत्रो ग्रामं गतवानित्यादावपि तृतीया चैत्रेण ग्रामो गत[191] इत्यादावपि[192] द्वितीया स्यात् कृतोऽनभिहितकर्तृकर्मसंख्याकत्वादिति[193] भावः। ननु[194] आख्यात एवायमुक्तानुक्तविभागः[195] कृत्तद्धितसमासेषु[196] कर्त्रादेरभि-धानानभिधानाभ्यां नियमो भविष्यति। आख्यातकृत्तद्धितसमासभेदेन[197] अनभिहिते[198] [पा. सू. 2-3-1]

इत्यादिसूत्रार्थभेदोऽपि इष्ट एवेत्यतः [आह-] **किंचे**ति। **न नियमः** कर्त्राख्याते कर्तुरेव, कर्माख्याते कर्मण एव संख्याभिधानमिति नियमाभावः। तदेवाह-**पदार्थे**ति। **पदार्थतावच्छेदकावच्छिन्नस्य** एकत्वावच्छिन्नस्य।[199] **कर्तृकर्मसाधारण्येने**ति। तथाच तण्डुलं पचतीत्यत्रापि कदाचिदाख्यातेन तण्डुलसंख्याभिधाने तण्डुलः पचतीति स्यात्, चैत्रेण पच्यते तण्डुल इत्यत्रापि

कर्तृसंख्याभिधाने चैत्रः पच्यते तण्डुल इति च[200] स्यादिति भावः। ननु कर्त्रेकत्वत्वादिना[201] शक्तिबोधादेव[202] न कर्मादिसाधारण्यम् अत आह–**कर्त्रेके**ति[203]। न च मैत्रं ग्रामं नयति चैत्र[204] इत्यादौ कर्मणोऽपि कर्तृत्वात् कथं न[205] साधारण्यमिति वाच्यम्। तत्तत्क्रियाकर्त्रेकत्वत्वादिना[206] शक्यत्वात् एव[207] शक्त्यानन्त्यस्येष्टत्वात्[208]। **अभिधेयत्वं** विशेषणतयैवेति[209] शेषः। **शक्तौ गौरवं** कर्त्रेकत्वत्वेन कर्मैकत्वत्वेन[210] च विभिन्नशक्तिकल्पनात् एकत्वत्वापेक्षया[211] कर्त्रेकत्वत्वस्य शक्यतावच्छेदकत्वे गौरवम्। अस्मन्मते एकवचनत्वं[212] तिप्त्वादिकं[213] वा शक्ततावच्छेदकं तन्मते तु कर्त्राख्यातैकवचनत्वादिकं कर्त्रादिविशेष्यकबोधजनकतिप्त्वादिकं वेति[214] शक्ततावच्छेदकमिति[215] गौरवमिति। ननु कर्त्रादिषु शक्त्यभ्युपगमेऽपि[216] कथं संख्यान्वयनियमः कथं वा न[217] गौरवमित्यत[218] आह–**तस्मादि**ति। **आत्मनेपदत्वेने**ति[219]। परस्मैपदस्य कर्मणि[220] कदाचिदप्यप्रयोगात्[221] इति[222]। **तत्तद्रूपेण** तिप्त्वादिना[223]। **एकपदे**ति। तथाच कर्त्राख्यातजन्यसंख्याप्रकारकबोधे[224] कर्माख्यातजन्यसंख्याप्रकारकबोधे[225] च तत्तदाख्यातजन्यकर्तृकर्मोपस्थितेः कारणत्वान्नान्यत्र संख्यान्वय इति भावः। **वाच्यगामित्वम्**[226] आख्यातवाच्यकर्तृकर्मविशेष्यकान्वयबोधविषयत्वम्। **अव्युत्पन्नमि**ति। आख्यातजन्ये कर्तृबोधे[227] कर्मतात्पर्यज्ञानस्य[228] तद्ग्राहकप्रकरणादेर्वा कर्मबोधे च[229] कर्तृतात्पर्यज्ञानस्य तद्ग्राहकप्रकरणादेर्वा[230] विरोधित्वं फलबलात् कल्प्यते इति भावः। यद्वा तदाख्यातजन्ये कर्तृबोधे[231] कर्मबोधकविभक्तिसमभिव्याहृताख्यातजन्यकर्त्रुपस्थितेः कर्मबोधे च तृतीयान्तपदसमभिव्याहृताख्यातजन्योपस्थितेः[232] कारणत्वम्, चैत्रश्चैत्रेण तण्डुलं तण्डुलः पक्ष्यत इत्यादिप्रयोगस्त्विष्ट एव उभयवाक्यार्थतात्पर्ये सर्वैरेवावृत्त्या तादृश- समूहालम्बनबोधोपगमादिति। **चैत्रः पक्ष्यते तण्डुल** इति। पक्ष्यत इत्यस्य कर्तरि कर्मणि च साधुत्वात् उभयस्याभिधाने[233] उभयत्र प्रथमा स्यात्। चैत्रः[234] पाककर्ता तण्डुलः पाककर्म इत्याकारकश्चान्वयबोध इति भावः। ननु तथापि मैत्रः पच्यते तण्डुलमिति कर्तृमात्रबोधकत्वेन प्रयोगः स्यात् अत आह–**कर्तरी**ति। यथा च तथाविधकर्तृबोधे यगाद्यसमभिव्याहृताख्यातजन्यकर्त्रुपस्थितेः कारणत्वात् न तथाप्रयोग इति भावः।।

७. लाघवेन आख्यातस्य[235] यत्नमात्रशक्तौ कर्तृकर्मसंख्याभिधानानभिधानाभ्याम्[236] उक्तानुक्तविभागे संख्यायाः कर्तृकर्मसाधारण्येनान्वयबोधोपपादनमेव मूलबाधकमुद्धरति[237]–**भावने**ति। **समानपदे**ति। इदं चासत्तिकल्पने[238] उपजीव्यम्। एकस्यार्थस्यान्वयबोधानुरोधेनाव्यवधानेनान्वयप्रतियोगिनः[239] पदार्थान्तरस्योपस्थितेरावश्यकत्वे अर्थान्तरेणापि सामग्रीसत्त्वात् अन्वयबोध[240]

इति भावः। न च कृतिसाध्यत्वादिविशेष्यधात्वर्थे[241] संख्यान्वय इति[242] वाच्यम्, आख्यातजन्यसंख्यान्वयबोधे तज्जन्यभावनाप्रकारकसामग्र्या[243] एव नियामकत्वे तात्पर्यात्। भावनाया एवान्वये[244] किं नियामकं तद्दर्शयति–**भावनायाश्चे**ति। भावनायां विशेषणतया धात्वर्थस्यान्वयेन उक्तं नियामकमतो[245] **विशेष्यत्वेने**ति। कर्मत्वाद्यनवरुद्धं तदर्थविशेषणं[246] तेन तण्डुलादिव्युदासः। धात्वर्थस्य व्युदासायाह[247]–**प्रथमान्ते**ति। न च तदेवास्त्विति वाच्यम्, प्रथमान्तपदोपस्थाप्यत्वस्य नीलो घटोऽस्तीत्यादौ तादात्म्येन घटादिविशेषणे नीले चन्द्र इव मुखमस्तीत्यादौ च[248] चन्द्रे तत्सादृश्ये च सत्त्वात। तत्र च भावनान्वयविरहेण तद्बाधकत्वात् इतराविशेषणत्वरूपस्य[249] कर्मत्वाद्यनवरुद्धत्वस्य तत्राभावादिति। मन्मते अव्ययात् प्रथमैव तन्मते स्वस्तिष्ठति देव इत्यादावधिकरणत्वावरुद्धस्वर्गादिवारणाय तदिति कश्चित्। वस्तुतश्चैत्रः पचति तण्डुल इत्यादौ[250] प्रथमायां कर्मत्वशक्तिभ्रमेण तण्डुलकर्मकपाकानुकूलकृतिमानिति अन्वयबोधात् तण्डुलादिवारणाय **कर्मत्वाद्यनवरुद्ध** इति[251]। तथाचाख्यातजन्यभावनाप्रकारकबोधे समानविशेष्यत्वप्रत्यासत्त्या प्रथमान्तपदजन्योपस्थितिः कारणं विशेषणतया तदन्वयबोधजनकसमभिव्याहारस्य सहकारीति भावः[252]। ननु प्रथमान्तपदोपस्थाप्यत्वस्य[253] विशेषणत्वेनैव कुतो नान्वय इत्यत आह–**तथैवे**ति। विशेष्यत्वेनैवेत्यर्थः। तथैवानुभवादिति भावः। धात्वर्थस्यापि[254] भावनायामन्वितत्वात्[255] स एव विशेष्योऽस्त्वत आह–**धात्वर्थस्ये**ति। तथा च विशेषणतया धात्वर्थान्वयबोधे[256] आख्यातार्थभावनोपस्थितेः भावनाप्रकारकबोधे च प्रथमान्तपदजन्योपस्थितेः कारणत्वस्य क्लृप्तत्वात् अन्यत्र तदन्वये नियामकाभावादिति[257] भावः। नन्वनन्यगत्या भावाख्यात- जन्यभावनाप्रकारकबोधे[258] धात्वर्थोपस्थितेरेव कारणत्वरूपं व्युत्पत्त्यन्तरं[259] कल्प्यमत आह–**भावनाया** इति[260]। भावना आख्यातार्थः। स च प्रकृते आश्रयता, चैत्रः स्वपितीत्यादौ[261] कृतिव्यापारयोरप्रतीतेः। तथाच चैत्रेण सुप्यते इत्यादौ चैत्रवृत्त्याश्रयताया निरूपकत्वसम्बन्धेन[262] स्वापेऽन्वये चैत्रेण सुप्यते न मैत्रेणेत्यादौ[263] नञर्थान्वयानुपपत्तिः, निरूपकत्वसम्बन्धस्य अभावप्रतियोगितावच्छेदकत्वाभावात्।[264] एवं च चैत्रादिनिरूपिताश्रयताया धात्वर्थस्वापादौ[265] आश्रयत्वसम्बन्धेनान्वयो वाच्यः। तथाच **बाधात्**[266] चैत्राश्रयतायाः स्वापे गगनाश्रयतायाः स्थितौ बाधादित्यर्थः। **विशेष्यविरहात्** विशेष्यत्वेनान्वयधीविषयविरहात्[267]। **अतएव** संख्याया अनन्वितत्वादेव। **औत्सर्गिकं** प्रथमोपस्थितम्[268], तथैव साधुत्वादिति भावः[269]। **एवं** भावनाया अनन्वितत्वे। **यथायथमि**ति। वर्तमानत्वं लटः इष्टसाधनत्वं लिङ इत्यर्थः[270]।

इष्टसाधनत्वमपि भावप्रत्ययार्थं[271] इति बोधयितुमिदमुपन्यस्तम्। तदर्थस्तु[272] मणिकारमते तु[273] **धात्वर्थ एवे**ति। **आदिभ्याम्**[274] अतीतत्वादिकृति-साध्यत्वपरिग्रहः। चैत्रेण सुप्यते इत्यादौ चैत्रवृत्तिवर्तमानस्वाप[275] इत्यन्वय-बोधः। वृत्तित्वं तृतीयार्थः। चैत्रेण[276] सुप्येत चैत्रेण पच्येत इत्यादौ च चैत्रवृत्तिस्वाप इष्टसाधनं चैत्रवृत्तिकृतिसाध्यः पाक[277] इष्टसाधनमिति रीत्यान्वयबोधः[278]। **तदबोधकानां** वर्तमानत्वाद्यबोधकानाम्। **प्रयोगे**ति। पाक इत्यादौ केवलधातोरसाधुत्वादिति। नन्वाश्रयत्वसम्बन्धेन भावनाविशेष्यत्वस्य संख्यान्वयनियामकत्वे पच्यते तण्डुल इत्यादौ कथं तदन्वय इत्यत आह–**भावनाया** इति[279]। **अन्यथा** वक्ष्यमाणक्रमेण। तथाच साक्षात्परम्परासाधारणं भावनाविशेष्यकत्वमात्रं[280] नियामकमिति भावः। **तव** वैयाकरणस्य[281]। यथा त्वन्मते परस्मैपदेन कर्मणोऽनभिधानं[282] तथा मन्मते कृतेः[283] कर्मणि नान्वयः। यथा तव कर्तरि[284] यकोऽसाधुत्वं तथा **मम**ाश्रयत्वसंसर्गेण[285] कृतेरन्वये यकोऽसाधुत्वम्। यथा तवैकदा उभयाबोधकत्वं[286] तथा ममैकदा उभयत्रान्वयबोध[287] इत्यर्थः। इति[288] क्रमेणोदाहरति–**मैत्रेणे**ति[289]। कृतेर्विषयतया तण्डुलेऽन्वये तण्डुलवृत्तिसंख्याया[290] उक्तत्वात् तत्र प्रथमा, मैत्रवृत्तिसंख्याया अनुक्तत्वात् तत्र तृतीया, मैत्रवृत्तिपाकभावनाविषयस्तण्डुल[291] इति चान्वय-बोधः[292]। एवमन्यत्राप्यूह्यम्। **व्यापारे**ति आश्रयत्वादेरप्युपलक्षणं[293] तेन जानातीत्यादिपरिग्रहः[294]। कर्त्रादिशक्तौ वैयाकरणयुक्तिं[295] दूषयति–**भिन्नाभ्यामि**ति। घटो घट[296] इत्यादौ सामानाधिकरण्याव्यवहारात् भिन्नाभ्यामिति। **बोधकत्वं** शक्तिलक्षणान्यतरसम्बन्धनप्रतिपादकत्वम्, न तु शाब्दधीजनकत्वम्, कृतिशक्तत्वेऽप्यविरोधादिति। **सिद्धमि**ति। तथाच तदनुरोधात् न कर्तरि शक्तिसिद्धिरिति[297] भावः। **अन्यादृशम्** एकवृत्तिधर्मद्वयबोधकत्वादिरूपम्। **न वार्यते** कृतिशक्त्येति शेषः। चैत्रपदेन चैत्रत्वस्याख्यातेन[298] तद्वृत्तिकृतेश्च बोधनादिति भावः[299]।।

८. कथं भावनाविशेष्यः[300]? अत्र[301] समाधानं शङ्कते–**विषयतयेति चेदि**ति[302]। तदपि खण्डयति[303]–**सविषये**ति[304]। तत्र[305] गमनानुकूलव्यापारस्य नोदनाख्यसंयोगस्य विषयाप्रसिद्धेरिति भावः। सविषयनिर्विषयकव्यापा-राभिधाने[306] भेदेनान्वयबोधभेदं दर्शयन्नाह–**अत्रे**त्यादिना। **भावनाविषय** इति। अत्र विषयत्वं संसर्गः, भावनाया एव साक्षादन्वयः कर्माख्यातस्थले[307] कर्मत्वबोधस्यानुभविकत्वादाह–**मैत्रनिष्ठे**त्यादि। **साक्षादि**ति प्रथमे। **परम्परये**ति द्वितीये। तत्र धात्वर्थादिना[308] व्यवधानादिति। **रथनिष्ठगमनानुकूलव्यापारे**ति। रथनिष्ठत्वं व्यापारान्वितं तत्रापि[309] कर्मत्वप्रत्ययानुरोधात्[310] रथनिष्ठ-व्यापारजन्यगमनजन्यफलशाली[311] ग्राम इति क्रमेणान्वयबोधः बोद्धव्यः[312]।।

९. प्राचां मतं दूषयितुं तद्रीत्यैव[313] वाक्यार्थं विवेचयति–**नव्यास्त्व**ति[314]। कर्त्राख्याते आश्रयत्वस्य संसर्गत्वात् कर्माख्यातस्थले आधेयत्वस्य तृतीयार्थत्वे कर्त्राख्यातकर्माख्यातयोर्विशेषणविशेष्यभाववैपरीत्येन[315] तुल्यत्वात्[316] तथाविध-पदार्थबोधस्यानुभविकस्यानुपपत्तिगौरवं चेत्यत आह[317]–**संख्यामात्रं वे**ति। मात्रपदेन[318] आधेयत्वादिव्यवच्छेदः। **सम्बन्धः** पाकानुकूलकृतौ मैत्रस्य सम्बन्धः। **वाक्यार्थ** इति। नामार्थस्य धात्वर्थेनैवान्वयस्याव्युत्पन्नत्वात् न त्वाख्यातार्थेनापीति भावः। **तथा** वाक्यार्थः। **तदपि** फलमपि। **प्रकारी**ति। तथाचानुभवविरोधेन[319] न[320] तथेत्यर्थः। ननु धातोः फलावच्छिन्नक्रियावाचकत्वे[321] तत एव फललाभो भविष्यतीत्यत आह–**फले**ति। **विशेषणे**ति[322]। फलस्य क्रियाविशेषणतयैव धातुशक्यत्वेन फलविशेष्यकक्रियाविशेषणकबोधस्याशक्यत्वात्[323] तस्य[324] धातुतोऽसाध्यत्वादिति भावः[325]। **इत्थं चे**ति। फलस्य आत्मनेपदार्थत्वे[326] चेत्यर्थः[327]। **न लभ्येते**ति। कर्माख्यातस्थले परसमवेतक्रियाजन्यफलत्व-प्रकारकप्रतीतेः[328] सर्वानुभवसिद्धत्वादिति भावः। **भावनाया** इति। तथाच मैत्रनिष्ठभावनाविषयपाकजन्यफलशाली तण्डुल इत्यन्वय इति भावः।[329] सुबर्थभावनायां धात्वर्थस्य विशेषणत्वात्[330] इत्यत आह[331]–**तिङुपस्थापिते**ति। तिङुपस्थापिवर्तमानत्वादौ धात्वर्थस्य विशेषणत्वादाह[332]–**भावनाया** इति[333]। **अन्यत्र**[334] पचतीत्यादौ। **भज्येते**ति। कृत्यर्थकाख्यातान्तधातुजन्यपाकप्रकारक-बोधे[335] आख्यातजन्यकृत्युपस्थितेः कारणत्वम्। आख्यातार्थान्तरे वर्तमानत्वादौ तदन्वयबोधातिप्रसङ्गवारणार्थं[336] **क्लृप्तमि**ति। फले तदन्वये तद्भङ्गः। कार्यकारणभावान्तरकल्पनागौरवं[337] चेति भावः। प्राचां मतं दूषयित्वा स्वमतमाह–**तस्मादि**ति[338]। मैत्रेण गतम्[339], चैत्रेण[340] पक्वास्तण्डुला इत्यादौ कृतेरन्यतोऽलाभात् तृतीयायां तत्र[341] शक्तिकल्पनमावश्यकमिति भावः। **व्युत्पन्नत्वादि**ति। तृतीयाजन्यकृतिप्रकारकधातुजन्यपाकविशेष्यकबोधे[342] तृतीयाजन्यकृत्युपस्थितेः कारणत्वस्य च[343] चैत्रेण पक्वास्तण्डुला इत्यादौ कल्पनान्न व्युत्पत्तिविरोध इति भावः। **कर्तृकर्मवत्** कर्तृकर्मणोरिव **नातिप्रसङ्गः** चैत्रेण पचति तण्डुलस्तण्डुलं पक्ष्यते[344] चैत्रेण[345] इत्यादौ नातिप्रसङ्गः[346]। **न वे**ति। एकदा कृतिफलयोरबोधकत्वादिति भावः। ननु[347] कर्माख्यातेन भावनानभिधाने भावनान्वयित्वस्य संख्यान्वयित्वनियामकत्वात्[348] तत्र किं नियामकमत आह–**तिङुपस्थाप्याया** इति। **भावनाया इवे**ति। संख्यान्वयित्वमेव भावनान्वयित्वनियामकत्वं[349] किं न स्यादिति प्रतिबन्धिसूचनायाह[350]–**प्रथमान्ते**ति। संख्यायाः कृतेश्चान्वये प्रथमान्त-पदोपस्थाप्यत्वमेव नियामकमिति भावः। ननु अचेतनानुरोधात् आख्यातार्थ-विशेष्यत्वं संख्यान्वयनियामकं तथाख्यातार्थे फलविशेष्येऽपि संख्यान्वये

प्राचीनव्युत्पत्तिबोध इति चेत्, न[351]। तथा सति वर्तमानत्वादिविशिष्टधात्वर्थेऽपि[352] संख्यान्वयापत्तेः। तृतीयार्थाख्यातजन्यसंख्यान्वयबोधे[353] कृतिप्रकारकबोधजनक-सामग्र्याः[354] एवं व्यापाराश्रयाद्यर्थकाख्यातस्थले[355] व्यापारप्रकारकबोधजनक-सामग्र्या[356] विशिष्टैकहेतुत्वकल्पनाया आवश्यकत्वात्। कर्माख्यातस्थले फलप्रकारकबोधजनकसामग्र्या एव तादृशबोधजन-कहेतुत्वकल्पने गौरवादिति[357]। नन्वेवामाख्यातवत् लाघवादिना कर्तृकर्मकृतोरपि कृतिफले एव[358] शक्ये स्यातामतस्तत्र धर्मिणि शक्तिं व्यवस्थापयति-**चैत्रो गन्ते**त्यादिना[359]। कर्तरि[360] कर्मणि च शक्तिप्रदर्शनाय[361] उदाहरणद्वयम्। उक्तरूपसामानाधिकरण्यस्य साधकत्वम्[362]। समानवचनलिङ्गत्वमपि[363] दर्शयति-**मित्रा पक्त्री**ति। समानलिङ्गकत्वमपि[364] आनुशासनिकं साधुत्वायैव[365] अभेदान्वयसाधकमिति[366] यदि ब्रूयात् तदा तन्मतनिराकरणाय अन्वयानुपपत्तिं दर्शयति-**भोक्ते**ति। अत्र[367] चैत्रादिपदस्यादिपदस्य[368] चार्थवशात्[369] नियमतोऽध्याहारे मानाभावात्[370]। भोजनानुकूलकृतिस्तृप्यति[371] पाकजन्यफलानि भुङ्क्ते पाककृतिरपसार्यताम् इत्यत्रानन्वयाद्धर्मिणि शक्तिरिति भावः। **सामानाधिकरण्ये**त्यादिना[372] भोक्ता तृप्यतीत्यादावन्वयबोधपरिग्रहः। ननु कर्तृकर्मशक्तौ कथं तदेकदेशकृतौ[373] कर्मत्वे च धात्वर्थस्यान्वय इत्यत आह-**चैत्रस्ये**त्यादि[374]। नप्तृपदस्य पुत्रपुत्रशक्तेस्तत्र[375] विशेष्य- चैत्रसम्बन्धान्वयात्[376] पुत्रेऽपि[377] तथा प्रयोगः स्यात्, पुत्रस्य चैत्रसम्बन्धवत्त्वात्[378]। अतो विशेषणीभूतपदार्थस्य[379] जन्यपुरुषस्यैकदेशे[380] जन्यत्वे चैत्रसम्बन्धान्वयः। तथाच चैत्रसम्बन्धिजन्यत्वाश्रयबोध इति भावः[381]। ननु तत्र जन्यत्वे पुरुषे च नप्तृपदशक्तिद्वयम्[382]। तथाच चैत्रस्य सम्बन्धस्य जन्यत्वे चैत्रसम्बन्धि-जन्यत्वस्य पुरुषे तादृशपुरुषस्य पुनर्जन्यत्वे तादृशजन्यत्वस्य पुनः[383] पुरुषेऽन्वये विनैव एकदेशान्वयं प्रागुक्तान्वयबोधो भवत्येव। एकपदोपात्तयोरप्यन्वयः कृतिवर्तमानत्वयोरिव व्युत्पत्तिविशेषबलान्नानुपपन्नोऽतः[384] स्थलान्तरमाह-**मैत्रादन्य**[385] इति। **तत्रान्यादि**पदानां[386] भेदादिकमेव शक्यतावच्छेदकं न तु भेदाद्याश्रयत्वम्[387], गौरवात्, अननुभवाच्च। अतो न तत्र खण्डशक्तिसम्भावना। तत्रावधित्वे[388] पञ्चम्यर्थः। मैत्रावधिमत्त्वा-श्रयभेदवानित्यन्वयबोध इति भावः[389]। एवमन्यत्राप्यूह्यम्। **अपर** इति तत्रासुरादिवत्[390] पर्युदासनञा परत्वविरोधिगुण-वानित्यन्वयः[391] बोध्यते। तादृशविरोधिगुणे परत्वे[392] पञ्चम्यर्थान्वय इति भावः[393]। **अवच्छेदकेनैवे**त्येवकारेण पदार्थीभूतकर्त्रादिव्यवच्छेदः। ननु चैत्रस्य नप्ता सुन्दरः मैत्रादन्यो नित्य इत्यादौ विशेषणस्य[394] सुन्दरस्य नित्यस्य चान्वयात्। तत्र इतरपदार्थान्वये तद्विशेष्यकवृत्तिज्ञानजन्यतदुपस्थितेः[395] कारणत्वस्य कल्पनात् कथमेकदेशे तदन्वय इत्यत आह-**तथैवे**ति। एकदेशेनैवेत्यर्थः।

तथाचानुभवानुरोधादनन्यगतिकतया[396] च[397] षष्ठ्यादिभिन्न–पदार्थान्वयेऽतथोपस्थितेः[398] कारणत्वम्। नप्त्रादिपदार्थान्वये[399] विशेषणत्वेन[400] तदुपस्थितेरेव हेतुत्वम्। अतएव विशेष्ये[401] कदापि न तदन्वयः। एवं कर्त्रुपस्थापकतृजन्तधात्वर्थान्वयेऽपि विशेषणत्वेन कृत्युपस्थितेरेव हेतुत्वम्। अतः कर्तरि कदापि न[402] तदन्वयः। एवमन्यत्राप्यूह्यम्। क्लृप्तकार्यकारणभावस्य सङ्कोचे[403] कार्यकारणभावान्तर–कल्पने[404] च[405] गौरवादाह–**अस्तु वे**ति। कृतौ धात्वर्थानुकूलत्वभानस्यानुभ–विकस्योपपादनायाह[406]–**कृत्यादिघटित** इत्युक्तम्। **आदिभ्यां** फलतच्छालिनोः संग्रहः[407]। इत्थं च **पक्ते**त्यादौ पाकीयः[408] कर्तेत्याकारको बोधः[409]। सम्बन्धश्च स्वजनककृतिमत्त्वम्[410]। एवं च[411] चैत्रस्य नप्ता मैत्रादन्य इत्यादौ षष्ठीपञ्चम्यर्थयोः[412] स्वाश्रयजन्यतावज्जन्यताश्रय–पुरुषत्वेन स्वाश्रयभेदवत्त्वसम्बन्धेन भेदवति चान्वयो वाच्यः[413]। इत्थं च न कुत्राप्येकदेशान्वय इति। कर्माख्यातेन कृतेरबोधने फलस्य बोधने चानुगुणान्तरमाह[414]–**मुख्ये**ति। मुख्यकर्मत्वं फलवत्त्वात्[415] पच्यते तण्डुल इत्यादौ। भाक्तं तु विषयत्वादिरूपं ज्ञायते घट इत्यादौ। एवं मुख्यकर्तृत्वं चैत्रः[416] पचतीत्यादौ। भाक्तं च[417] स्थाली पचतीत्यादौ, जानातीत्यादौ च। आदिना[418] विषयत्वादिकरूपस्य[419] भाक्तकर्मत्वस्य व्यापाराश्रयत्वादिरूपस्य[420] भाक्तकर्तृत्वस्य संग्रहः। **विशेषणस्यापी**ति। विशिष्टस्यानतिरिक्तत्वात् विशेष्यतयैवाभिधानस्यानुक्तत्वात् विशेषणतयाभिधानेऽप्यभिधानमेवेति[421] भावः। चैत्रेण भुक्त्वा[422] गम्यते इत्यादौ क्त्वाप्रत्ययेन कृतेरभिधानेऽप्याख्यातेन[423] तदनभिधानात् तृतीया, तादृश–कृत्यभिधानस्य अप्रयोजकत्वात्। वस्तुतश्चैत्रेण भुक्त्वा गम्यत इत्यादौ भोजनानन्तरगमनानुकूलकृतिरेव मुख्यं कर्तृत्वम्[424], तस्य च[425] कृता आख्यातेन[426] वाऽभिधानमेव। अतएव भोक्त्रा पक्त्वा चैत्रेणान्नं[427] भुज्यत इत्यादौ कृता[428] भोजनकृतेरेवाभिधानेऽपि[429] भोक्त्रभिन्न- चैत्रवृत्त्यन्नभोजनकृतेः[430] प्रधानकर्तृत्वस्य भोक्त्रेत्यनेनानभिधानान्न तृतीयानुपपत्तिरेव[431]। एवमन्यत्राप्यूह्यम्॥

१०. **धातूत्तरे**ति। आख्यातक्त्वावुन्तुमादिषु प्रत्ययेषु[432] कृतिशक्तिकल्पनसमये आख्यातत्वादिकमपहाय लाघवादुक्तरूपेणैव तत्र[433] शक्तिः कल्प्यते इत्याशयः। **भावकृतोऽपी**ति। कर्मप्रत्ययेष्वपि कृतिशक्तिरस्त्येव। कृतिबोधे समभिव्याहार–विशेषो नियामकः। उभयबोधकसमभिव्याहारे च एकदा उभयबोध–कत्वान्नातिप्रसङ्गः इति **तन्नो**क्तम्। भावकृतः कृतिशक्तत्वेऽपि समभिव्याहारविशेषभावान्न तद्बोधः इत्यस्यापि सुवचत्वादाह–**धातुत्वादी**ति[434]। धातुत्वं प्रत्ययत्वञ्चाभियुक्तानां तादृशपरिभाषाविषयत्वं तदपेक्षया लघुरूप–स्याख्यातत्वस्य लघुत्वादित्यर्थः। धातुत्वं प्रत्ययत्वं च[435] तावदन्यतमत्वं तदपेक्षया आख्यातत्वस्य[436] तिबाद्यन्यतमत्वरूपस्य[437] लघुत्वादित्यर्थः इति

तु[438] कश्चितु।

११. ये तु कर्तृकृतामपि विशेष्यशक्तिकल्पने[439] कृतावेव शक्तिः सामानाधिकरण्यानुरोधाद्विशिष्टे[440] लक्षणेति तन्मतं दूषयति[441]–**यदपी**ति। **कर्तृकृतोऽपी**ति। अत्र तृत्त्वादिकमेव शक्ततावच्छेदकमतो न गौरवमिति भावः। स्वयं वक्ष्यमाणस्य[442] **विशिष्टान्तराणामि**त्यत्र **अन्तर**पदस्य व्यावृत्तिं दर्शयितुं[443] गवादिपदे विशिष्टशक्तिं व्यवस्थापयति-**यतो विने**त्यादि। **शक्यत्वासम्भवादि**ति। शक्तेरवच्छिन्नत्वनियमात्। निर्विकल्पकोपस्थिते तद्ग्रहासम्भवाच्चेति भावः[444]। गोत्वत्वादिकमेव तथास्त्वत आह–**गोत्वत्वादी**ति। गवेतरासमवेतत्वादिघटितस्यातिगौरवात्[445]। एवमपि विशेषणतया गोत्वविशिष्टे शक्तेरेवापरीहाराच्चेति[446] भावः। **विशिष्टान्तराणां** किञ्चिद्विशिष्टविशेषणकानां यथाकाशपदे शब्दवतः महदादिपदे च[447] महत्त्वादिमतः शक्यत्वे लाघवाच्छब्दस्य महत्त्वादेश्च[448] शक्यत्वापत्तिरिति भावः[449]। **केवले** इति। विशेषणतानापन्न[450] इत्यर्थः। महदादिपदस्य केवलमहत्त्वादौ स्वारसिकप्रयोगाभावात् तत्र यदि[451] विशिष्टे[452] शक्यमिति तदा[453] केवलकृतावप्यप्रयोगात्[454] तत्रापि कृतिविशिष्टे शक्तिरिति भावः। **स्वारसिके**ति। तेनाधुनिकलक्षणया[455] प्रयोगेऽपि न क्षतिः।।

१२. **एवंचे**त्यारभ्य **केचिदि**त्यन्तमेकं मतम्। फलस्य कृदात्मनेपदलभ्यत्वव्यवस्थापने[456]। **व्यापारविशेषो** गमनत्वादिविशिष्टः। **द्वितीयादेरि**ति। स्वत्वादाविव स्वारसिकप्रयोगात् षष्ठ्या अपि कर्मत्वमर्थः। स च शक्त्या निरूढलक्षणया वेत्यन्यदेतत्। फले द्वितीयाद्यर्थैकदेशे तज्जनकत्वं तु धात्वर्थ एवाश्रयतयाऽन्वेति। इत्थं च समानवित्तिवेद्यतया धात्वर्थजन्यत्वस्यापि फले लाभात् परसमवेतधात्वर्थजन्यफलशालित्वरूपं कर्मत्वं कर्तृप्रत्ययस्थले लब्धं भवतीति भावः। **फलमात्रं वे**ति[457]। तथाच शक्यतावच्छेदके न गौरवम्[458], न वैकदेशान्वयः इति भावः[459]। **अलाभादि**ति। **फलविशेषे**त्यादौ हेतुः, **इतरथा** शुद्धव्यापारस्यैव[460] धात्वर्थत्वे[461]। **पर्यायते**ति। त्यजतीत्युक्ते यादृशार्थबोधो[462] गच्छतीत्युक्ते तद्विलक्षणार्थबोधस्यानुभविकत्वात्[463]। तच्चोभयोः शुद्धस्पन्दार्थकत्वे नोपपद्यते इति संयोगावच्छिन्नस्पन्दे गमेर्विभागावच्छिन्नस्पन्दे च त्यजेः शक्तिः। एवमन्यत्रापि इति भावः।।

१३. गूढाभिसन्धिः[464] शङ्कते–**तवापी**ति। फलविशेषावच्छिन्नव्यापारस्यैव[465] धात्वर्थत्ववादिनोऽपीत्यर्थः। ग्रामं गच्छतीत्यादौ तु[466] धात्वर्थतावच्छेदकसंयोगादौ द्वितीयार्थवृत्तित्वान्वयेन तथान्वयबोधसम्भवात्[467] तन्नोक्तम्। **संयोगादी**त्यादिना। त्यज्यत इत्यादौ[468] विभागादिपरिग्रहः[469]। स्पन्दविशेषणतया धातुशक्यस्य

संयोगादेर्विशेष्यतया[470] बोधासम्भवात् कर्मप्रत्ययस्य फलसामान्यबोधकत्वादिति भावः। यदि च[471] कर्माख्यातादेरेव संयोगत्वादिरूपेण शक्तिस्तदा ममापि द्वितीयादेः संयोगत्वादिना रूपेण शक्तिरित्यभिसन्धिः। **तदवच्छिन्ने**ति। संयोगाद्यवच्छिन्नेत्यर्थः। सामान्यशक्तस्य विशेषबोधकसमभिव्याहारेण विशेष-बोधकत्वमित्यत्र दृष्टान्तमाह–**यथे**ति। **स्वर्गजनकत्वं**[472] **प्रतीयत** इति पूर्वेणान्वयः। **अन्यदेतदि**ति। यदीष्टतारूपेणैव[473] स्वर्गरूपेष्टबोधकत्वं तदा तत्रापि[474] फलतारूपेणैव[475] संयोगादिबोधकत्वम्[476]। यदि च तत्र व्युत्पत्त्यन्तराश्रयणेन[477] इष्टस्वर्गयोरभेदान्वयबोधेन वा स्वर्गरूपेष्टसाधनत्व-बोधकत्वं तदा ममापि धात्वर्थतावच्छेदकसंयोगादिकम् अस्याभेदान्वयात् व्युत्पत्त्यन्तराश्रयणात्[478] वा[479] संयोगादिरूपफलबोधकत्वमिति[480] भावः।।

१४. ननु फलत्वेन फलस्य[481] शक्त्या संयोगत्वादिरूपेण बोधजनकत्वं व्युत्पत्ति-सहस्रेणाप्यशक्यं तेन रूपेण पदादनुपस्थितेः। नापि धात्वर्थतावच्छेदकसंयोगस्य फलेऽभेदान्वयधीः, इतरविशेषणतया उपस्थितस्य संयोगस्य फलादौ विशेषणतया[482] अन्वयासम्भवात्। स्वर्गजनकत्वादिना[483] स्वर्गजनकत्वधीस्तादूप्येण शक्तौ सामान्यशक्तौ तु[484] स्वर्गजनकत्वादिबोधो[485] मानस एव इत्यत आह–**अस्तु वे**ति। यथा तदादिपदं बुद्धिप्रकारवति शक्तमित्याकारकशक्तिग्रहेऽपि[486] यदा[487] घटत्वादिरूपेण वक्तृबुद्धिप्रकारवत्ता गृह्यते तदा तेन रूपेण[488] बोधकत्वम्[489], तथात्मनेपदं कर्मकृत्पदं वा प्रकृत्यर्थतावच्छेदकवति फले[490] तच्छालिनि वा शक्तमित्याकारकशक्तिग्रहेऽपि[491] संयोगत्वादिरूपेण प्रकृत्यर्थतावच्छेदकत्वग्रहे आख्यातादेरेव[492] संयोगत्वादिना[493] बोधकत्वमित्यर्थः। **फलतच्छालिनी**त्याख्यातकृतोर्यथासंख्यमन्वयः। न च घटत्वांशे अन्याप्रकारकघटत्वप्रकारकशाब्दे तादृशशक्तिग्रहस्याहेतुत्वात्[494] कथमेवमिति वाच्यम्, तादृशशाब्दे तादृशपदार्थोपस्थितेर्हेतुत्वस्यावश्यकत्वे शक्तिज्ञानस्य उक्तरूपेण हेतुत्वे मानाभावात्। प्रकृते च[495] बुद्धिप्रकारवति[496]। शक्तमित्याकारेण गृहीतशक्तिकपदज्ञानस्यापि घटोऽस्य बुद्धिप्रकारवानितिज्ञानसहकारेण घटत्वांशेऽन्याप्रकारकघटत्वप्रकारकबोधजनकत्वसम्भवात्[497]। अतएव मनस्त्वांशेऽन्याप्रकारकमनस्त्वप्रकारकबुद्धिस्थत्वज्ञानासम्भवात् तत्पदादितो न तादृशमनस्त्वप्रकारकधीरिति।।

१५. नन्वेवंविधानन्तव्युत्पत्तिकल्पने गौरवादाख्यातादेरेव संयोगत्वादिना[498] शक्तिरस्तु, शुद्धस्पन्दादिबोधकगमधातुयोग एवाख्यातस्य संयोगबोधकत्वं[499] तादृशत्यज-धातुयोगे च विभागबोधकत्वमिति क्रमेण नियमोऽस्तु। न च[500] लक्षणया त्यागतात्पर्येण यत्र ग्रामं गच्छतीत्यादिप्रयोगः तत्रापि संयोगबोधकतापत्तिरिति

वाच्यम्। तत्र धातोरेव[501] विभागावच्छिन्नस्पन्दे लाक्षणिकतया शुद्धस्पन्दाबोधकत्वात्। अतः प्रकारान्तरेण फलस्य धात्वर्थतावच्छेदकत्वं व्यवस्थापयति–**अपि चे**ति। विभागस्यापि गमनपतनजन्यत्वात् तच्छालिनि पूर्वदेशे गमिपत्योः कर्मत्वं स्यात्। एवं संयोगस्यापि त्यागजन्यत्वात् तच्छालिनि[502] उत्तरदेशे त्यजेः कर्मत्वं स्यात्। एवं स्पन्दजन्यसंयोगविभागयोः[503] पूर्वोत्तरदेशयोः सत्त्वात् उभत्रैव तत्कर्मत्वं[504] स्यात्। स्वमते च[505] उत्तरसंयोगावच्छिन्नस्पन्दे[506] गमेरधःसंयोगावच्छिन्ने[507] पतेर्विभागावच्छिन्ने च त्यजेः शक्तत्वात्, स्पन्देश्च धात्वर्थतावच्छेदकफलाभावान्नातिप्रसङ्गः[508] इति भावः।।

१६. ननु सामान्यतः कर्मत्वानिरुक्तावपि न क्षतिः। स्वजन्योत्तरदेशसंयोगशालित्वं गम्यादेः कर्मत्वमित्यादिना[509] विशिष्यैव[510] तन्निर्वचनसम्भवात्, स्पन्दधातोश्च[511] कर्मव्यवहाराभावेन तथा निरुक्तिविरहात् अत आह–**फले**ति। **व्यवहार** इति[512]। मुख्य इति शेषः। कथं तर्हि शुद्धज्ञानाद्युपस्थापके[513] जानाति इत्यादौ तद्व्यवहार इत्यत आह–**भाक्तस्त्वि**ति। सकर्मकत्वव्यवहार इत्यनुषज्यते। नन्वनुगतरूपेण सकर्मकत्वानिर्वचने का क्षतिरित्यत[514] आह–**तादृशधात्वि**ति। तथाप सकर्मकधातुयोगे कर्मप्रत्ययविधानस्य सकर्मकत्वाननुगमेनाननुगमापत्तिरतोऽनुगमनिर्वचनमपेक्षितमिति[515] भावः। **कर्मप्रत्यया** द्वितीयादयः। **यद्यपि** जानातीत्यादौ अनुगतसकर्मकत्वाभावेऽपि, तत्तद्धातुयोगे[516] सकर्मकत्वविधानवत्[517] अत्रापि गम्यादिधातुयोगे कर्मप्रत्ययविधानं नानुपपन्नम्[518]। न च स्पन्दधातुयोगे कर्मप्रत्ययापत्तिः **तवा**पि स्पन्दधातुयोगे[519] तदापत्तिः[520]। अथ जानातीत्यादौ विभक्त्यर्थविषयित्वावच्छिन्नस्वार्थप्रतीतिजनकत्वं गौणसकर्मकत्वमनुगतं[521] घटं करोतीत्यादौ द्वितीयार्थविषयित्वप्रकारकयत्नविशेष्यकबोधजनकत्वस्य करोतीत्यादौ सत्त्वात्। कस्यचिद् धातोस्तथा बोधकत्वं कस्यचित् नेत्यत्र शब्दशक्तिवैचित्र्यस्य नियामकत्वादिति चेत्, तर्हि विभक्त्यर्थफलावच्छिन्नव्यापारबोधकत्वं गम्यादौ सकर्मकत्वमनुगतं गम्यादिधातोरेव तादृशफलप्रकारकान्वयबोधजनकत्वं[522] न स्पन्देरित्यत्र शब्दवैचित्र्यस्य[523] नियामकत्वादिति क्रमेण सर्वदोषोद्धारः सम्भवत्येव। तथापि त्यजिगम्योः पर्यायतापत्तिरेव[524] दोषः। न हि कर्मासमभिव्याहृतयोस्त्यजति गच्छतीति शब्दयोरेकार्थबोधकत्वं[525] कश्चिदनुभवतीति[526] ध्येयम्। धात्वर्थतावच्छेदकफलस्य नामार्थे कथं साक्षादन्वयबोध[527] इत्यत आह–**तत्र चे**ति[528]। तादृशसकर्मकधातुयोगे[529] चेत्यर्थः। तेन घटं जानातीत्यादौ द्वितीयाया अर्थभेदेऽपि[530] न क्षतिः। नन्वेवं

कर्मणि द्वितीया [पा. सू. 2-3-2]

इति पृथक् सूत्रकरणानुपपत्तिः[531],

सप्तम्यधिकरणे च [पा. सू. 2-3-36]

इत्यत्र द्वितीयासप्तम्योरधिकरणे चेति करणे[532] एकेनैव सूत्रेण तद्विधानसम्भ-वादत आह–**अतएवे**ति। धात्वर्थतावच्छेदकफलाहिताधेयत्वबोधकत्वादेवेत्यर्थः[533]। स्थाल्यां पचति इत्युक्ते स्थाल्याधेयत्वं नियमतः पाके प्रतीयते, तण्डुलं पचतीत्यत्र[534] तण्डुलाधेयत्वं तदवच्छेदकफल एव प्रतीयते, न पाके इति व्युत्पत्तिविशेषज्ञापनार्थं पृथक्सूत्रप्रणयनमिति भावः। यद्यपि ग्रामे गच्छतीत्यादौ सप्तम्यर्थस्याप्याधेयत्वस्य[535] तादृशफलेऽन्वयस्तथापि तत्रापि गमन एवाधेयत्वविवक्षयैव तथाप्रयोगादिति[536] ध्येयम्।।

१७. नन्वेवं द्वितीयाया आधेयत्वार्थकत्वे कर्माख्यातस्य फलार्थकत्वे च[537] चैत्रः पचति तण्डुलं[538] चैत्रेण[539] पच्यते तण्डुलः[540] इत्यनयोः विशेषणविशेष्यभाववैप-रीत्येन[541] तुल्यवत् पदार्थबोधस्य सर्वानुभवसिद्धस्यानुपपत्तिः, एकदेशान्वयविरोधश्च इत्यत आह–**अस्तु वे**ति। **कर्माख्यातस्ये**ति। तत्र[542] धात्वर्थतावच्छेदकफलस्य विशेषणविशेष्यभावविपर्ययस्याशक्यत्वेनान्वये पूर्वयुक्त्या[543] फलबोधक-त्वस्यावश्यकत्वादित्यर्थः[544]। अत्रापीच्छादिवत्[545] व्युत्पत्तिविशेषादेव द्वितीयायाः फलविशेषबोधकत्वं विशिष्टशक्तिस्वीकारेणैवेति[546] ध्येयम्[547]। नन्वेवं ग्रामं गच्छतीत्यत्र ग्रामवृत्तिसंयोगजनकसंयोगावच्छिन्नस्पन्दानुकूलकृतिमानित्यन्वयबोधो[548] वाच्यः[549]। तत्र च[550] संयोगावच्छिन्नस्पन्दे[551] द्वितीयार्थसंयोगान्वयः प्राचीननये पौनरुक्त्यादसम्भवी। दण्डवान् रक्तदण्डवान् इत्यन्वयबोधो[552] नव्यैरेवोपगमात् तादृशसंयोगद्वयबोधेऽननुभवश्चेत्यत आह–**स्ता**[553] वेति। अत्र च[554] कल्पे द्वितीयाया आधेयत्वं कर्माख्यातस्य चाश्रयत्वमर्थः[555]। कर्तृप्रत्ययस्थले धात्वर्थस्य फलस्य[556] स्वार्थव्यापारविशेषणतया, कर्मप्रत्ययस्थले तु विशेष्यतयान्वयः। एवंच ग्रामं गच्छति चैत्र इत्यत्र ग्रामाधेयसंयोगानुकूल–स्पन्दानुकूलकृतिमांश्चैत्रः, चैत्रेण गम्यते ग्राम इत्यत्र च[557] चैत्रकृतिजन्य–स्पन्दजन्यसंयोगाश्रयो[558] ग्राम इत्यन्वयधीः[559]। तत्र कर्तृप्रत्ययान्तगमधातुजन्य–संयोगप्रकारकबोधे धातुजन्यव्यापारोपस्थितेः[560]। तादृशधात्वर्थस्य स्पन्दप्रकारकबोधे[561] आख्याताद्यर्थोपस्थितेः कारणत्वस्य कल्पनात्[562]। एवं कर्मप्रत्ययस्थले[563] कर्मप्रत्ययान्तगम्यादिधातुजन्यस्पन्दप्रकारकबोधे-तदर्थसंयोगोपस्थितेरिति[564]। तादृशधात्वर्थसंयोगप्रकारकबोधे आख्यातजन्या-श्रयत्वाद्युपस्थितेः कारणत्वस्य कल्पनान्न नियमेनान्वयबोधप्रसङ्ग[565] इति ध्येयम्। परसमवेतत्वस्य फलेऽन्वये संयोगविभागरूपस्य फलस्य[566] परनिष्ठत्वात्[567] आत्मानं प्रयातीत्यादेः प्रसङ्गः। न स्याच्च तण्डुलं पचतीत्यादि, तत्र च[568] तण्डुलवृत्तिविक्ळृत्तिरूपफलस्य तण्डुलान्यावृत्तित्वादित्यत[569] आह **क्रियान्वयी**ति। तादृशपरसमवेतत्वप्रकारकबोधे कृतिजन्यस्पन्दादिरूपव्यापारो-पस्थितेरेव[570] कारणत्वस्य कल्पनात्[571] नान्यत्र तदन्वय इति भावः।।

१८. परत्वं[572] यदि सर्वत्र प्रकृत्यर्थापेक्षिकं प्रत्याय्यते[573] तदा कर्माख्यातस्थले चैत्रेण स्वमात्मा[574] गम्यते इति प्रयोगापत्तिरित्यत[575] आह–**इयांस्त्व**ति। **तिङादिने**त्यादिना[576] कर्मकृतः परिग्रहः। स्वार्थं यत् फलं तदाश्रयापेक्षयेत्यर्थः। फलाश्रयस्य शक्यत्वे विशेषणतया फलस्यापि आख्यातार्थकर्मकृत्यर्थानुपपत्तिः। इदं च पूर्वकल्पानुसारेण **स्तां वा फलव्यापाराव**िति[577]। कृतिकल्पे[578] तु आश्रयत्वापेक्षयेति[579] बोध्यम्। इत्थं च ग्रामं गच्छतीत्यत्र ग्रामान्यसमवेतो ग्रामवृत्तिसंयोगानुकूलो यः स्पन्दस्तदनुकूलकृतिमानित्यन्वयधीः गम्यते ग्राम इत्यत्र ग्रामान्यसमवेततादृशस्पन्दजन्यसंयोगाश्रयो ग्राम इत्यन्वयधीः। अत्र चोभयकर्मजसंयोगस्थलेऽपि मल्लो मल्लान्तरं गच्छतीतिवत् स्वमात्मानं[580] गच्छतीति न प्रयोगः, स्वात्मसमवेता या स्वात्मवृत्तिसंयोगजनिका क्रिया, सा न परसमवेता। परत्वं प्रकृत्यर्थापेक्षया, परत्वं च भिन्नत्वम्। **व्यापाराव**िति आत्मभेदस्य स्वात्मन्यभावात् स्वात्मापेक्षया परत्वं मल्लान्तरेऽप्यस्ति। तत्समवेता क्रिया कर्म भवत्येव। एतन्मल्लेति मल्लान्तरं एतन्मल्लः सवात्मानं गच्छतीत्यादिप्रयोग इति [न] काचिदनुपपत्तिः। **कर्मप्रत्ययेने**ति। घटं जानातीत्यत्र ज्ञाननिष्ठं विषयित्वं घटो ज्ञायत इत्यत्र विषयत्वं सर्वत्रैव तन्मते विशेष्यवृत्तेरेव सम्बन्धत्वादिति। अत्र च परसमवेतत्वमनर्थकतया न निवेश्यम्। एवम् आत्मानं जानातीत्यादिकमपि सूपपदमेव। **एकत्र** कर्तृस्थले। **अन्यत्र** कर्मस्थले। कुतो धर्मिबोधकत्वस्य व्यवस्थापनादाह–**ज्ञात** इति। ननु यत्र धातोरपि यत्नवाचकत्वेन तत्रापि भाक्तं सकर्मकत्वं स्यादित्यत आह–**यतत** इति। तथाच यत्र विषयत्वेनान्वयस्तत्रैव सकर्मकत्वमिति भावः। **अतएवे**ति। यत उद्देश्यत्वेनान्वयः अतएवेत्यर्थः। अन्यथा भोजनं करोतीतिवत् तदानीमेव भोजनं यतते इति स्यात्। अतएव करोतेरपि नोद्देश्यत्वेनान्वयः। तेन भोजनाय करोतीति न प्रयोगः।।[581]

१९. मण्डनमतमुपन्यस्यति–**धातोरि**ति। **धातोः** पच्यादिधातोः। **फलं** विक्लृत्त्यादि। यद्यत्फलावच्छिन्नव्यापारवाचकत्वं यद्यद्धातोर्नैयायिकैरभ्युपेतं[582] तत्तद्धातोस्तत्–फलमित्यर्थः। एवंच पचेर्विक्लृत्तिः त्यजेर्विभागः गमेरुत्तरसंयोगोऽर्थ इति न त्यजिगम्योः पर्यायत्वमिति भावः। अनुकूलत्वान्तर्भावेन शक्तौ गौरवादेकदेशान्वया–पाताच्चाह–**व्यापारमात्रं वे**ति। आख्यातस्यार्थ इत्यनेनान्वयः[583]। ननु फलस्य धात्वर्थत्वे लिङाद्यर्थस्येष्टसाधनत्वादेस्तत्रैवान्वयात्[584] व्यापारगोचरे[585] इष्टसाधनत्वादिबोधस्य[586] विध्यजन्यत्वात्[587] विधेः प्रवर्तकता न स्यात्[588] [इत्यत] आह–**लडादी**ति। यथासंख्यं **वर्तमानत्वादी**त्यनेनान्वयः[589]। **लडादी**त्यादिना वर्तमानत्वादिना[590] भविष्यत्वादेश्च परिग्रहः[591]। **लिङादी**त्यादिना विध्यर्थकाख्यातस्य **इष्टसाधनत्वादि**ना[592] कृतिसाध्यत्वबलवदनिष्टानु–

बन्धित्वयोः[593] परिग्रहः।[594] **तत्रैव** व्यापार एव। पचतीत्यत्र अस्मन्मत-सिद्धधात्वर्थोऽधःसन्तापनादिरूपः[595] एव[596]। भवन्मते[597] आख्यातार्थविधेयतया[598] कृत्यादिघटितपरम्परासम्बन्धेन चैत्रादौ भासते, न तु कृतिरेव तादृशफलानुकूलत्वेन चैत्रादौ भासते। तथा सति पचेत इत्यादौ कृतिसाध्यत्वस्य लिङर्थस्य कृतावनन्वयात्[599]। एवं गच्छतीत्यादावपि बोध्यम्। ननु भावकृतां प्रयोगमात्रसाधुत्वात् पाक इत्यत्र फलमात्रलाभेऽसङ्गतिरतो न धातोः फलमात्रमर्थ इत्यत्र आह–**भावे**ति। भावाख्यातस्याप्यनुकूलव्यापारोऽर्थः। **तेन** कर्माविवक्षायां चैत्रेण पच्यते इत्यादौ तादृशव्यापारस्येष्टसाधनत्वबोधोपपत्तिः, तृतीयार्थव्यापारस्येष्टसाधनत्वबोधोपपत्तिः[600]। तृतीयार्थव्यापारे तदन्वयबोधे[601] पृथग्व्युत्पत्तिकल्पनापातादिति। **व्यापारसत्त्व** इति। तदानीं पाको विद्यते इति प्रयोगो न स्यादित्यपि द्रष्टव्यम्। **व्यापारविगम** इति। तदानीं पाकोऽतीत इति प्रयोगो न स्यादित्यपि द्रष्टव्यम्। **मिथोगमनमि**ति[602]। संयोगस्य द्विष्ठत्वेऽपि संयोगानुकूलव्यापारस्य गमनपदार्थस्याद्विष्ठत्वादिति भावः। ननु एतन्मते[603] धात्वर्थतावच्छेदकफलशालित्वं न कर्मत्वं[604] फलस्यैव धात्वर्थत्वात्। नापि परमात्रसमवेतव्यापारजन्यधात्वर्थफलशालित्वं[605] भूमिं प्रयाति विहग इत्यादौ आत्मानं[606] प्रयातीत्यादेः प्रसङ्गात्, विहगस्यापि आपेक्षिकपरस्वावय-वसमवेतात्मकव्यापारजन्यधात्वर्थशालित्वादत[607] आह– **प्रत्ययोपनीते**ति। तादृशस्वात्मव्यापारस्तु[608] न प्रत्ययोपनीतं गमनात्मकव्यापारस्यैव प्रत्ययो-पनीतत्वात्, स च न परसमवेत इति नातिप्रसङ्गः। व्यापारत्वेन प्रत्ययोपनीतत्वप्राप्तये **व्यापार**पदम्, अन्यथा कालस्यापि वर्तमानत्वादिना प्रत्ययोपनीतत्वात् तज्जन्यधात्वर्थशालित्वेन स्वस्मिन्नपि कर्मत्वापत्तिः इति[609]। गच्छतीत्यादौ तादृशविभागादिशालित्वेन पूर्वदेशादौ कर्मत्वापत्तिरतो **धात्वर्थे**ति।

अत्र च[610] परसमवेतत्वं कर्मप्रत्ययार्थः। कर्त्राख्यातस्थले आख्यातार्थव्यापारे, कर्माख्यातस्थले तु निष्कृष्टमते तृतीयार्थव्यापार एवान्वेति। परत्वं तु धात्वर्थाधिकरणतया यदन्वीयते तदपेक्षयेति बोध्यम्। इत्थं च ग्रामं गच्छति चैत्र इत्यत्र ग्रामवृत्तिसंयोगजनकग्रामभिन्नसमवेतव्यापारवांश्चैत्रः, चैत्रेण ग्रामो गम्यत इत्यत्र चैत्रवृत्तिग्रामभिन्नसमवेतव्यापारजन्यसंयोगशाली ग्राम इति बोधः[611]। नन्वाख्यातस्योभत्र व्यापारबोधकत्वे कथमेकत्र कर्तृप्रत्ययः कर्मप्रत्यय इति व्यवहारः, अत आह[612]–**फलव्यापारयो**रिति। फलस्य विशेषणत्वे व्यापारस्य विशेष्यत्वे[613] च कर्तृप्रत्यय इति, वैपरीत्ये च कर्मप्रत्यय इति व्यवहार इत्यर्थः। पचतीत्यादावाख्यातार्थव्यापारे धात्वर्थस्य विशेषणतयैवान्वयस्य व्युत्पत्तिसिद्धत्वात्।।

२०. एवं कर्माख्यातस्थले धात्वर्थस्य फलस्य नामार्थे साक्षादन्वये कर्त्राख्यातस्थले

द्वितीयादिना वृत्तित्वप्रतिपादनात् तुल्यवत्पदार्थबोधस्यानुभविकत्वस्य[614] भङ्गो व्युत्पत्तिविरोधश्चेत्यत आह–**वस्तुतस्त्व**ति। **अधिकरणत्वमि**त्यादि प्रथमान्तत्रयस्यार्थ इति पूर्वोक्तेनान्वयः। कर्मकृतः फलाश्रयबोधकत्वे[615] धात्वर्थफलेनान्वय इति तस्यापि शक्यमाह–**कर्मकृत** इति[616]। **फलस्ये**ति कर्तृकृतो यत्नाश्रयबोधकत्वे रथो गन्तेत्यादावनुपपत्तिस्तुल्यप्रकारकबोधजनक-त्वरक्षार्थम्[617] आख्यातस्यापि यत्नशक्तत्वापत्तिरत आह–**कर्तृकृत** इति। **जानातीत्यादिप्रयोगे**[618] इति। आख्यातकर्मकर्तृकृतामिति शेषः। **पूर्वोक्तैवे**ति। कर्तृकर्माख्यातयोराश्रयविशेषत्वे कर्तृकर्मकृतोराश्रयविषयत्वार्थः[619]। एवं नश्यतीत्यादावपि प्रतियोगित्वादिकमर्थो बोध्य इति भावः। **सुबर्थ एवे**ति। आख्यातार्थस्य व्यापारस्य[620] तत्रानन्वयात् धात्वर्थफले च[621] वर्तमानत्वान्वये[622] व्यापारसत्त्वदशायां[623] फलसत्त्वकाले च[624] पच्यत इति प्रयोगापातादिति भावः। **आदि**ना चातीतत्वभविष्यत्त्वयोः[625] परिग्रहः[626]। **अनायत्ये**ति। तत्र सामानाधि-करण्याद्यन्यथानुपपत्त्या, व्यापारमात्रस्य शक्यत्वासम्भवादिति भावः। **तदन्वयः** वर्तमानत्वाद्यन्वयः। कर्तृकृदाद्युपस्थाप्यवर्तमानत्वप्रकारकबोधे[627] व्यापारे कर्तृकृदादिजन्योपस्थितिप्रकारकत्वं[628] तन्त्रम्। **व्यापारे** इतराश्रयबोधे[629] व्यापारविशेष्यकवृत्तिज्ञानजन्योपस्थितेस्तन्त्रतायां[630] पदार्थतावच्छेदकान्वय-बोधबाधिकायां[631] तादृशवर्तमानत्वादि[632] कार्यतावच्छेदककोटौ निवेश्यमिति भावः। अतएवारुचेराह **स्तां वे**ति। कथं तर्हि व्यापाराश्रयरूपविशिष्टार्थलाभ इत्यत आह–**विशिष्टमि**ति। **अन्वयबले**ति। स्वार्थव्यापारस्याश्रयत्वसम्बन्धेना-श्रयेऽन्वयबोधे स्वजन्योपस्थितेस्तन्त्रमिति[633] कार्यकारणभावकल्पनादिति भावः[634]। इदं तु बोध्यम्। आश्रयस्य स्वातन्त्र्येण शक्यत्वेऽप्याश्रयत्वे निरूपितत्वसम्बन्धेन व्यापारान्वयबोधे तथैव एकदेशान्वय इति आश्रय एव[635] आश्रयत्वसम्बन्धेन व्यापारस्यान्वय इति आश्रयो व्यापारवानिति बोधस्त्विष्ट एवेति। एकपदोपात्तयोः एव[636] परस्परमन्वयेन विशिष्टलाभे दृष्टान्तमाह–**एवकारस्ये**ति। तत्र विशिष्टस्य शक्यत्वेऽनुपपत्तिं दर्शयति–**अन्ययोगप्रतियोगिके**ति। **अतिप्रसक्तत्वादि**ति। पार्थ एव धनुर्धर इतिवत्[637] पार्थ एव द्रव्यमित्यादिप्रयोगप्रसङ्गादिति[638]। पार्थान्यगुणादितादात्म्ययोगव्यवच्छेदस्य[639] द्रव्यत्वावच्छेदेन सत्त्वादित्यर्थः। **शक्याप्रसिद्धि**रिति। तादात्म्यरूपान्ययोगस्थलेऽन्यतादात्म्यस्य केवलान्वयित्वात्[640] तद्व्यवच्छेदाप्रसिद्धिरिति भावः[641]। अन्यसमवेतत्वरूपान्ययोगस्थले गुरुधर्मस्यावच्छेदकत्वेनान्यसमवेतत्वाद्यवच्छेदस्य[642] शक्यस्य प्रसिद्धावपि[643] पृथिव्यामेव गन्ध इत्यादौ[644] च गन्धादौ तदन्वयो बाधित इत्याह[645]–**बाधितत्वं चे**ति। दूषणान्तरमाह–**पार्थ एवेत्यादावि**ति। **तस्य पार्थान्ययोगत्वाद्यवच्छिन्न-व्यवच्छेदस्य** ततोऽन्ययोगत्वाद्यवच्छिन्नव्यवच्छेदात्[646] पार्थस्यैव[647]

आकाङ्क्षादिवशात् संसर्गविशेषलाभसम्भवात् लभ्यं पदार्थस्येति[648] भावः।।

२१. ननु स्वोपस्थापकपदसमभिव्याहृतैवकारस्य स्वान्ययोगव्यवच्छेदे[649] शक्तिरिति नोक्तदोष इत्यत आह–**स्वान्ये**ति। **शक्त्यानन्त्यमि**ति[650]। स्वत्वस्यैकस्याभावात् पार्थान्ययोगत्वावच्छिन्नव्यवच्छेदत्वादिना शक्यत्वस्य वाच्यत्वादिति भावः। नन्वन्ययोगव्यवच्छेदयोः शक्यत्वे कथं पार्थान्ययोगत्वावच्छिन्नव्यवच्छेदलाभ इत्यत आह–**नीलमि**ति[651]। अत्रापि पार्थेन[652] समं अन्ययोगस्यान्वये[653] पार्थान्ययोगत्वावच्छिन्नस्य[654] लाभे तेन समं व्यवच्छेदस्यान्वये विशिष्टव्यवच्छेदलाभ इत्यर्थः। ननु सुबर्थव्यापारे पदार्थतावच्छेदकव्यापारे च वर्तमानत्वाद्यन्वयबोधे व्युत्पत्त्यन्तरकल्पना। एवंच[655] व्यापाराश्रययोः पृथक्शक्यत्वे व्युत्पत्त्यन्तरकल्पना[656] तयोः परस्परमन्वये च व्युत्पत्त्यन्तरकल्पना च[657] <u>मण्डनमते</u> दोष इत्यत आह–**समानमि**ति। आख्यातस्य कृतिशक्तत्वे कर्तृकृदादेश्च[658] कृत्याश्रयशक्तत्वेऽपि[659] तादृशकल्पना आवश्यकीति भावः। **कालान्वये**ति।[660] वर्तमानत्वादिकालान्वयेत्यर्थः[661]। ननु व्यापारतदाश्रय-योराख्यातकर्तृकृदर्थत्वे[662] संयुज्यते[663] संयुक्त इत्यादौ तदभावादसङ्गतिरित्यत आह[664]–**धात्वर्थे**ति[665]। ननु अदृष्टवदात्मसंयोगस्य[666] संयोगानुकूलक्रियादेर्वा साक्षात् परम्परया वा[667] सर्वत्र सम्भवान्न तादृशव्यापाररहितत्वम्[668] अत आह–**संयोगत्वमात्रे**ति[669]। **न सकर्मकत्वमिति**[670]। व्यापारे प्रत्ययोपनीतत्वादिति[671] भावः। एतेन कर्मलक्षणे प्रत्ययोपनीतत्वविशेषणस्य[672] व्यावृत्तिर्दर्शिता। ननु भावे [पा. सू. 3-3-18]
घञ् इत्याद्यनुशासनात्[673] **घञादेः प्रयोगसाधुतामात्रं** प्रतीयते[674], भावो हि धात्वर्थः इति[675]। तस्य च[676] धातुनैवाभिधानात् तन्मात्रविवक्षायां भावे[677] घञिति[678] <u>सूत्रार्थ</u>पर्यवसानात्। तथाचानुशासनविरोध इत्यत आह–**संयोग इत्यादावि**ति[679]। तथाच एतदभिधायकमेवानुशासनमिति[680] भावः। **प्रसङ्गादि**ति। लक्षणयाऽनुभवस्योपपादने तु लाघवात्[681] यत्नत्वमेव[682] शक्यतावच्छेदकमिति भावः। लाघवस्यापेक्षायां[683] त्वाह–**फले**ति। असाधारण-जनकत्वविवक्षायां[684] न[685] दोष इत्यह आह–**विभागादी**ति। चलतीष्टापत्तिरतो **निश्चलादावि**ति[686]। **त्यजतीत्यादेरि**त्यादिना अभिघाताख्यसंयोगानुकूल-स्पर्शादिमत्यपि निश्चले[687] गच्छतीत्यादिप्रयोगप्रसङ्गः[688] परिगृहीतः। न तु[689] तत्राख्यातस्य[690] स्पन्दत्वरूपेण व्यापारे शक्तिः। एवं धातोः[691] नानार्थस्यावश्यकत्वे आख्यातस्य तत्कल्पनायां गौरवादिति[692]।।

२२. <u>गुरुमत</u>माह–**तत्र तत्रे**त्यादिना। तत्र तत्र त्यजति[693] गच्छतीत्यादौ[694]। **तत्तत्फले**ति। संयोगविभागादीत्यर्थः[695]। तेन पर्यायतापत्तिर्निरस्ता[696]। व्यापारविशेषः स्पन्दादिरूपः, तेन विभागानुकूलपूर्वसंयोगादिमति[697] त्यजतीत्यादिप्रसङ्गो[698]

निरस्तः। **क्वचिदाश्रयत्वादिकमपी**ति। भावाख्यातस्थले आश्रयत्वादेरभावात् **क्वचिदि**ति। इत्थं[699] च मध्यस्थं पूर्वत्राप्यन्वयि तेन च[700] तत्र[701] प्रथमान्तपदाभावात् संख्यावर्तमानत्वाद्यविवक्षायां च वर्तमानत्वादेरन्वयेऽपि न क्षतिः[702]।।

।। इति महामहोपाध्यायश्रीश्रीयुतसिद्धान्तवागीशभट्टाचार्यविरचिता आख्यातवादटिप्पनी समाप्ता इति[703]।।

सन्दर्भसंकेतः

1. आख्यातस्येति, आख्यातं यत्नत्वावच्छिन्नशक्यताकमित्यर्थः · · · आख्यातत्वं च सङ्केतविशेषसम्बन्धेन आख्यातपदवत्त्वम्, न तु जातिः तित्वादिना साङ्कर्यात् मानाभावाच्च। शक्ततावच्छेदकं च न तत्, किन्तु प्रत्येकं तित्वादिकमेव, आख्याततत्वप्रकारेणाज्ञानदशायां तित्वादिना ज्ञानात् शाब्दबोधमात्रस्य शक्तिभ्रमजन्यत्वप्रसङ्गात्, तित्वादिना प्रकारेणाज्ञानदशायां तत्प्रकारेण ज्ञानात् शाब्दबोधानुदयस्य सर्वसिद्धत्वात् AVR, p. 868
2. यत्नत्वं च प्रवृत्तित्वम्, प्रवृत्तित्वं च रागजन्यतावच्छेदकतया सिद्धम्, अहं यते अहं प्रवृत्तोऽस्मि अहं करोमीत्यनुव्यवसायसाक्षिको निवृत्तिजीवनयोनिव्यावृत्तो जतिविशेषः, निवृत्तिजीवनयोनियत्नयोः रागाजन्यत्वात् तथानुव्यवसायविरहाच्च। AVR, p. 868
प्रवृत्तिश्च निवृत्तिश्च तथा जीवनकारणम्।। 149।।
एवं प्रयत्नत्रैविध्यं तान्त्रिकैः परिदर्शितम्।
चिकीर्षाकृतिसाध्येष्टसाधनत्वमतिस्तथा।।150।।
उपादानस्य चाध्यक्षं प्रवृत्तौ जनकं भवेत्।
निवृत्तिस्तु भवेद् द्वेषाद् द्विष्टसाधनताधियः।।151।।
यत्नो जीवनयोनिस्तु सर्वदातीन्द्रियो भवेत्।
शरीरे प्राणसञ्चारे कारणं तत् प्रकीर्तितम्।।152।। BP, p. 351-2
3. Rāmabhadra differs: सर्वैः प्रामाणिकेराख्यातस्य विवरणादित्यर्थः। न तु सर्वाख्यातस्य विवरणादित्यर्थः, पाकं करोतीत्यनेन अपचदित्यादेरविवरणात्। AVV, p. 1
4. Different ways of apprehending denotative power of a word:
शक्तिग्रहं व्याकरणोपमानकोशाप्तवाक्याद् व्यवहारतश्च।
वाक्यस्य शेषाद् विवृतेर्वदन्ति सान्निध्यतः सिद्धपदस्य वृद्धाः।। BP, p. 230. Also in AVR, p. 873
5. A: ०हितव्यापकस्य. Cf. ननु गमनोपहितव्यापार एव गच्छतीत्यस्यार्थो · · · AVT (R), p. 876
6. A: अत्र प्रतीतेश्च। Cf. · · · अप्रतीतेः AV, p. 880
7. A: ०व्यापाराभावस्तु
8. A: सिद्धान्तः०। AVR (p. 878): मेध्याख्यनाडीविशेषावच्छेदेनात्ममनः संयोगो निद्रा।
9. A: सिद्धान्तः०
10. A: सिद्धान्तः०
11. C starts from त्यर्थः। · · · ·
12. A: ०पेक्षगौर०
13. C: ०त्यादौ चैत्रे ज्ञाना xxxxxx दन्वयोऽस्तु।
14. C adds किंलक्षणम्वा before अतएव.
15. C lacks अपि.

16. A: इत्यादिना
17. A: संसर्गविधया. C: ०संसर्गवि xxxxxx नुकूल.
18. C: ०त्याद्ये
19. C: मैत्र for चैत्र
20. C: मैत्रीय for चैत्रीय, ०का xxxxxx जन्य.
21. C: द्वितीये
22. C: सा xxxxx त०
23. A: पचतीत्यादौवित्यर्थद्वारा, C: पचतीत्यत्र विभक्त्यर्थद्वारा
24. A: ०न्वयासाक्षा०
25. C: ०भानस्य तेन सम्बन्धेनाभे०
26. C: अत्र तण्डुल० बो xxxx जन्या वा
27. C: तदुप०
28. A: करणं
29. C: ०शेष्यत्वं
30. C: तेन for तादृश
31. C: ०ल xxxxxxxxx प्रकारकक xxxxxxx दजन्यबोधं
32. C: ०न्यकर्मतोपस्थितिः
33. C omits the sentence.
34. C omits न.
35. C: न कल्प्यते
36. C: यद्वा एवं कर्तृत्वादौ विभक्त्यर्थे xxxxx न्धेन तन्डुल०
37. C: ०बोध xxxxx प्रकारकबोधं
38. C: प्रति समान · · · सत्त्या विभक्तिजन्योपस्थितेः धातुजन्यपाकप्रकारककृतिविशेष्यकबोधं प्रति वा विभक्त्यादिजन्यकृत्याद्युपस्थितेः कारणत्वं बोध्यम्।
39. C: नाम xxxxx या
40. C omits पुनः०
41. C: चैत्रः पचति तण्डुल इत्यादौ
42. C: तादृशान्वयबो.
43. A: नानार्थस्य
44. A: ०वारकः
45. A: ०कारणता वास्तु
46. C: चैत्रो ज xxxxx स्य नामार्थे
47. C: साक्षाद् भाने.
48. C omits the word.
49. C omits the word.
50. C: क्वचिदन्वय
51. C: ०ज xxxxx ति
52. C: ०पदजन्योपस्थि०
53. A omits अनयथा. A: ०वादिनापि
54. C: ०भ्युपे xxxxx
55. A: कर्मत्वानभित्वानभिधानात्, C: कर्मत्वस्यानभिधानात्
56. C: च for एव, असाधुत्वात् असाधुत्वज्ञानादेव
57. C: नैतादृश xxxx
58. C: कर्मतातत्०
59. C: अतस्तत्संर्गकबोधे
60. C: प्रसक्तिरि xxxxx

61. C: xxxxx कत्वं
62. C omits the word.
63. The second hemistich is यत्न एव कृतिः पूर्वा परस्मिन् सैव भावना।। vide TCM, p. 820. AVT (R), p. 890 records the hemistich as कृञो यत्नाभिधायित्वं न व्यापारप्रसक्तता।।
64. A: ०व्यवहारात्, C: अङ्कुरस्यxxxxxxव्यवहाराच्च
65. C: ०न्तानुधावनं
66. C: कर्तृकृतः। Cf. कर्तरि कृत्।। पा. सू. 3-4-67
67. C omits बोध.
68. C: भावः xxxxx समभिव्याहृतकर्तृकृतामाश्रय
69. C: ०लक्षणाया
70. C: omits अपि
71. C: तृचश्चाश्रयार्थकत्वे
72. C: यत्नाश्रय एव कर्तृ०
73. C: क्रिया xxxxx दाश्रयः
74. C: अङ्कुरादिः
75. C: ०यत्नजन्यत्व०
76. C: ०पत्तिसम्भ०
77. C: ०दि xxxx दी०
78. C omits अपि.
79. C: इति
80. C: ०व्यापा xxxxx माह
81. C: ०कत्वासिद्धौ
82. C: ०मत्त्वमात्रप्रती०
83. C: सिद्धत्वात् for सम्मतत्वात्
84. C: जनकव्यापा xxxxx त्वं च
85. C: जन्यत्वं
86. C: संयोगादिलक्षणव्यापारद्वाराप्रसङ्गः. Reading appears to be corrupt.
87. C: पाकानुकूलव्या०
88. C: पच xxxx पत्तिं
89. A: यत्नाबोधकत्व
90. C omits इति.
91. Cf. पाकादेस्तादात्म्यसम्बन्धेन हेतुत्वम्। AVV, p. 6
92. C omits इतरथा तु.
93. C: विवर xxxx यत्न०
94. C omits वा.
95. C adds a long passage before it: अनुमानलभ्येप्यर्थे प्रयोक्तुस्तात्पर्यस्य सत्त्वात् धूमोऽस्तीति वाक्ये वह्निपरत्ववत्त्वमिति भावः। अन्यथान्यलभ्य xxxxx शविव[र]णात् शक्यत्वे धर्मिणः यत्नवतः। तथाच तस्य प्रथमान्तपदलभ्यत्वार्थशक्यत्वम्। तथा यत्नस्यापि
96. C: ०कत्वे
97. C: ०हृतेऽ xxxx दार्थे
98. C: वा यत्ने आख्यातार्थवर्त०
99. Mathurānātha appears to have referred to Bhavānanda: केचित्तु नन्वध्याहृतपदाद् यत्नोपस्थितौ वर्तमानत्वस्यान्वयो भविष्यतीत्यत आह, अन्यत्रेत्याहुः। AVR, p. 889
100. C: xxxxx पदार्थेऽपि
101. C: ०प्रकारकान्वयबोधे
102. C: ०ख्यातपदजन्यवर्त xxxx बोधे

103. C: हेतुत्वस्य कल्पनात्
104. C: ०रीत्यास्यापि
105. C omits the word.
106. C: ०व्यापारयोश्च xxxxx
107. A: ०व्यापारबोधिते
108. C: ०विगमे xxxx
109. C: ०ष्यतीति
110. C: दूषणान्तर.
111. A: धर्मिविशेष इति
112. A: ०करणस्येति
113. A omits the word.
114. C: यत्नव्यधिxxxxx
115. A omits अपि.
116. C omits न.
117. C omits वर्तमान.
118. C omits वर्तमान
119. A: ०मूलकानुमाशङ्कस्त्रय
120. C: चैतन्येति
121. C: ०प्रतीतावपि
122. Cf. चैत्रत्वादीति। चैत्रत्वं स्वरूपतो विशेषणं तेन चैत्रत्वत्वेन चैत्रत्वस्य शब्दानुपस्थितत्वे न क्षतिः। AVR, pp. 902-3
123. A: ०मापकमितिः, शोभनत्वस्य स्थाल्यादिसाधारणतया शोभनत्वे सति तादृशव्यापारवत्त्वं न यत्नानुमापकमिति भावः। AVR, p. 903
124. A: ०न्वयेपि
125. C: घटत इति for सुघट एवेति
126. C: व्यापारशक्तावपि सर्वत्र न शक्त्या · · · पत्तिरिति।
127. C ? ज्ञातमिं०
128. C: ०त्यादिना।
129. Cf. लाघवेनेति जन्यत्वं धर्मत्वं वा व्यापारत्वं अपेक्ष्य यत्नत्वस्य लघुत्वेनेत्यर्थः। AVT (R) p. 903
130. C: यत्नत्व
131. C omits the word.
132. C: लाघवात्
133. A: यत्नशक्तावति
134. C: यत्न for कृति
135. A: प्रतीति०, C: ०प्रयोगं
136. A:०त्यादिनात्वयमपि, C omits त्वयमपि
137. A: कृतीतसा · · · कृतेश्च
138. A: ०कत्वं वेदेनैव
139. C: तेनापि
140. जनकसामान्ये शक्तिवादिना। AVR, p. 905; जनकमात्रे आख्यातशक्तिवादिना। AVT (R), p. 905
141. A: विषयत्वम्। AVR (p. 906): विषयित्वं। AVT(R) (p . 906): विषयित्वं संसर्गः।
142. C: तच्च स्वरूप · · · न्यदेव वास्तु
143. C: तद्भानं
144. C: विलक्षणजनकत्वं
145. A: ०त्यादि न प्रसङ्गः। C: पचतीति न प्रयोगः।
146. A: सामानाधिकरण्यमिति।

147. A: द्वितीयातृतीययो:। AVR (p. 910): तयो: तृतीयाद्वितीययो:।
148. C totally omits the sentence starting with अनभि.
149. A: नदनुरोधेन
150. C: कर्तृशक्ति० for कर्तरि शक्ति०
151. A: कृतेभिधान इति।
152. A omits कर्तृ०
153. C omits तु.
154. C: तृतीयैवात्र कृत्यभिधानादिति
155. C: ०हितायां
156. C: इति
157. A: पदाहारे। C: अस्तीतिक्रियाध्याहारे।
Mathurānātha's reference to Bhavānanda: केचित्तु क्रियारहितं वाक्यमेव नास्तीतिमते घट इत्यत्र क्रियापदाध्याहारस्यावश्यकत्वे अस्तीत्यादितिङन्तमेवाध्याहर्तव्यम्। तथाच विनिगमनाविरह इति कदाचित् ब्रूयादतस्तदुपेक्ष्य सक्रियमेव वाक्यमुदाहृतम्। · · · तिङ: संख्याशक्तिनिराकरणाशक्यत्वात् इत्याहु:। AVR, p. 913
158. C: न च तत्रैक for न चैक
159. A: लक्षणा असाधुत्वात्, C: लक्षणासाधुत्वात्
160. A: इत्यादिसूत्रं
161. C: नियमबोधकतया
162. C: इति for इत्यादिकं
163. C: तु
164. A: ०रूपोपस्थितचैत्रमैत्रे for: रूपेणो · · · त्रे
165. A: तिङ् for तिबु
166. C: ०तत्वेऽप्येको
167. A: बाधकभावादिति for बाधका · · · भाव:
168. C: नन्वेवमप्येक०
169. A: तिङा for तिबा
170. C: एकत्वे न शक्ति:
171. C: सिध्येदित्यत
172. A: सुप्त्वेन, C: सित्वेन
173. C omit च.
174. A: तिङे for तिबे
175. C: शक्ति: सिध्यतीति
176. A: तिङेकवचनसुबेकवचनानां
177. A: ? तदग्रहे
178. A : नैकत्वबोधकत्वबोधकत्वं
179. A: लक्षणावादिना
180. यद्यप्येकवचनत्वं नैकत्वशक्तत्वत् आत्माश्रयात् नाप्येकत्वबोधकत्वं पदमात्रस्यैव लक्षणादिना एकत्वबोधकत्वात् · · · AVR, p. 915
181. A: उपस्थितकर्तरि for उपस्थिते कर्तरि
182. A: तिङन्तादिनैव
183. C: न्यायनये
184. C: यत्नेऽपि
185. C omits इति.
186. C: एकत्वशक्त्येत्याहु: for एकत्वे · · · हु:
187. AV: कर्तृकर्मसंख्या · · · ·

188. C: तदपि
189. A omits न.
190. A omits तथाच.
191. C: गम्यत
192. A: इत्यत्रापि
193. A: ०संख्यासत्त्वादिति, C: ०हितसंख्याकत्वादिति
194. C omits the word.
195. A: आख्या एवायदुक्तानुविभाग: for आख्यात · · · ग:, C: एवोक्तानुक्तविभाग:
196. C adds च after ०समासेषु.
197. A omits समास.
198. C: ?अभिहिते
199. C omits the sentence.
200. A omits च.
201. C: कर्त्रेकत्वादिना
202. A: शक्तौ बाधादेव
203. C: कर्त्रेकत्वेति
204. A: and C: चैत्र
205. A : तत् for न
206. A: ०क्रियाया: कर्त्रैक.
207. C omits शक्यत्वात् एवं.
208. Reading accepted here according to A (fol 16a 3). A (fol 5a6): तत्तत्क्रियाकर्त्रैकवत्त्वादिना शक्त्या.
209. Reading accepted here according to A (fol 16a3). A (fol 5a6): अभिधेयत्वं विशेषतयेति। C: विशेषणतयेति
210. C omits the word.
211. Reading accepted here according to A (fol 16a4). A (fol 5a6): oशक्ति एक०
212. A : ? एकत्वंतवत्वं
213. C: तिप्तस्त्वादिकं
214. A omits वेति०
215. C omits the word.
216. C: शक्त्युपग०
217. C omits न.
218. C omits इति०
219. C: आत्मनेपदेनेति
220. A and C omit कर्मणि.
221. C: कदाचित् कर्मण्यप्रयोगात्
222. C omits the word.
223. C: तिप्तस्त्वादिना
224. A: ०संख्याप्रकारकान्वयबोधे
225. A omits the word.
226. C omits the word.
227. Reading accepted here according to A. A: ०जन्यकर्तृ. C: तदाख्यातजन्यबोधे
228. A omits कर्म०
229. A omits कर्मबोधे च.
230. C omits all the words starting with कर्मबोधे up to ०देर्वा०
231. C: ०जन्यकर्तृ०

232. C: ०जन्यकर्मोपस्थिते:
233. C: उभयाभिधाने
234. C: मैत्र:
235. A omits the word.
236. A omits कर्म.
237. C: मूलं बाध०
238. A: चाशक्तिकल्पनम्
239. C: ०रोधेन व्यव०
240. C: अन्वयधी:
241. C: ०विशेष्ये धात्वर्थे
242. C: ०विशेष्यत्वत्वेर्थे संख्यायन इति। C: कुतो न संख्या०
243. C: ०प्रकारकबोधजनकसामग्र्या
244. C: एव तथान्वये
245. A: उक्तनिया०
246. C: तद्विशे०
247. C: धात्वर्थव्युदासार्थमाह for धात्व · · · याह
248. A omits च.
249. A: तद्वाचकत्वात् भावनाविशेषण० for तद्बाधक · · · विशेषणत्व.
250. A: इत्यत्र
251. Cf. अत्र प्रथमान्तपदोपस्थाप्यत्वमात्रोपादाने तण्डुल: पचति चैत्र इत्यादौ प्रथमाया: कर्मत्वे शक्तिभ्रमेण लक्षणाज्ञानेन वा यदा तण्डुलकर्मकेत्यादिबोधस्तदापि तण्डुले भावनान्वयापत्तिरत: कर्मत्वाद्यनवरुद्ध इति कर्मत्वाद्यविशेषणीभूत इत्यर्थ:। AVR, p. 926. C: कर्मत्वाद्यनवरुद्धेति
252. A: ०व्याहारा: सहकारीति भाव: for व्यावहारस्य · · · भाव:। C: ०प्रकारकबोधे प्रथमान्तपदजन्योपस्थिति: कारणं समानविशेष्यकत्वं प्रत्यासत्ति: विशेषणतया तदन्वयबोधसमभिव्याहारस्य सहकारीति भाव:।
253. C: ०स्थाप्यस्य
254. A omits अपि.
255. C: समन्वितत्वात् for अन्वितत्वात्
256. A: ०न्वये
257. C: ०भाव इति
258. C: भावनाख्यातजन्य० for भावाख्यातजन्य०
259. A: व्युत्पत्त्यनन्तरं
260. A:भावनेति for भावनाया इति
261. A:? स्वपितैपत्यादौ
262. A: ०श्रयतानिरूपक०
263. C: चैत्रेणे०
264. C: निरूपकत्वादिसम्बन्धस्य अभावप्रतियोगितानवच्छेदकत्वात् for निरूपक · · · त्वाभावात्
265. C: धात्वर्थे स्वापादौ
266. C: बाध:, Source text: बाधितत्वात्
267. A: विशेष्यत्वेनान्वयान्वयधी०, C: विशेष्यत्वान्वयधी०
268. Cf. औत्सर्गिकं प्रथमोपस्थितमित्यपि कश्चित्। AVR, p. 933, C: प्रथमोपस्थितिं
269. A omits भाव:०
270. C: लिङोऽर्थ: for लिङ इत्यर्थ:
271. C: भावनाप्र०
272. C: तदन्वयस्तु
273. A: अपि for तु
274. C: आदिना

275. C: ०मानः स्वाप
276. C: मैत्रेण
277. C: मैत्रवृत्तिकृतिसाध्यपाक for चैत्रवृत्तिकृतिसाध्यः पाक
278. C: ०मित्यन्वय० for मिति रीत्यान्वय०
279. A: भावनेति for भावनाया इति
280. A: ०विशेष्यत्वं मात्रं
280. C: नैयायिकस्य
282. C: ०स्मैपदस्य करणेऽभिधानं for ०स्मैपदेन ··· नभिधानं
283. C: कृते
284. C: कर्तरि तव for तव कर्तरि
285. C: सम्बन्धेन for संसर्गेण
286. C adds a word अव्युत्पन्नं after उभयाबोधकत्वं.
287. Cf. यथा तव एकदा न कर्तृकर्मबोधकत्वं तथा ममाप्येकदा न कर्तर्याश्रयत्वेन कर्मणि चान्यथान्वयबोधकत्वमिति भावः। AVR, p. 937
288. C omits इति.
289. A: चैत्रेणेति
290. C: ०वृत्तित्वसंख्याया
291. C omits वृत्ति.
292. C omits च.
293. A: ०लक्षकं, C: ०त्वादावप्युपलक्षणं
294. A: तेन जातीत्यादि०, AVR (p. 939): व्यापारेत्युपलक्षणं आश्रयत्वप्रतियोगित्वमपीति बोध्यम्। शब्दैक्यस्यानुपादेयत्वात् तेन चैत्रो जानाति घटो नश्यतीत्यादेरपि संग्रहः।
295. C: वैयाकरणोक्तयुक्तिं
296. C: अयमिति घट for घटो घट
297. A omits शक्ति.
298. A adds चैत्रत्वादिना before this word.
299. Cf. केचित्तु अन्यादृशं यत्राख्यातेन कृतिर्बोध्यते तत्र चैत्रादिपदेनापि चैत्रादिकं बोध्यते इत्येवंरूपमित्यर्थः, इत्याहुः। AVR, p. 940
300. C: कथमिति भावनाविशेष्यः इति पूर्वेणान्वयः।
301. C omits the word.
302. C omits चेदिति.
303. C: दूषयति
304. C: रथेनेति for सविषयेति. Source text: सविषयकव्यापार changed according to A
305. C: अत्र
306. A: सविषयक for सविषय, C: ०व्यापाराभिधान
307. A: स्थाने
308. C: धात्वर्थत्वादिना
309. C: अत्रापि
310. C: कर्म for कर्मत्व
311. C omits गमनजन्य०
312. A omits the word.
313. C: उत्तर
314. C: ०स्त्वित्यादिना
315. A: ०विशेष्यविशेषणभाव०
316. A: तुल्यवत्
317. A: ०नुपपत्तिगौरवद्धेतुत्यत आह

318. A: मात्रशब्देन
319. C omits च.
320. C omits न, but then the prior word shoud be split as ०नुभवविरोधे न.
321. A: ०वाचकत्वात्
322. A: विशेषण इति
323. C omits क्रियाविशेषणतयैव धातुशक्यत्वेन फलविशेष्यक०
324. C omits the word.
325. C: इत्यर्थ: for इति भाव:
326. A: चात्मने०
327. C: अपि for च
328. C: ०फलरूपकर्मत्वप्रकारक०
329. A omits the full portion from भावनाया
330. C: विशेष्यत्वात्
331. A omits इत्यत आह.
332. C: विशेष्यत्वादाह
333. A: भावनायामिति
334. C: तथाच
335. C: कृत्यर्थाख्याता.
336. C: ०वारकं
337. A: ०कल्पने गौरवं
338. C: तस्मात् कृत्यनभिधायकेति
339. C: चैत्रेणानीतं for मैत्रेण गतम्
340. C: मैत्रेण
341. A: तृतीयायास्तत्र
342. C omits धातुजन्य.
343. C omits च.
344. C: पच्यते
345. C: चैत्र
346. C: इत्यादेर्न प्रसङ्ग:
347. C: नन्वेवं
348. C: ०न्वयेऽनिया०
349. C: भावनान्वयनियामकं
350. C omits आह.
351. C: न चाचेतनत्वानुरोधात् आख्यातार्थविशेष्यत्वं संख्यान्वयनियामकं तथा चाख्यातार्थफलविशेष्येऽपि संख्यान्वये प्राचां न व्युत्पत्तिविरोध इति वाच्यं for the sentence ननु · · · न।
352. C: ०विशेष्ये धात्वर्थेऽपि
353. C: कृत्यर्थका for तृतीयार्था
354. C omits जनक०
355. C omits आश्रयादि.
356. C: व्यापारादिबोध.
357. C: अपि हेतुत्वकल्पने गौरवादिति for the entire portion विशिष्टैक · · · गौरवादिति
358. C omits the word.
359. C: गन्तेत्यादि
360. A adds न before कर्तरि.
361. C: शक्तत्व for शक्ति
362. C: साधकं

363. C: समानफललिङ्गकत्वमपि
364. A omits the portion starting from दर्शयति upto ०त्वमपि०
365. C: भेदाभावं
366. A adds न before अभेदा.
367. C adds च after अत्र.
368. C: ०पदस्यैदेनादिपदस्य
369. C: स्मरणात्
370. C adds च before मानाभावात्.
371. C: भोजनकृतिस्तृप्ति
372. C: ०करण्यादिना
373. C: तदेकदेशे कृतौ
374. C omits आदि.
375. C: पुत्रपुत्रे शक्तिस्तत्र
376. A: विशेष्ये चैत्र ··· न्वये
377. C: चैत्रपुत्रेऽपि
378. C: पुत्रपुत्रस्य तस्य चैत्रसम्बन्धित्वात् for पुत्र ··· त्वात्
379. C omits पदार्थ.
380. A: पुरुस्यैकदेशे, C: पुंरूपस्य एकदेशे
381. C: चैत्रसम्बन्धित्वादतः पुंसः एकदेशेन चैत्रसम्बन्धिजन्यत्वाश्रयपुंजन्यपुरुष इत्यन्वयबोध इति भावः for the entire portion चैत्रसम्बन्धान्वयः ··· इति भावः
382. C: ०पदस्य शक्ति०
383. C omits the word.
384. A: ०विशेषः नानुत्पन्न इति for ०विशेष ··· ऽतः
385. A: चैत्रादन्य
386. C: अत्र for तत्र
387. A: भेदाश्रयत्वं, C: भेदाद्यश्रयत्वं
388. C: घटादित्यत्रावधिमत्त्वं for तत्रावधित्वं
389. C omits इति भावः.
390. C: अत्र for तत्र
391. C omits इत्यन्वयः०
392. C: ०गुणपरत्वे
393. C: बोध्यं
394. C: विशेषणे
395. C: धी for ज्ञान
396. C omits च.
397. C omits च.
398. A: ०पदार्थान्वयेतथो., C: ०पदार्थान्वयबोधोऽतथो०
399. C: न नञादिपदसमभिव्याहृतशक्त्याद्यर्थान्वये
400. C: तु विशेषणत्वेन
401. C: विशिष्य
402. C omits न०
403. C: ०भावसङ्कोचे
404. C: ०न्तरस्य कल्पने
405. C omits च०
406. A: ०भविकत्वस्यापादनायाह
407. A: ग्रहः

408. C: पाकीय
409. C: अन्वयबोध:
410. C: स्वजन्यकृति०
411. C omits च०
412. C: षष्ठ्या for षष्ठी
413. C: आश्रयजन्यतावत् पुरुषजन्यत्वे स्वाश्रयभेदवत्त्वसम्बन्धेन च चैत्रे भेदवति चान्वयो बोध्य: for the entire portion स्वाश्रयजन्यता · · · वाच्य:
414. A: ०गुणान्तरमाह
415. A: मुख्यकर्मत्वं फलकत्वात्, C: मुख्यत्वं फलरूपं
416. C: मुख्यं कर्तृत्वं
417. C: भाक्तस्तु for भाक्तं च
418. C: आदिभ्यां
419. C omits आदिक.
420. C omits आदि.
421. A omits अपि.
422. A: पक्त्वा
423. A: कृतेरप्यभिधाने
424. C: मुख्यकर्तृत्वं
425. A omits च
426. C: कृता वा आख्यातेन
427. C: भुक्त्वा चैत्रेणान्नं for भोक्त्रा · · · न्नं
428. A: तृजा
429. C: भोजनानुकूलकृतेरभिधानेऽपि
430. C: ०कृतेश्च
431. C omits एव.
432. C: ०क्त्वातुम्वुनादिप्रयोगेषु for क्त्वावुन् · · · येषु
433. C omits the word.
434. C: धातुत्वेति
435. A omits the word.
436. A: कतिपयघटितस्य
437. C omits the word.
438. A: अपि for तु
439. C omits शक्ति.
440. C: कृतिविशिष्टे for विशिष्टे
441. C omits the entire portin कर्तृकृतापीति · · · वक्ष्यमाणस्य.
442. C omits व्यावृत्तिं दशयितुं०
443. C: तद्ग्रहत्वासम्भ०
444. A omits the word.
445. A: ०वेतत्वघटित०
446. C omits एव०
447. A omits the word.
448. A: शब्दमहत्त्वा० for शब्दस्य महत्त्वा०
449. A omits the word.
450. A: ? विशेषणभावापन्न
451. C: तत्तद् for यदि
452. C: विशिष्टत्वं

453. C adds यदि ब्रूयात् before तदा.
454. C: ०कृतामप्य०
455. A: तेननाधु०
456. A omits फलस्य and adds a sentence एवं फले द्वितीयाद्यर्थैकदेशे। तज्जनकत्वं तु धात्वर्थ एवाश्रयस्य before कृदात्मने०
457. C: फलमात्रेति for फलमात्रं वेति
458. C: न शक्यतावच्छेदकगौरवम् for शक्यता · · · गौरवम्
459. A omits इति भावः०
460. C: शुद्धस्पन्दव्यापा०
461. A: धात्वर्थे
462. C: यावदर्थे०
463. A: ०भविकत्वाच्च
464. A: गूढावसन्धिः, C omits the word.
465. C omits एव.
466. A: च
467. C omits अन्वय.
468. A: त्यजत इत्यादौ
469. A: संग्रहः for परिग्रहः
470. A: विशेषण for विशेष्य
471. C omits यदि च.
472. AV (K): स्वर्गादिजनकत्वम्
473. A adds यदि after this word. C: यदि तत्रेष्टत्वरूपेणैव
474. C: अत्र for तत्र
475. C: फलत्व for फलता
476. A: संयोगादिबाधकत्वं
477. A: ०न्तराश्रयेण
478. C: ०संयोगादिरूपफलस्याभेदान्वयव्युत्पत्त्य० for ०संयोगा · · · व्युत्पत्त्य०
479. A omits the word.
480. A: ०बोधकत्वादिति
481. A omits the word.
482. A omits the wrod.
483. A: स्वर्गत्वादिना
484. C: च
485. A omits स्वर्ग०
486. A: आदि for आकारक
487. A: यथा for अपि यदा
488. A adds च after the word.
489. A: ?बाधकत्वं
490. A omits the word.
491. A omits आकारक०
492. A:?०तादौ एव
493. C: संयोगादि
494. A: ०ग्रहस्य हेतुत्वात्
495. A omits the word.
496. A: बुद्धिप्रकारेति
497. C: स्मृति for बोध

498. A omits the word.
499. A: संयोगादिबोधकत्वं
500. C omits न च॰
501. C omits एव॰
502. C: एतच्छालिनि
503. A: ॰विभागसंयोगयो:
504. C omits तत्॰
505. C omits the word.
506. C: ॰च्छिन्ने स्पन्दे
507. A omits गमे:, adds च after ॰छिन्ने॰
508. C: ॰भावात् नोक्ताति.
509. A:?गम्यादिकर्मत्वं नित्यादिना for गम्यादे · · · दिना
510. A: विशिष्यापि
511. A omits च॰
512. C omits the word
513. C: ॰स्थापक
514. C omits इति॰
515. A: अनुगत for अनुगम, C: कर्मत्वा for सकर्मकत्वा
516. A: तत्र for तत्तद्
517. C: कर्मप्रत्ययविधानवत्॰
518. A: कर्मप्रत्ययाविधानं वानुपपन्नं for कर्म · · · पन्नम्
519. C omits कर्म · · · योगे.
520. C: तदापत्ते:
521. C: ॰जनकमनुगतं सकर्मकत्वं for ॰जनक · · · मनुगतं
522. C omits तादृश॰ ॰प्रकारकस्वार्थबोध॰ for ॰प्रकारकान्वयबोध॰
523. A: शक्ति for शब्द
524. C: ? पर्यापत्ति॰
525. A: एककार्यकत्वं for एकार्थबोधकत्वं
526. C: कस्यचिन्मते भवतीति
527. C omits बोध॰
528. A:?अतएवेति for तत्र चेति
529. A: ॰सकर्मकत्वधातुयोगे
530. A: द्वितीयार्थभेदेऽपि for द्वितीयाया अर्थभेदेऽपि
531. C: सूत्रप्रणयणा॰
532. C omits चेति करणे.
533. C:?फलार्थान्विता for फलाहिता. Omits इत्यर्थ:॰
534. A: इत्युक्ते for इत्यत्र
535. C: सप्तम्यर्थाधेयत्वस्य
536. C: ॰प्रयोग इति
537. C omits the word.
538. C: तण्डुलं पचति for पचति तण्डुलं
539. C: मैत्रेण
540. C: तण्डुल: पच्यते for पच्यते तण्डुल
541. A विशेष्यविशेषणतावन्मात्रवैपरीत्येन
542. C omits the word.
543. C: पूर्वोक्तयुक्त्या

544. A: फलबोधस्याशक्यत्वादित्यर्थ:
545. A: अत्रापीष्टादिवत्
546. A: विशेष for विशिष्ट
547. A: भावधेयं
548. C omits संयोगजनक.
549. C: बोद्धव्य:
550. C omits the word.
551. C: ०च्छिन्ने स्पन्दे
552. C: इत्यन्वयस्य
553. C: आस्तां
554. C omits the word.
555. C omits च.
556. C: धात्वर्थफलस्य for धात्व · · · स्य
557. A omits the word.
558. C: चैत्रवृत्तिकृतिजन्यसंयोगाश्रयो
559. C: इति चान्वयधी:
560. A: ०स्थिति:, C: तज्जन्यस्पन्दोपस्थिते:
561. A: ०धात्वस्यस्पन्दप्रकारकबोधे, C: ०धात्वर्थप्रकारकबोधे
562. C: ०णत्वकल्प० for ०णकत्वस्य कल्प०
563. C omis the word.
564. A omits इति.
565. C: कारणत्वकल्पनान्नान्वयबोधप्रसिद्ध for कारणत्वस्य · · · प्रसङ्ग
566. C: ०रूफलस्य for ०रूपस्य फलस्य
567. C: द्विष्ठतया
568. C omits तत्र च.
569. A: ? तण्डुलावृत्ति.
570. C: ०प्रकारकशाब्दबोधात् तज्जन्य० for ०प्रकारकबोधे · · · जन्य०
571. C: करणत्वकल्पनात् for कारणत्वस्य कल्पनात्
572. C omits the word.
573. A omits the word.
574. C: स्वात्मा
575. C omits इति०
576. A: लिङ for तिङा
577. Vide unit no. 17.
578. A omits कृति.
579. A: स्वाश्रयापेक्षाया
580. C: स्वात्मानं
581. A:आत्मभिन्नस [म] वेतात्मवृत्तिसंयोगजनिकायामान्तरवृत्तिक्रियातदनुकूलकृतिमत्त्वस्य अस्मिन्नभावादेव नातिप्रसङ्ग:
for the entire portion स्वात्मसमवेता या स्वात्म · · · न प्रयोग:
582. C: ०भ्युपेयते
583. A: इत्यन्वय:
584. C: ०द्यर्थेष्टसाध०
585. A: व्यापारावागोचर
586. C: ०साधनतादि.
587. A: विधेजन्यत्वात्
588. C omits विधे: · · · स्यात्०

589. C: वर्तमानादित्य.
590. A omits the word.
591. A: ग्रह. AdosQ a sentence after परिग्रहः–वर्तमानत्वात्यादिना अतीतत्वादे ग्रहः०
592. A adds च after ०त्वादिना. C: ०त्वादीत्यादिना
593. A adds इष्टसाधनत्व before कृतिसाध्यत्व०
594. A: संग्रहः
595. A: अस्मन्मतासिद्ध., C: स्वतसिद्ध.
596. A omits the word.
597. A: तन्मते
598. A: ? ०विधया
599. A: कृतावन्वयात्
600. A omits तृतीयार्थ · · · पपत्तिः.
601. A: तदन्वये
602. C omits मिथोगमनमिति
603. A ननु तन्मते for एतन्मते
604. A: कर्मत्वात्
605. A omits मात्र०
606. C: स्वात्मानं
607. A: समवेतस्वात्मक for समवेतात्मक, C: स्वापेक्षिक for आपेक्षिक, धातु for धात्वर्थ
608. C: स्वावयवात्मक for स्वात्म
609. A omits इति.
610. C omits the word.
611. C: ?ग्रामवृत्तिसंयोगजनकग्रामभिन्नसमवेतव्यापारजनकसंयोगशाली ग्राम इति बोधः for the entire portion ग्रामवृत्ति · · · बोधः
612. A: एव
613. A: विशेषणत्वेन
614. A : ०नुभविकस्य
615. A: फलान्वयबोधकत्वे
616. A: इत्यादि
617. C: गच्छति for गन्ता, यत्न for तुल्य
618. C omits आदि०
619. C: कर्तृकर्माख्यातयोराश्रयविषयावर्थः for the entire portion कर्तृकर्माख्यातयोराश्रयविशेषत्वे कर्तृकर्मकृतोराश्रयविषयत्वार्थः
620. C: ०तार्थव्यापारस्य
621. C omits च०
622. C: वर्तमानत्वाद्यन्वये च
623. A: व्यापारासत्त्व०
624. C omits च०
625. C omits च०
626. A: संग्रहः
627. A: कर्तृकृताद्यु०
628. A: कर्तृकृतादि, ०प्रकारत्वं
629. A: इतरान्वयबोधे
630. C: ०तन्त्रतायां तु
631. C omits बोध.
632. C: ०वर्तमानादि०

633. C: स्वजन्याश्रयोन०
634. C omits the word.
635. A omits आश्रय एव०
636. A omits एव०
637. A omits वत्०
638. C: इत्यादेरपि प्रसङ्गात्
639. C omits योग.
640. C: ०न्वयित्वेन
641. A omits तद्. C: इत्यर्थ: for इति भाव:
642. C: ०च्छेदकत्वेऽन्यसमवेतत्वाद्यवच्छिन्नव्यवच्छेदस्य
643. C adds असमवेते before प्रसिद्धावपि०
644. C omits च गन्धादौ०
645. C omits बाधित इत्याह०
646. A omits आदि०
647. A omits the word
648. A: ०संसर्गविशेषणलाभ०,? ०सम्भवात् न तु०
649. C: स्वान्ययोगे
650. C omits the word.
651. Source text needs amendment?
652. A: पदार्थेन
653. A omits the word.
654. A: नील for पार्थ
655. A omits the word.
656. A: शक्य for व्युत्पत्ति
657. From the word च, we have got the opportunity for verifying the text with another nanuscript of hand-made paper having only a singl folio. Ms no. 7764, fol no 16. Here 16a1-16b2 contains आख्यातवादटिप्पनी of Bhavānanda. The manuscript has actual perforation at the centre. This manuscript is assigned as B.
658. A: ०कृतादेश्च, B and C: ०कृदादे:
659. C omits अपि.
660. C: कालान्वयीति
661. C: वर्तमानादिकालान्वयीत्यर्थ:
662. B: व्यापाराश्रय०
663. A: युज्यते
664. B & C: ०तिरत आह
665. A: धात्वर्थ इति
666. B: omits संयोगस्य०
667. B: omits वा०
668. B: ०पारविरहित्वं
669. A: संयोगवत्त्वमात्रेति
670. A and B: सकर्मत्वमिति
671. B: ०नीतत्वाभावादिति
672. B: ०नीतवि., C omits विशेषणस्य०
673. A and C: ०घञित्यनु.
674. C: ०साधुत्वमात्रप्रतीते: for ०साधुतामात्रं प्रतीयते

675. A and C omit इति०
676. B omits च०
677. B and C omit भावे०
678. A: घत्रि
679. B: इत्यादि
680. A: ०भिप्रायिक०, B: ०भिप्रायक०
681. C: ०स्योपपादनत्वलाघवात्
682. C: ?आत्मत्वमेव
683. C: ०लाघवस्योपेक्षायां
684. C: ०जनकविवक्षायां
685. B omits the word.
686. B: निश्चलेति
687. B: ०मति निश्चलेऽपि for ०मत्यपि निश्चले
688. A: ०प्रयोग: सम्बन्ध: च, B omits प्रयोग० C omits आदि०
689. A: च
690. C: कर्त्राख्यातस्य
691. A and C omit धातो:०
692. C: नानार्थत्वमिष्टमेवेति वाच्यं, धातोर्नानार्थत्वमिष्टमेवेति वाच्यं, धातोर्नानार्थस्यस्यावश्यकत्वे आख्यातस्य तत्० for नानार्थस्या . . . तत्०
693. A omits तत्र तत्र त्यजति. C omits त्यजति.
694. A adds तु after ०त्यादौ.
695. C: विभागसंयोगा.
696. A: सपर्यायता.
697. B: कर्तृ for पूर्व
698. B omits आदि.
699. A: इदं
700. A omits the word.
701. A adds च after तत्र०
702. B ends here with a colophon. But A repeats a long portion which already takes place in fol 5a5-5b3 as dittography. (Fol 16a2) ननु एकत्वादिना शक्तौ बाधादेव न कर्मादिसाधारण्यं अत आह (3) कर्त्रेवेति न च मैत्रं ग्रामं नयति चैत्र इत्यादौ कर्मणोऽपि कर्तृत्वा कथं न तत्साधारण्यमिति वाच्यं तत्तत्क्रियाया: कर्त्रैकत्वत्वादिना शक्यत्वात् एवं शक्त्यानन्त्यस्येष्टत्वात् अविधेयस्त्वविशेषणतैवेति शेष:। शक्तौ गौरवं कर्त्रैकत्वत्वेन कर्मैकत्वत्वेन च विभिन्नशक्तिकल्पनात् एकत्वत्वापेक्षया कर्तैकत्वत्वस्य शक्यतावच्छेदकत्वे गौरवं अस्मन्मते एकत्वं तवत्वं तिप्त्वादिकं वा शक्ततावच्छेदकं तन्मते तु कर्त्राख्यातैकवचनत्वादिकं कर्त्रादिविशेष्यकबोधजनकतिप्त्वादिकं शक्ततावच्छेदकमिति गौरवमिति। ननु कर्त्रादिषु शक्त्यभ्युपगमेऽपि कथं संख्यान्वयनियम: कथं वा न गौरवम् अत आह-तस्मादिति। आत्मनेपदत्वेनेति। परस्मैपदस्य कदाचिदपि अप्रयोगादिति। तत्तद्रूपेण तिप्त्वादिना एकपदेति तथाच कर्माख्यातजन्यसंख्याप्रकारकान्वयबोधे च तत्तदाख्यातजन्यकर्तृकर्मोपस्थिते कारणत्वान्नान्यत्र संख्यान्वय इति भाव:। वाच्यगामित्वं आख्यातवाच्यकर्तृकर्मविशेष्यकान्वयबोधविषयत्वं अव्युत्पन्नमिति तदाख्यातजन्ये कर्तृबोधे तात्पर्यज्ञानस्य तद्ग्राहप्रकरणादेवाकर्तृतात्पर्यज्ञनस्य तद्ग्राहप्रकरणादेर्वा विरोधित्वं फलबलात् कल्प्यत इति भाव:।।
703. B records the colophon: इति सिद्धान्तवागीशविरचिताख्यातवादटीप्पनी समाप्ता।।

    A adds post colophon: रामशर्मण: पुस्तकमिदं स्वाक्षरञ्च।। समाप्तोऽयं ग्रन्थ:। शुभमस्तु। शकाब्दा 1607, 10 वैशाख।। वैशाखमासस्य दशमदिवसे समाप्तोऽयं ग्रन्थ:।। After this some deities and a series of the letter श्री have been mentioned to make the lines (16b3-4) complete.

    C records the colophon: इति महामहोपाध्यायश्रीभवानन्दसिद्धान्तवागीशभट्टाचार्यविरचिता

शिरोमणिकृताख्यातवादसारमञ्जरी समाप्ता।।

Post colophon:

पापपुञ्जयुते रुद्रे न्याय्यमेवाशुभं त्वया।
किन्तु मातरिदं चिन्त्यं शिवाख्याते जगत्श्रुता।।
मलाख्ये श्रावणे मासि रुद्रः क्षुद्रमतिः पुनः।
लिलेख ग्रन्थमेनं तु ज्वरसन्तापसंयुतः।।

।।श्रीनारायणाय नमो नमः।।

List of authorities and quotations in the Text and Commentary

Authorities mentioned in the *Ākhyātavāda*

Quotation in the *Ākhyātavāda*

Authorities and text mentioned in the *Ākhyātavādatippanī*

Page Nos.

Quotations in the *Ākhyātavādaṭippanī*

Bibliography

Ākhyātavāda. Raghunātha Śiromaṇi. Also called *Ākhyātaśaktivāda*. Vide TCM, pp.867–1009.

Ākhyātavāda. Raghunātha Śiromaṇi. With the commentary *Ākhyātavādavyākhyā* of Rāmabhadra Sārvabhauma. Ed. Prabal Kumar Sen, Sanskrit Pustak Bhandar, Kolkata, 1979.

Ākhyātavādarahasya. Mathurānātha Tarkavāgīśa. Vide TCM, pp. 867–1009.

Ākhyātavādaṭippanī. Rāmacandra Nyāyavāgīśa. Vide TCM, pp. 867–1009.

Ākhyātavādavyākhyā. Rāmabhadra Sārvabhauma. Vide *Ākhyātavāda*, edited by Prabal Kumar Sen.

Bhāṣāpariccheda. Ascribed to Viśvanātha Siddhāntapañcānana. With *Bhāṣāparicchedamuktāvalī*. Ed. Dr. Anamika Roy Chowdhury. Distributor: Sanskrit Pustak Bhandar, Kolkata, 2004.

Bhattacharya, B. : *A Study in Language and Meaning*, Calcutta, 1962.

Bhattacharya, Dinesh Chandra: *Vaṅge Navya-nyāya Carcā*. Bangiya Sahitya Parishat, Kolkata, 1952.

Chatterjee, K. N.: *Word and its Meaning*. Chowkhambha Orientalia, Varanasi, 1979.

Mazumdar, Pradip Kumar: *The Philosophy of Language*. Sanskrit Pustak Bhandar, Calcutta, 1977.

Pandeya, R.C.: *The Problem of Meaning in Indian Philosophy*. Motilal Banarsidass, Delhi, 1963.

Potter, Karl: *The Encyclopedia of Indian Philosophies*. Vol. VI (Indian Philosophical Analysis. Nyāya-Vaiśeṣika from Gaṅgeśa to Raghunātha Śiromaṇi). Motilal Bararsidass, Delhi, 1993

Raja, K. Kunjunni: *Indian Theories of Meaning*. The Adyar Library and Research Centre. Adyar, Madras 20, 1977.

Shastri, Gaurinath: *The Philosophy of Word and Meaning*. Calcutta Sanskrit College Research Series No.5, 1959.

Tattvacintāmaṇi of Gaṅgeśa Upādhyāya. Vol IV, Part 2 (containing Śabda section). With explanatory notes on *Ākhyāta* and Nañ-samāsa by Raghunātha Śiromaṇi. Ed. Pt. Kamakhyanatha Tarkavagisa. Oriental Book Centre, Delhi, 1990.

PART II

Nañvāda of Raghunātha Śiromaṇi

with
NAÑVĀDAṬIPPANĪ
of
BHAVĀNANDA SIDDHĀNTAVĀGĪŚA

Critically edited by
Sanjit Kumar Sadhukhan

Contents

Introduction

The meaning of the negative particles had long been a topic of discussion in Indian philosophy. The Vaiyākaraṇas, Mīmāśakas and the Naiyāyikas and sometimes others have contributed so much to the topic that it led Raghunātha to compose a separate treatise entitled *Nañvāda.* The negative particle *nañ* here stands for *na* and *mā* used separately in a sentence and *na, a* and *an* in compound words. But sometimes the words meaning difference (i.e. mutual absence) or the like also come under the purview of *nañ.* But what does the *nañ* mean in different types of sentences or words? The Vaiyākaraṇas are found to have examined in detail, the meaning of *nañ* occurring in the Pāṇini sūtras to match the case with the meaning of the sūtras. (Cf. *anaci ca* 8.4.47, *nañ* 2.2.6, etc.). In the topic of Nañ-tatpuruṣa, the meaning of *nañ* is a very important matter of discussion. Apart from this, the Vaiyākaraṇas have also contributed to the topic separately in later independent works. We may mention, by way of example, at least two great grammatico-philosophical works: *Vaiyākaraṇabhūṣaṇasāra* of Kauṇḍa Bhaṭṭa and *Paramalaghumaiijuṣā* of Nāgeśa Bhaṭṭa. The meaning of *nañ* in the word *abrāhmaṇa* is of much interest to the Vaiyākarasṇas. Anyway, they hold two kinds of *nañ:* (i) Paryudasa and (ii) Prasajyapratiṣedha. The first one is affirmation through negation and the second one is negation absolute. The well-known verses in this regard are as follows:

प्रधानत्वंविधेर्यत्रप्रतिषेधेऽप्रधानता।
पर्युदासः सविज्ञेयोयत्रेतरपदेननञ्॥
अप्रधान्यंविधेय त्रप्रतिषेधेप्रधानता।
प्रसज्यप्रतिषेधोऽसौक्रियययायत्रनञ्॥

Simultaneously the Vaiyākaraṇas also refer to a verse where the six meanings of *nañ* have been enumerated:

तत्सादृश्यमभावश्चतदन्यत्वंतदल्पता।
अप्राशस्त्यंविरोधश्चनञर्थाषट्प्रमीर्तिताः॥

The Mīmāṣakas also are found to have been very much concerned to find out the meaning of *nañ* as they have had to explain

numerous Vedic ritualistic injunctions. In particular, the Prābhākara Mimpsakas are the pioneers in this field.

The Naiyāyikas also became a participant in this contentious debate. In the fifth chapter of the *Nyāyamañjarī* of Jayanta Bhaṭṭa there is the discussion on the meaning of nañ, *vis-a-vis* the conflicting views thereon. In the Samāsavāda of the *Tattvacintāmaṇi* of Gangeśa, *nañ* has been discussed.

Raghunātha has discussed the topic in a separate treatise, *Nañvāda.* Though in volume it appears a small work, it is not small at all in the quality and importance of its content. It surveys a wide range of discussions on the topic and the incorporation of the same within the space of such a small work has been made possible by his wonderful power to convey a lot in a terse manner, with utmost economy in words. According to the Naiyāyikas, absence is four-fold, prior absence *(prāgabhāva)*, posterior absence *(pradhvalsābhāva)*, absolute absence *(atyantābhāva)* and mutual absence *(anrnyābhāva)*. The first three are called relational absence *(samsrgābhāva)*. Of these four varieties of absence, the first two do not come under the purview of linguistic consideration. The other two, viz. mutual absence and absolute absence, have a linguistic basis, and they can be expressed only with the help of the negative particle *na.* (Cf. *Negative Words,* p. 35).

At the very beginning of the discussion, Raghunātha declares that the denotative meaning of *nañ* is two types of absence, Relational absence and Mutual absence. And those, being true to the meaning of *nañ,* will have the counterpositiveness *(pratiyogitā),* which must in turn be 'limited by the property of that which is syntactically connected to absence by the relation of counterpositiveness' *(anvayitāvacchedakāvacchinna)*. This conclusion is attested by our verbal knowledge. Let us take an example for illustration: *bhūtale na ghaṭaḥ* (There is no pot on the ground). Here the *neñ* denotes relational absence. Absence is always determined with reference to some positive entity. So in *na ghaṭaḥ,* the absence is with reference to *ghaṭa*. This *ghaṭa* is the counterpostive *(pratiyogin)* of absence. The property of being counterpositive is counterpositiveness *(pratiyogitā)*. The *nañ* in *na ghaṭaḥ,* cannot simply denote an absence 'having counterpositive-ness,' but that counterpositiveness must be limited by some property. And in the present case that counterpositiveness must be limited by the property of that *(ghaṭa)* which is syntactically connected to absence. So *nañ* denotes an absence having (i.e. reflecting) counter-

positiveness which is limited by the property of that which is syntactically connected to absence. Here *ghaṭatva* is the desired property. If the expression would be *bhūtale na nīlaḥ ghaṭaḥ* then the absence, i.e. the meaning of *nañ* would mean absence whose counterpositiveness is limited by the property of that which is syntactically connected to absence. Here not simply *ghaṭa,* but *nīla ghaṭa,* is syntactically connected to absence. Therefore the property called *anvayitā* will be *nṣlaghaṭatva* and not *ghaṭatva.* Raghunātha establishes his view by citing the example of our verbal usages in the cases of two types of absence: We do not say *nīlagharṭavati na ghaṭaḥ* (There is no pot in a place where there is a blue pot); rather we say, *nīlaghṭavati na pītaḥ ghaṭaḥ* (There is no yellow pot in a place where there is a blue pot). It indeed is the case of relational absence. On the strength of this verbal usage, we affirm that the absence must reflect the counterpositiveness limited by the property of that which is syntactically connected to absence by the relation of counterpositiveness. Here *pīta ghaṭa* (i.e. yellow pot) is connected to absence. So the property of that, i.e. *pītaghaṭwtva* will be the limiting factor of that counterpositiveness of that absence. After this, the case of mutual absence is demonstrated. We never say *nīaḥ ghaṭaḥ na ghaṭaḥ,* rather we say *nṣlaḥ ghaṭaḥ na pītaḥ ghaṭaḥ.* On the strength of this verbal usage, we affirm that in the case of mutual absence also *nañ* denotes the absence which reflects the counterpositiveness limited by the property *(pītaghaṭatva)* of that which is syntactictically connected to absence.

Now Raghunātha proceeds to explain the meaning of *nzñ* used with a verb and with a word with sixth case-ending. In course of discussion, he criticises the Vaiyākaraṇa view according to which the meaning of sixth case-ending is possessorship *(svāmitva)* etc. belonging to a person meant by the word with the sixth case-ending. According to the Naiyāyikas, the meaning of the sixth case-ending is the property of being-possessed *(svatva)* etc.

In the second section, Raghunātha mentions the views of two different schools of philosophers on the moot point at issue. One is referred to by *kecit* and the other by *kaścit.* These philosophers could not be identified, as Bhavānanda did not say anything on it. Anyway, according to the first, in a negative sentence *nañ* denotes the absence of the qualifier *(viśeṣaṇa)* in a qualificand *(viśeṣya),* but according to the other, absence denoted by *naā* is connected to the meaning of the seventh case-ending, and then this absence is connected to the counterpositive as a qualifier. For example, *bhūtale*

na gha: According to former philosophers, the verval knowledge will be 'the absence of occurrence-on-ground in the pot. And according to the latter, the pot *(pratiyogin)* is possessed with the absence of occurrence-on-ground. Raghunātha obviously is against these two views, but he did not put across his opinion very explicitly. Bhavānanda, however, in his commentary, has given the exposition as to the contention of the author.

In the third section, Raghunātha explains the cases in which *nañ* denotes mutual absence. When in a case there is no knowledge of *nañ* and the two entities are connected by the relation of identity, then if in that case *nañ* is added, the mutual absence is known by that *nañ*.

In the fourth section, Raghunātha criticises the view of the Smārtas (i.e. the Mimāmsakas). The Smārta view is explained with reference to a sentence: *yajatiṣu ye yajāmaham karoti nānuyajeṣu* (In sacrifices, one utters the *mantra 'ye yajāmaham,'* but not in an *Anuyāja* sacrifice). It is a single sentence. If we determine the meaning as conveying that the *nañ* here negates the action, then it will allow the option of action. That is, when the utterance of *mantra* is prohibited, it means that there is the chance of prescription to utter the *mantra.* And this prescription is granted by *yajatiṣu ye yajāmaham karoti.* So in a single matter *(anuyāja),* there are the options, prescription and prohibition. But such a dichotomy is inconsistent. So to avoid it, *nañ* in *nānuyajeṣu* involves a mutual absence. But this view is untenable according to Raghunātha. It is a common experience that when some particular is prohibited, the general prescription will proceed to all setting aside that particular. There is a well-known example also. *Bhrāhmaṇebhyaḥ dadhi dātavyam kauṇḍbnyāya na* (Yogurt should be given to brāhmaṇas, but not to Kauṇḍinya). It means yogurt should be given to all brāhmaṇas excepting Kauṇḍinya. Where is the question of option of giving or not-giving yogurt to Kauṇḍinya? Then there is the discussion on the *nañ* in a sentence like *rātrau śrāddham na kurvīta.* Important here is the view of Raghunātha that the prohibition must not always presuppose the occurrence. With characteristically effective sarcasm, he poses the rhetorical question: should the verbal knowledge 'there is no fire in a lake' lead us to expect a fire to occur on a lake! If the opponents say that—if there is no chance of occurrence of fire on the lake then the prohibition is futile, they are to be answered: the reason for offering the prohibition is because of the possibility of misunderstanding and nothing else. If two

conflicting scriptural statements involve a single object, only then there comes the question of option. For example, the conflicting statements that one is to use a certain kind of cup called ṣoḍaśī in certain kind of ceremony (called *Atirātra* sacrifice), and that one is not to use that particular kind of cup in that ceremony. Given the validity of the logic, the Prābhākaras explain the prohibitory injunction in the similar way. There is a Vedic injunction: *na kalañjam bhakṣtyet* (one must not eat *kalañja). Kalanja* is the meat of a bird or animal killed by a poisoned arrow. The *liṇ* suffix *yat* denotes action *(kārya)*. The *kalañja-eating* is connected to the meaning of *nañ*-absence, and then this absence is connected to the meaning of *liṅ*-action. And then again, the power *(apūrva)* to be generated by prohibition is to be connected as object *(viṣayatvena)*. Therefore, in view of some result (as the Vedic injunctions cannot be futile), one has to guess this distinct type of verbal knowledge. Action should be done in respect of absence of *kalañja-eating*.

In the fifth section, Raghunātha narrates the relation between relaters involved. In *bhūtale na ghaṭaḥ* (There is no pot on the ground), the relation between the pot and its absence is counterpositive-Iocus relation *(pratiyogi-anuyogi-bhāva)*, and the relation between the 'absence of the pot' and the ground is locus-located relation *(ādhāra-ādheya-bhāva)*. But in *bhūtalam na ghaṃaḥ*, (the ground is not the pot), the relation between the 'absence of the pot' and the ground cannot be *ādhāra-ādheya-bhāva*, as here with the word *bhūtala* there is no sixth or seventh case-ending, and furthermore there appears no knowledge of *ādhāra* as object-attribute *(prakāra)* in the knowledge. Had the hearer heard the sixth or seventh case-ending, then only he could have known the *ādhāra* as object-attribute. Again no type of relation (conjunction etc.) between the ground and the pot can be known there, since the meaning of the two words *(nāṁa)* are different with the same case-ending in two words, and direct relation between them is not comprehended. But in regard to *nipāta* like *iva, eva* etc. the case is different. Even if there is the same case-ending with the two words, the knowledge of *pratiyogin* and *anuyogin* do appear. As for example, *candraḥ iva mukham* (the face is like the moon). Here *iva* means similarity. *Candra* is counterpositive, and *mukha* is the locus. So they are related. Therefore, except in the case of *nipāta*, where there is the knowledge of relation of separate entities appearing from words, the fundamental prompter *(tantra)* of that knowledge is the presence of meaning of case-endings, being object attribute in the

knowledge. So in the case where there is the connection with the meaning of *iva* etc. there is no dependence on sixth case-ending or its like. In the case of *aghaṭam bhūtalam* or *asamaḥ deśaḥ* etc., in view of identical locushood *(sāmānādhikaraṇya)* in a compound, *nañ* obviously means absence.

In the sixth section, Raghunātha mentions the view of a group of philosophers. Bhavānanda comments that these philosophers did not admit the exclusion of *nipāta* in the case wherein the occurrence of the meaning of case-ending as an object-attribute in the knowledge of syntactical connection of differences between the meanings of two words is needed. But he does not say any more about their explanation on *pratiyogitā* and *anuyogitā* in a sentence with the *nipātaṟiva, eva* etc. Anyway, in *ghaṭasya abhāvaḥ the* sixth case-ending used with the counterpositive word *ghaṭa* means locushood *(anuyogitva)*. There the *ghaṭa* is connected as conditioned *(nirūpita)* and *abhāva* is connected as locus *(adhikaraṇa)*. The meaning of the sixth case-ending is neither counterpositiveness, and nor the *ghaṭa* is connected as located, nor *abhāva* as conditioner. *Nañ* cannot have the strength to produce the knowledge of mutual absence of the meaning of the case-ending, or to produce the knowledge of relational absence in the case where the word denoting *pratiyogin* has the same case-ending as the *anuyogin* word. For example, let us take the first one: *na pacati na rājñaḥ*. Here the *nañ* cannot denote the mutual absence of the meanings of *tip* and sixth case-ending. The example for the next one: *būalam na ghaṭraḥ*. Since the word *ghaṭa* has the same case ending as with the word *bhūtala,* the *nañ* has no strength to denote the relational absence of *ghaṭa* on *bhūtala*. Raghunatha apparently accepts the views of these philosophers as he has not criticised them.

Commentaries on the *Naāvāda*

Nañvāda has been commented upon by a humber of Naiyāyikas. A list of the commentaries is given below:

1. *Nañvādaīkā* by Sārvabhauma Bhaṭṭācārya (Ṛamabhadra Sārvabhauma). Ms available in the Asiatic society (Ms no. III. G. 148).
2. *Nañvādaṭippana* by Kūsadāsa Sārvabhauma. Ms available at the repository of Raghunathji Temple of Jammu. (Stein's Cat. p. 147).
3. *Nañvādṭīkā* by Viśvanātha Siddhāntapañcānana. Ms available at Pune (Ms no. 117 of A. 1879–80).
4. *Nañvādaṭippanī* by Bhavānanda Siddhāntavāgīśa. Edited

presently. Partly printed.

5. *Nañvādaṭīkā* by Rudra Nyāyavācaspati. Appears to be lost. (Vide *Vange Navyanyāy Carcā,* p. 274).
6. *Nañvādādīdhitiraudrī* by Rudra Tarkavāgīśa. Appears to be lost. (Vide *Vange Navyanyāy Carcā,* p. 145).
7. *Nañvādaṭīkā* by Raghudeva Nyayālaṇkāra. Ms available at Tanjore. (Vide Tanjore Cat. P. 4568). Ms available also at the Asiatic Society (Ms no. 7832).
8. *Nañvādaṭippanī* by Rāmacandra Tarkavāgīśa. Ms available in the Sanskrit Sahitya Parish at. Ms nos. 3525, 3609, 8272, 12006.
9. *Nañvādaṭīkā* by Jagadguru Rāmakṛṣṇa Bhaṭṭācārya Cakravartin. Ms available in Ulwar Palace library. (Vide Peterson: Ulwar Cat. pp. 29+55).
10. *Nañvādavyākhyā* by Gadādhara Bhaṭṭācārya. Printed in the *Tattvacintāmaṇi,* vol. IV, Part 2 under the editorship of MM Kamakhyanath Tarkavāgisa. Oriental Book Centre, Delhi, 1990
11. *Nañvādaviveka* by Jagannātha, son of Vidyānidhi. Two copies of this treatise were available at the Raghunathji Temple of Jammu. (Stein's Cat. p. 147). It appears to be a commentary on the *Nañvāda* of Raghunātha Śiromaṇi.
12. *Naṇvādavyākhyā* by Jagadguru Jayarāma Nyāyapañcānana. (Vide *Vange Navyanyay Carcā,* p. 280)
13. Ingalls reports a *Vyākhyā* by Mathurānātha Tarkavāgīśa on Raghunātha's *Nañvāda.* (Vide *Encyclopaedia of Indian Philosophies,* vol. I).
14. A commentary by Rāmanātha. (Vide *Encyclopaedia of Indian Philosophies,* vol. I).
15. *Viveka* by Paṭṭābhirāma. (Vide *Encyclopaedia of Indian Philosophies,* vol. I).

Printed edition and the manuscripts utilized to prepare the edition of the *Nañvāda*

A: *Nañvāda:* Printed in the Appendix in the *Tattvacintāmaṇi,* vol. IV, Part 2 (pp. 1010–86). Oriental Book Centre, Delhi, Reprint, 1990.

B: *Nañvāda* manuscript no. 8737, preserved in the manuscript library of Sanskrit Sahitya Parishat, Kolkata. Partly damaged at the left end. Running title : (नञ्वाद शि Square-shaped space is left blank at the centre but no perforation is there.
No. of folios: 3

Lines per page: 4
Letters/line: 55 approx.
Size: 39 x *6Y2* cm
Script: Bengali

C: *Nañvāda* manqscript no 8193, preserved in the manuscript library of Sanskrit Sahitya Parishat, Kolkata. Square-shaped space is left blank at the centre with actual perforation. The text of *Nañvāda* is followed by पदार्थतत्व of Raghunat the centre but no performation is there.

No. of folios : 3
Lines per page: 4
Lettes/line : 55 approx
size : 39 61/2 cm
Script : Bengali

C: *Nañvāda* manuscript no 8193, preserved in the manuscript lubrary of Sanskrit Sahitya Parishat, Kolkata, Square-shaped space is lift blank at the centre with actual perforation. The text of *Nañvāda* is followed by of Raghunātha.

No. of folios: 3 (lbl-3bl)
Lines per page: 5-6
Letters/line: 80 approx.
Size: x *6Y2* cm
Script: Bengali

Printed edition and the manuscripts utilised to prepare the edition of the *Nañvādamippanī*

P: *Nañvāda* commentary of Bhavānanda. Incomplete text printed in the Appendix in the *Tattvacintāmaṇi,* vol. IV, Part 2 (pp. 1010-1086), Oriental Book Centre, Delhi, Reprint, 1990. There is no mention of the name of the commentator. Sri Dinesh Chandra Bhattacharya in his *Vange Navya-Nyāy Carcā* (p. 135) identified the commentator as Bhavānanda on the basis of the colophon in a manuscript of the Madras library. Anyway the Asiatk society, Kolkata had a com men tary on this *Nañvāda* of Raghunātha Śiromaṇi named *Naāvādārthapradṣpa.* This manuscript also has colophon stating the name of the commentator. But Sri Bhattacharya did not mention this manuscript. Moreover he did not mention the incompleteness of the text in the Printed edition either.

Q: Manuscript (no. 7764) of *Nañvādaṭippanṣ* of Bhavānanda. Preserved in the manuscript library of Sanskrit Sahitya Parishat, Kolkata.Fol no 16al-16b2. Contains *ākhyātavādarṭippanṣ* of

Bhavānanda; then starts the *Nañvādaṭippanī*. Square-shaped space is left blank at the centre with actual perforation.

No. of folios: 11 (l6b2-26b8)
Lines per page: 6–7
Letters/line: 78 approx.
Size: 40x *6Y2* cm
Script: Bengali

R: Manuscript (no. G 5926) of *Nañvādarthapradīlpa* of Bhavānanda. Preserved in the manuscript library of the Asiatic Society. The manuscript has no square-shaped blank space left at the centre. It has a number of scribal errors.

No. of folios: 10
Lines per page: 13–14
Letters/line: 78 approx.
Size: **11** x 5 inch
Script: Devanagari.

Bhavabhuti. Here starts the Nandī-śloka. Square shaped space is left blank at the centre with actual perforation.

No. of folios: 11 (1682 Śaka)

Lines per page: 6-7

Letters/line: 78 approx.

Size: 40 x 6.2 cm

Script: Bengali

R: Manuscript (no. G 2980) of Mahāvīracarita of Bhavabhuti. Preserved in the manuscript library of the Asiatic Society. The manuscript has no square-shaped blank space left at the centre. It has a number of scribal errors.

No. of folios: 10

Lines per page: 13-14

Letters/line: 75 approx.

Size: 11 x 5 inch

Script: Devanagari

रघुनाथशिरोमणिकृतः नञ्वादः

१. संसर्गाभावोऽन्योन्याभावश्च[1] नञोऽर्थः। तत्र चान्वयितावच्छेदकावच्छिन्न-प्रतियोगिताकत्वं[2] व्युत्पत्तिबललभ्यम्, नीलघटवति न घटः, नीलो[3] घटो न घट इत्याद्यव्यवहारात्, इह नीलघटवति[4] न पीतो[5] घटः, नीलो[6] घटो न पीतो[7] घट[8] इत्यादिव्यवहाराच्च[9]। प्रतियोग्यभावान्वयौ च[10] तुल्ययोगक्षेमौ। तेन यत्पदोपस्थाप्यस्य[11] प्रतियोगिनो[12] अनुयोगिन्याधाराधेयभाव-सम्बन्धेनान्वयस्तत्र[13] तत्संसर्गाभावस्यापि[14] तथा, यथा पचति चैत्रः, न पचति चैत्रः, चैत्रस्येदम्, नेदं[15] चैत्रस्य इत्यादौ[16] तिङाद्यर्थस्य कृत्यादेः प्रथमान्तपदोपस्थापित[17] एव तत्र[18] तथेति तदभावस्यापि तथा[19] इति[20]। षष्ठ्यादेश्चैत्रादिनिरूपितं स्वत्वादिकमर्थो[21] न तु तन्निष्ठं[22] स्वामित्वादिकम्[23]। तस्य धनाद्यवृत्तित्वेन चैत्रीयेऽपि धने नेदं चैत्रस्येति प्रसङ्गात् निरूपकत्वादेः सम्बन्धस्य प्रतियोगितानवच्छेदकत्वादित्येषा[24] दिक्। यत्र चाधाराधेयभावो न संसर्गमर्यादया[25] लभ्यस्तत्रानुयोगिपदे[26] सप्तम्यपेक्षा, यथा भूतले घटः, भूतले न घट[27] इति। अत्र च[28] तात्पर्यवशात्[29] कदाचिद्भूतलादौ[30] घटाभावः[31] कदाचिच्च[32] घटादौ भूतलवृत्तित्वाभावः प्रतीयते[33]। अतएव पृथिव्यां गन्धो न जले इत्यादौ प्रतीतेरेकविशेष्यकत्वानुभवः[34]।।

२. केचित् तु सर्वत्र विशेष्ये विशेषणस्याभावो नञा प्रत्याय्यते। अतएव भूतले घटो नास्ति घटौ न स्तः घटा न सन्ति[35] इत्यादौ घटोऽस्तीत्यादाविव वचनैक्यनियम[36] इत्याहुः[37]। तेषां मते[38] जातौ न सत्तेत्यत्र गतिश्चिन्तनीया जातिसमवेतत्वस्याप्रसिद्धत्वात्,[39] सम्बन्धान्तरेण जातिवृत्तित्वस्य सत्तायामपि[40] सत्त्वात्।। सप्तम्यर्थान्विताभावस्य विशेषणतया प्रतियोग्यन्वय इति कश्चित्[41]।।

३. यत्र च[42] विशेषणविशेष्ययोरभेदेनान्वयो[43] व्युत्पन्नस्तत्रान्योन्याभावो नञा[44] बोध्यते, यथायं घटो नीलः, नायं घटो नील इति। अत्र[45] विशेषणविशेष्यपदयोः, समानविभक्तिकत्वं विरुद्धविभक्तिविरहो[46] वा तन्त्रम्। अतएव

"यजतिषु ये यजामहं करोति नानुयाजेषु" [ ]

इत्यादावेकवाक्यतानुरोधात्[47] ये यजामहमित्यादेरनुषङ्गगौरवाच्च यजतीष्वनुयाजभेदो बोध्यते। विशेषणविभक्तिस्तु प्रयोगसाधुत्वाय[48]। नामार्थयोर्भेदेनान्वयबोध[49] एव प्रकारीभूतविभक्त्यर्थोपस्थितेस्तन्त्रत्वात् लाघवेन तयोरन्वयबोधमात्र[50] एव तथात्वम्। विशेषणविभक्तिस्तु अभेदार्थिका। नीलोत्पलं चित्रगुरित्यादौ लुप्ताया[51] विभक्तेरनुसन्धानमिति मते तु न राज्ञ इत्यत्र षष्ठ्यर्थसम्बन्धस्येव[52] अत्रापि सप्तम्यर्थाभेदस्याभावो[53] बोध्यताम्।।

४. यत्तु करणनिषेधे विकल्पापत्तेर्भेदपरतेति, तदसत्। विशेषनिषेधे सामान्यविधेस्तदितरपरतायाः[54] "ब्राह्मणेभ्यो दधि दातव्यं कौण्डिन्याय[55] न दातव्यम्" इत्यादौ व्युत्पत्तिसिद्धत्वात्[56] विकल्पानवकाशात्। न च तत्रापि[57] कौण्डिन्यभेदो बोध्यः। कौण्डिन्यपदस्य विरुद्धैकवचनावरुद्धत्वात्[58]। न खलु महतो राज्ञः न महतो राज्ञः इत्यत्रेव महतां राज्ञो न महतां राज्ञ इत्यत्रापि राजनि[59] महदभेदभेदौ प्रतीयेते। एको न द्वावितिवत्[60] कथञ्चित् तत्समर्थनेऽपि[61] द्वितीयस्य दातव्यमित्यस्यानन्वयप्रसङ्गात्। अतएव "रात्रौ श्राद्धं न कुर्वीत" इत्यादौ करणनिषेधेऽपि न विकल्पावकाशः। न हि[62] तत्रापि रात्रीतरपरता। रात्रिभिन्ने श्राद्धविधावपि "अमावास्यायां[63] पितृभ्यो दद्यात्" इत्यादितो रात्रिश्राद्धप्रसक्तत्वस्य[64] दुर्वारत्वात्। न खलु क्रियारहितं[65] श्राद्धविधायकं वाक्यान्तरमस्ति येनेदं तेन समम्[66] एकवाक्यतामासादयेत्। नापीदं नानुयाजेष्वितिवत् पृथक् क्रियारहितम्। अथ रात्रौ श्राद्धस्य[67] प्रसक्तौ विकल्पापत्तिरप्रसक्तौ निषेधानुपपत्तिः[68], प्रसक्तं हि प्रतिषिध्यत[69] इति चेत्, साधीयानयं मन्त्रपाठो यद्बलात् जलह्रदे दहनो[70] नास्तीत्यादौ शाब्दबोधेऽपि परमयत्नेन[71] तत्र दहनप्रसक्तिरुपादीयते[72]। निषेधवैयर्थ्यमिति[73] चेत्, तात्पर्यानवबोधनिबन्धनरात्रिश्राद्धकरणवारणस्य[74] तदर्थत्वात्। एकविषयतया पुनरनन्यगत्या षोडशिग्रहणाग्रहणयोर्विकल्प[75] इति। अत्र च षोडशिग्रहण[76] नेष्टसाधनमित्यादिकं नार्थस्तत्र[77] ग्रहणविधिविरोधात्, अपि तु षोडशिग्रहणाभाव[78] इष्टसाधनमित्यादिकम्। व्युत्पन्नश्च नञ्समभिव्याहृतधात्वर्थस्याभावेऽपि विभक्त्यर्थान्वयः।। अतएव[79] <u>प्राभाकराः</u>–

न कलञ्जं भक्षयेत् इत्यादिश्रुतेः[80] कलञ्जभक्षणाभावविषयकं कार्यमित्यर्थमाहुः[81]। नियमस्तु[82] तात्पर्यादिवशात् मुख्यफलाजनकत्वेऽपि अङ्गस्य[83] परमापूर्वरूपोपकारसाधनत्वम्[84] अविरुद्धम्। ग्रहणविध्यन्यथानुपपत्त्या षोडशिग्रहणादतिशयितं[85] परमापूर्वम्। तस्माच्चातिशयितं मुख्यं फलं[86] कल्प्यत इति सर्वसमञ्जसम्।

५. प्रतियोग्यभावयोः प्रतियोग्यनुयोगिभावो अभावाधिकरणयोराधाराधेयभावश्च सम्बन्धविधया भासते। निपातातिरिक्तस्थले एव प्रातिपदिकार्थयोर्भेदान्वये[87]

प्रकारीभूतविभक्त्यर्थोपस्थितेस्तन्त्रत्वात्।[88] अतएव इवाद्यर्थान्वये[89] न षष्ठ्याद्यपेक्षा। अघटं भूतलम् असमो देश इत्यादौ समासे सामानाधिकरण्यानुरोधात्[90] नञोऽभाववत्परता।।

६. केचित तु प्रतियोगिपदोत्तरसुपः[91] प्रतियोगित्वे अनुयोगित्वे वा नञुत्तरस्याधिकरणत्वे[92] नञो वा अभाववति[93] लक्षणा विभक्त्यर्थानुयोगिसमानविभक्तिकार्थयोरन्योन्याभावसंसर्गाभावयोर्बोधने[94] नञो न सामर्थ्यम्।[95] तेन न पचति न राज्ञ इत्यादौ कृतिसम्बन्धादेरन्योन्याभावो[96] भूतलं न घट इत्यादौ घटादेः[97] संसर्गाभावो न प्रतीयत इत्याहुः।। इति।।

।।महामहोपाध्यायश्रीरघुनाथशिरोमणिभट्टाचार्यविरचितं नञ्वादरहस्यं सम्पूर्णम्।।[98]

संदर्भसंकेतः

1. C (1b1) notes a benediction: ओं नमो गणेशाय
2. B (1a1) omits च.
3. A (p. 1033): नील
4. C (1b1): पीत for नील
5. C (1b1) नीलो for पीतो
6. A (p. 1033), C (1c1): पीतो
7. A (p. 1033): नीलः, C (1b1): नीलो
8. A (p. 1033) omits the word.
9. B (1a2): इति for इत्यादि
10. B (1a2) omits the word.
11. A (p. 1035), B (1a3), C (1b2) and D (p. 1034): यत्पदोपस्थापितस्य: Changed according to E and F.
12. A (p. 1035) omits the word.
13. B (1a3): ० धेयभावान्वयबोधस्तत्र
14. C (1b2) omits तत्.
15. B (1a4): न for नेदं
16. C (1b3): इत्यादि
17. C (1b3) omits पद.
18. A (p. 1036) omits the word.
19. A (p. 1036), B (1a4): तत्र तथा
20. A (p. 1036), C (1b3) omit the word.
21. B (1a5): सत्त्वादि० C (1b3): निरूपितसत्त्वादि०
22. B (1a5): तन्निष्ठ
23. B (2a5), C (1b4): स्वामित्वादि

24. B(1b1): प्रतियोगित्वानव०
25. C (1b4): सम्बन्धमर्याद
26. B (1b1): omits पदे.
27. A(p. 1039): भूतले घटो न घट for भूतले घटः, भूतले न घटः
B(1b1): भूतले न घटः भूतले घट for भूतले घटः,भूतले न घटः
28. Addedaccording to Q and R manuscripts.
29. B(1b1): तात्पर्यादिवशात्
30. C (1b5) omits कदाचित्.
31. C (1b5): घटाद्यभावः
32. A(p. 1041), C (1b5) omit च.
33. C (1b5): भासते
34. B(1b3) omits प्रतीतेः.
35. C (2a1): न सन्ति घटा for घटा न सन्ति
36. C (2a1) ० नियमा
37. A(p. 1046): इत्यप्याहुः
C (2a1): इति प्राज्ञः (?इति प्राहुः)
38. A(p. 1046),B(1b4) omit the word.
39. A(p. 1046): प्रसिद्धेः for प्रसिद्धत्वात्
40. B(1b4), C (2a2) omit अपि.
41. C (2a2): केचित्
42. B(1b4) omits च
43. B(1b4): ० भेदान्वयो
44. B(1b4) reads नञा before अन्योन्याभावो.
45. A(p. 1049),B(2a1): तत्र
C (2a3): तत्र च
46. A (p. 1050),B(2a1): राहित्यं for विरहो
47. C (2a4): व्वाक्यानुरोधात्
48. A(p. 1052): योगसाधुः
C (2a4): प्रयोगसाधुः
49. C (2a4) omits बोध०
50. B(2a3) omits मात्र०
51. C (2a5): लुप्ताया एव
52. C (2a5): षष्ठ्यर्थस्य सम्बन्ध०
53. C (2a5): सप्तम्यर्थस्याभे०
54. C (2a6): ० परत्वस्य
55. B(2a5): तक्रकौण्डिन्याय
56. C (2a6): सिद्धत्वेन
57. C (2a6): omits अपि.
58. C (2b1): ० वचनविरुद्धत्वात्
59. B(2b1) omits अपि राजनि०
60. A(p. 1061): द्वावित्येत्रेव
61. C (2b1) omits तत्०

62. B(2b2): च
63. B(2b2): अमावस्यायां
64. B(2b2): ० प्रसक्तस्य
C (2b2): रात्रौ श्राद्धप्रसक्ते
65. C (2b3) क्रियारहितमपि
66. B(2b3): सहितं
67. C (2b3): श्राद्ध
68. A(p. 1067): कथंनिषेध:
B(2b4): निषेध: एवानुपपन्न:
69. C (2b5) omits प्रसक्तं हि प्रतिषिध्यत.
70. C (2b4): वह्नि:
71. A(p. 1069): परमप्रयत्नेन
C (2b4): परयत्नेन
72. C (2b3) omits दहन०
73. A(p. 1069): निषेधविधिवैयर्थ्यमिति
74. C (2b5) omits रात्रि
75. C (2b5) ग्रहणविकल्प
76. C (2b5) षोडशीग्रहणं
77. A(p. 1072): ० त्यादिकमर्थो for ० त्यादिकंनार्थस्तत्र
B(2b6): ० त्यादिकंनार्थो
78. C (2b5): षोडशीग्रहणा०
79. A(p. 1073): अत्र
80. C (3a1): इति for इत्यादि
81. A(p. 1074): ०कार्यमित्यर्थइत्याहु:
C (3a1): कार्यमर्थमाहु:
82. A(p. 1074), B(3a1): नियमतस्तु
83. C (3a1): चाङ्गस्य
84. B(3a, C (3a2): परमापूर्वरूपेष्टसाधनत्वम्
85. C (3a2): च षोडशीग्रहणा० · · · ०शयति (शयितं)
86. C (3a2): फलमिति
87. A(p. 1081): देनान्वये.
88. A(p. 1081),B(3a4): ० विभक्त्युपस्थिते०
89. C (3a4): इवार्थान्वये
90. A(p. 1082)B(3a5): ० करण्याद्यरोधात्
91. B(3a5): ० सुपश्च
92. A(p. 1084): ० करणत्वन
93. B(3a6) वाभवति for वा अभाववति
B(3a6) omits वा.
94. A(p. 1084): ० विभक्तिकस्यैवान्योन्या.
B(3a6): ० विभक्तिकयोरन्योन्या.
C (3a5): ० भावबोधने.
95. A(p. 1084): नञोऽसामर्थ्यम् for नञो न सामर्थ्यम्

96. A,B, C कृत्यादे But changed to कृतिसम्बन्धादेः according to the commentary.

97. B(3b1): घट

C (3b1): घटादेश्च

98. B(3b1): इति भट्टाचार्यशिरोमणिविरचितंनञ्वादरहस्यंसमाप्तम्।

C (3b1): इति नञ्वादः समाप्तः।

भवानन्दसिद्धान्तवागीशकृता नञ्वादटिप्पनी

१. **संसर्गाभाव** इति।[1] शक्यतावच्छेदकभेदेन शक्तिभेदस्य सूचनाय[2] उक्तिभेदः। तथाच संसर्गाभावत्वम् अन्योन्याभावत्वं[3] च नञः शक्यतावच्छेदकमित्यर्थः[4]। न च लाघवात् सर्वसाधारणमभावत्वमेव शक्यतावच्छेदकमस्तु तत्तत्समभि-व्याहारबलात्[5] समवायाद्यवच्छिन्नायास्तादात्म्यावच्छिन्नायाश्च[6] प्रतियोगितायाः[7] संसर्गतया भानादेव[8] बोधवैलक्षण्यमिति[9] वाच्यम्। घटो नास्तीत्यादौ संसर्गाभाव-त्वस्यैव[10] घटः पटो[11] न इत्यत्र भेदत्वस्यैव प्रकारतया[12] आनुभविकत्वेन तथाभिधानात्[13]। संसर्गाभावत्वं च ध्वंसप्रागभावयोरप्यनुभवबलाद् अनुगत-प्रतिबध्यप्रतिबन्धकभावबलाच्च सिद्धम्। भवति ह्यत्यन्ताभावस्येव[14] ध्वंसप्रागभावयोरपि बुद्धौ नियमतः तत्कालावच्छेदेन तद्देशे प्रतियोगिमत्ताधीप्रति-बन्धः, तत्र[15] समवायादिना तद्घटवत्ताबुद्धिं प्रति तद्घटत्वावच्छिन्नप्रतियोगिता-कात्यन्ताभावप्रागभावादिबुद्धित्वादिना[16] प्रतिबन्धकत्वद्वयकल्पने[17] गौरवात्। लाघवात्[18] समवायेन तद्घटत्वावच्छिन्नप्रतियोगिताकाभावबुद्धित्वमेव प्रति-बन्धकतावच्छेदकं[19] कल्प्यते, तच्च ध्वंसप्रागभावयोः समवायाद्यवच्छिन्न-प्रतियोगिताकत्वेनैव[20] निर्वहतीति[21] प्राचीनाः।

नवीनास्तु[22]—संसर्गाभावत्वं न संसर्गारोपजन्यप्रतीतिविषयाभावत्वं[23] संसर्गा-वच्छिन्नप्रतियोगिताकाभावत्वं[24] वा। आरोपस्याभावप्रत्यक्षहेतुतायां[25] मानाभावात्, अतीन्द्रियाभावाव्याप्तेः[26] संसर्गत्वावच्छिन्नत्वप्रतियोगित्वाद्यनिरुक्तेः[27] संयोग्यन्योन्याभावातिव्याप्तेश्च[28]। संयोगिता- दात्म्यस्य संयोगरूपतया तस्य फलतः संयोगावच्छिन्नप्रतियोगिताकत्वात् सम्बद्धतया[29] तादात्म्यतया वा[30] वैलक्षण्यस्य अवच्छेदकतया[31] निर्वक्तुमशक्य-त्वात्। एवमन्योन्याभावत्वमपि न तादात्म्यसम्बन्धावच्छिन्नप्रतियोगिताका-भावत्वम्[32] उक्तरीत्या संयोगेन संयोग्यत्यन्ताभावेऽतिव्याप्तेः। किन्तु अत्यन्ताभावादौ संसर्गाभाव इत्याकारानुगतप्रतीतिसाक्षिकमखण्डोपाधिरूपमेव[33] तत्। एवमन्योन्याभावत्वमपि तादृशप्रतीतिसिद्धमखण्डोपाधिरूपमेवेति[34] तदेव शक्यतावच्छेदकम्। यदि

च[35] घटो नास्तीत्यादावत्यन्ताभावत्वप्रकारेणैव[36] बोध आनुभविको न तु ध्वंसादिसाधारणसंसर्गाभावत्वेन, ध्वंसादिस्थलेऽपि अत्यन्ताभावमादायैव नास्तीत्यादिधीरबाधिता तदा अत्यन्ताभावत्वम् अन्योन्याभावत्वं च द्वयं[37] शक्यतावच्छेदकमितिप्राहुः[38]।

ननु यत्किञ्चिद्घटवति घटो नास्तीति यत्किञ्चिद्घटे वा घटो नेति धीः घटान्तरस्य संसर्गाभावम् अन्योन्याभावं वा अवलम्ब्य कुतो न स्यादत[39] आह–**तत्रे**ति। **तत्र** संसर्गाभावे अन्योन्याभावे च नञर्थे। **अन्वयिते**ति[40]। प्रतियोगितासम्बन्धेन[41] नञर्थे योऽन्वयी[42] तत्त्वावच्छेदकं[43] तादृगन्वयितावच्छेदकं[44] घटो नास्तीत्यादौ घटत्वादिकं तदवच्छिन्नप्रतियोगिताकत्वमित्यर्थः। **व्युत्पत्ती**ति। पदान्तरासमभिव्याहृतघटत्वविशिष्टघटवृत्तिमत्पदसमभिव्याहृतनञ्पदजन्यसंसर्गाभावोपस्थितेर्घटत्वावच्छिन्नप्रतियोगितासम्बन्धेनैव घटत्वविशिष्टप्रकारकान्वयबोधजनकत्वस्वाभाव्यं[45] **व्युत्पत्तिः, तद्बललभ्यं**[46] तद्बलात् सिद्धं शाब्दबोधविषय इत्यर्थः। तने नीलो घटो नास्तीत्यादौ न घटत्वावच्छिन्नाभावधीः, तत्र घटपदस्य नीलपदसमभिव्याहृतत्वात्[47] तदसमभिव्याहृतत्वं च तत्समभिव्याहृतत्वेनाज्ञाततत्वम्[48], तेन नीलो घटो नास्तीति प्रत्युक्ते[49] च[50] नील इत्यश्रुत्वा घटो नास्तीति यत्र शाब्दबोधः तत्रापि नानुपपत्तिः। अन्वयितावच्छेदकं च वैज्ञानिकम्। तेन लोहितो वह्निर्नास्तीत्यादौ लोहितवह्नित्वस्याप्रसिद्धावपि न क्षतिः। तत्र लौहित्यस्यानुयोगितावच्छेदकतया[51] भावत्वं वह्नित्वे[52] वह्नित्वस्यैवावच्छिन्नत्वे तादृशावच्छिन्नत्वस्य प्रतियोगिताकत्वे तस्य चाभावे सम्बन्धः संसर्गः[53] संसर्गविधया[54] भानेऽप्येतादृशः[55] परस्परोपश्लेषोऽनुभवबलात संसर्गविधयैव[56] विषयः। इयांस्तु[57] विशेषः–यत्र तादृशपरस्परोपश्लेष एव सम्बन्धताख्यविषयता पर्याप्ता तत्र तादृशावच्छिन्नत्वादीनां प्रकारता। यत्र च[58] तादृशविशिष्ट एव वैज्ञानिके पारमार्थिके वा सा पर्याप्ता तत्र न तादृशसम्बन्धघटकस्य प्रकारता[59] सा किन्तु सम्बन्धीभूततादृशविशिष्टप्रतियोगिन[60] एवेति। अतएव लोहितस्फटिक[61] इत्यादौ लौहित्यसमवायिप्रतियोगिकसंयोगस्य सम्बन्धत्वेन संयोगांशे[62] लौहित्यसमवायिनोऽपि प्रतियोगित्वस्य संसर्गतया भानेऽपि न लौहित्यसमवायिनः प्रकारतेति ध्येयम्। घटत्वमवच्छिन्नत्वं प्रतियोगिता[63] चेति विशकलितमेव[64] सम्बन्धः, न तु तेषां परस्परोपश्लेषोऽपीति <u>केचित्</u> तत् तुच्छम्। एतत् त्रितयं यदि घटत्वस्य सम्बन्धस्तदा[65] प्रतियोगितायामपि घटत्वस्य सम्बन्धभाने अनुभवविरोधः। अथ घटस्य सम्बन्धस्तदवच्छिन्नत्वेऽपि[66] घटस्य सम्बन्धभाने[67] घटत्वस्य च तदभाने[68] स एव विरोधः। घटत्वावच्छिन्नप्रतियोगिता अखण्डैवेति <u>केचित्</u>[69]। तदपि न।

लोहितवह्निर्नास्तीत्यादौ[70] तदसम्भवात्। घटो नास्तीत्यादौ[71] घटत्वादेरवच्छेद-कत्वभानस्य[72] आनुभविकत्वेन[73] तदनभ्युपगमे अनुभवविरोधात्। अत्र च घटो नास्तीत्यादौ घटः प्रतियोगितया घटत्वं च स्वावच्छिन्नप्रतियोगिताकत्वेन सम्बन्धेनाभावे[74] प्रकारीभूय भासते। घटत्वं च प्रतियोगिविशेषणतापन्नमेवाभावे प्रकारः, न तु स्वातन्त्र्येण, धूमवान् पर्वतो वह्निमान् इत्यादौ पर्वतविशेषणता-पन्नधूम[75] इव वह्नौ तेनाभावो घटीयः, घट इत्याकारो नेति नव्याः। अन्ये तु घटत्वावच्छिन्नप्रतियोगिताकत्वं घटस्यैव सम्बन्धः न तु घटत्वस्य इति नोक्तातिप्रसङ्ग इत्याहुः[76]। तादृशव्युत्पत्तौ अन्वयव्यतिरेकौ प्रमाणयति–**नीला घटवती**त्यादिना। यद्युक्तव्युत्पत्तिर्नाभ्युपेयते तदा नीलघटवत्यपि पीतघट-संसर्गाभावस्य नीलघटे[77] पीतघटान्योन्याभावस्य[78] सत्त्वात् घटप्रतियोगिकत्वेन तद्भानमपि नञा क्रियत इत्यर्थः। संसर्गान्योन्याभावभेदेनोभयत्र उदाहरणभेद-प्रदर्शनम्[79]। व्यतिरेकमुक्त्वान्वयमाह-**इह**[80] **नीले**त्यादिना। नीलघटवत्यपि क्वचित् पीतघटसत्त्वात् अवच्छेदकावच्छेदेनान्वये बाध[81] इति तद्वारणाय–**इहे**ति। इदं चात्र बोध्यम्[82]–**न पीतो**[83] **घट** इत्यादौ पीतगुणवतोऽभेदसम्बन्धे-नानुयोगितावच्छेदक[84]घटत्वम् अन्वयितावच्छेदकं नामार्थयोरभेदस्यैव संसर्गत्वात्। तच्च[85] समवायेन पीतगुणानुयोगितावच्छेदकं घटत्वमपेक्ष्य गुरुतरमतो नावच्छेदकम्, पीतगुणानुयोगितावच्छेदकं च घटत्वं नान्वयिता-वच्छेदकं तथा[86] तत्पदेनाबोधनात्[87]। अतो गुरुधर्मस्यावच्छेदकत्वकल्प एवैतादृशः शाब्दबोधो विशेषदर्शिनामिति। ननु भूतलं न घट इत्यादौ भूतलादौ घटादिसंसर्गाभावधीः स्यात्। न च संसर्गाभावबोधे अनुयोगिनि सप्तम्यपेक्षिता, चैत्रो न पचतीत्यादौ[88] तिङाद्यर्थस्य[89] कृत्यादेः संसर्गाभावबोधो न स्यादत आह–**प्रतियोगी**ति। **तुल्ये**ति। अभावान्वयः प्रतियोग्यन्वयेन तुल्ययोगक्षेमः, तेनानुयोगिनि प्रतियोग्यन्वयस्य यत्र सम्बन्धत्वं तत्र तदभावान्वयस्यापि तथात्वम्। यत्र च प्रतियोग्यन्वयस्य प्रकारत्वं तत्र तदभावान्वयस्यापि प्रकारत्वम्। तथाच उक्तपदोपस्थाप्यस्य[90] प्रतियोगिनोऽनुयोगिना अन्वयबोधे[91] यदपेक्षितं तत्र तदभावान्वयबोधेऽपि[92] तदपेक्षितमित्यर्थः पर्यवस्यति। एतदेव फलमुखेन दर्शयति–**तेने**त्यादिना। **यत्पदोपस्थाप्यस्ये**ति[93]। तथाच पदविशेषजन्यप्रतियोग्युपस्थित्यन्तर्भावेन कार्यकारणभावो बोध्यः। अन्यथा चैत्रो न पाककृतिरित्यत्रापि कृतिसंसर्गाभावधीः स्यादिति भावः। तिङाद्यर्थस्यापि कृत्यादेर्धात्वर्थे जनकत्वेन नञर्थे प्रतियोगित्वेनान्वयादाधारा- धेयभाव-सम्बन्धेनैवेत्युपपन्नमतः[94] **अनुयोगिनी**ति अधिकरणत्वेनान्वयबोधविषय इत्यर्थः। **तत्संसर्गाभावस्या**पि। तत्पदोपस्थाप्यस्य[95] प्रतियोगिनः संसर्गाभा-वस्यापि। **तथा** आधारधेयभावसम्बन्धेनैवान्वयः[96]। पचति चैत्र इत्यत्र प्रतियोग्य-

न्वयस्य सम्बन्धत्वं दर्शयित्वा तदभावान्वयस्य तद्दर्शयति–**न पचति चैत्र** इति। वैयाकरणमते कर्तुराख्यातवाच्यत्वात् तस्य च अभेद एव संसर्ग इत्यतः सुब्विभक्तिमुदाहरति–**चैत्रस्येदम**ित्यादिना। **तिङादी**ति **आदिना** षष्ठ्याः, **कृत्यादे**रिति **आदिना** स्वत्वस्य च[97] परिग्रहः[98]। **प्रथमान्ते**ति। तथाच विभक्तिजन्यकृत्युपस्थितिजन्यकृतिसंसर्गाभावस्याधाराधेयभावेनान्वयबोधे नञ्पदजन्याभावोपस्थितिः प्रथमान्तपदजन्याधिकरणोपस्थितिः[99] कारणमेवं रीत्या कार्यकारणभावो बोध्यः[100]। एवमुत्तरत्रापि। **तत्र** अनुयोगिनि चैत्रे धने च। **तथा** आधाराधेयभावसम्बन्धेनैवान्वयः[101]। **तदभावस्यापि** कृत्यादिसंसर्गाभावस्यापि। ननु षष्ठ्याद्यर्थः[102] स्वामित्वं तस्य च धने निरूपकत्वसम्बन्धेनैवान्वयो न त्वाधाराधेयभावसम्बन्धेनेत्यत आह-**षष्ठ्यादे**रिति। षष्ठ्यर्थस्वत्वे[103] प्रकृत्यर्थस्य चैत्रादेः केन सम्बन्धेनान्वय[104] इति तद्दर्शयति–**चैत्रादिनिरूपितम**िति। तथाच निरूपितत्वसम्बन्धेन तत्र प्रकृत्यर्थस्यान्वय इति भावः। **तन्निष्ठं** चैत्रादिनिष्ठम्। एतेन स्वामित्वस्य षष्ठ्यर्थत्वे प्रकृत्यर्थेन[105] समं तस्यान्वयबोधे निष्ठत्वमेव सम्बन्धः इत्युक्तम्। **तस्य** चैत्रादिनिष्ठ-स्वामित्वस्य। **धनाद्यवृत्तित्वेने**ति। तथाच वृत्तितानियामकेन सम्बन्धेन[106] स्वामित्वाभावबोधनेऽबाधित एवेति तथा प्रयोगः स्यादिति भावः। ननु स्वामित्वस्य षष्ठ्यर्थत्वे[107] तस्य निरूपकत्वसम्बन्धेनैव[108] धनेऽन्वयः। तत्सम्बन्धावच्छिन्नप्रतियोगिताक एव तदभावो नञा प्रत्याय्यते चैत्रीयं तु धनं तन्निरूपकमेवेति[109] कथं तत्र नेदं चैत्रस्येत्यादेः प्रसङ्गः इत्यत आह–**निरूपकत्वादे**रिति। निरूपकत्वादिसम्बन्धस्य प्रतियोगितावच्छेदकत्वे[110] किं बाधकमत[111] आह–**दिगि**ति। प्रमाणान्तरसिद्धमेवार्थं शब्दो बोधयति न तु शब्दबलादेव वस्तुसिद्धिः। वृत्त्यनियामकसम्बन्धपुरस्कारेणैव सर्वत्राभावप्रतीतिरस्ति एतद्धनस्वामित्वं चैत्रे नास्ति चैत्रस्वत्वमत्र नास्ति इत्येवाभावप्रत्ययात्, न तु निरूपकत्वादिसम्बन्धं प्रतियोगितावच्छेदकीकृत्य क्वचिदभावधीरस्तीति भावः[112]। **यत्र चाधारे**ति। यत्पदोपस्थाप्यस्य प्रतियोगिनोऽनुयोगिनीत्यनुषज्यते। अत्र च नामपदजन्यघटोपस्थितिजन्ये[113] नञ्पदजन्यघटसंसर्गाभावबोधे[114] अनुयोग्युपस्थापकपदोत्तरसप्तमी-समभिव्याहृतनञ्पदजन्या[115] नामपदोत्तरसप्तमीसमभिव्याहृत-नञ्पदजन्या वा[116] संसर्गाभावोपस्थितिः कारणम्, इत्थं च यावत् सप्तम्यन्तपदसमभिव्याहारो नञ्पदे न[117] जायते[118] तावन्न घट इत्यादितो घटसंसर्गाभावधीर्न भवत्येवेति। यद्वा[119] भूतले न घट इत्यत्र घटपदोपस्थाप्यस्य घटस्य नञ्पदजन्ये[120] भूतलाधेयत्वप्रकारकसंसर्गा- भावबोधे भूतलोपस्थापकपदोत्तर-सप्तमीसमभिव्याहृतनञ्पदजन्यसंसर्गाभावोपस्थितिः[121] कारणम्। भूतलं न घट इत्यादौ तु[122] फलाभावात् तथा विशेषसामग्री न

कल्प्यते सामान्यसामग्री च विशेषसामग्रीं विना न[123] कार्यजननीति एषा[124] दिक्। ननु सप्तम्यर्थस्यैवाभावो[125] नञा बोध्यते तस्य चानुयोगिनि घटे आध ाराधेयभाव:[126] सम्बन्ध एवेति पूर्वोदाहरणमेव तदा[127] आह—**अत्र चे**ति।[128] **कदाचिद् भूतलादावि**ति। तदानीमेव चरमोदाहरणमिति भाव:। चरम- बोधोपष्टम्भकमाह—**अतएवे**ति। **एकविशेष्यकत्वे**ति। पृथिवीवृत्तिर्गन्धो जलवृत्तित्वाभाववांश्च इति उभयत्रैव गन्धो विशेष्य:। आद्यकल्पानुसारेण[129] तु पृथिवीवृत्तिर्गन्धो जले गन्धाभाव इति बोधे भिन्नविशेष्यकत्वं स्यादिति भाव:।।

२. सप्तम्यर्थस्यैवाभावो भासते इति नियमवादिनां मतमाह[130]—**केचित्त्वि**ति[131]। नञोऽसमभिव्याहारे[132] यद्विशेष्ये यद्विशेषणतया भासते नञ्समभिव्याहारे[133] तद्विशेषणस्य तद्विशेष्येऽभावो नञा बोध्यते। तथाच भूतले घट इत्यादौ घट एव भूतलवृत्तित्वस्य विशेष्य इति तत्रैव भूतलवृत्तित्वाभावो नञा बोध्यत[134] इत्यर्थ:। **अतएवे**ति। यतएवाभावान्वयेऽपि घटस्यैव विशेष्यत्व- मित्यर्थ:। **वचनैक्यनियम** इति। अभावस्य विशेष्यत्वे विशेषणपदस्य विशेष्य- पदसमानवचनत्वनियमात् घटौ न स्त इत्यादौ द्विवचनादिकं न स्यात् किन्तु अभावस्यैकत्वेन[135] घटो नास्तीत्येकवचनमेव स्यात्, घटस्य विशेष्यत्वे च तस्य द्वित्वबहुत्वयो:[136] क्रियापदस्यापि द्विवचनादिकं युक्तमेवेति[137] भाव:। यद्यपि भूतले घटो नास्तीत्यत्र सप्तम्यर्थो निरूपितत्वं तच्च धात्वर्थे विद्यमानत्वे, तच्चाख्यातार्थे[138] आश्रयत्वे[139], तच्च नञर्थे अभावे स च[140] घटेऽन्वेतीति भूतलनिरूपितविद्यमानत्वाश्रयत्वाभाववान् घट इति अन्वयबोधेऽभाव[141]एव साक्षाद् घटे विशेषणम्, न त्वाख्यातार्थ:। तथापि परम्परया विशेषणस्यापि विशेष्यसमानवचनत्वमौत्सर्गिकं चैत्रो न पचतीत्यादौ दृष्टत्वादित्याशय:। न चैकघटवति भूतले घटौ न स्त इति न स्यात्, द्वित्ववद्घटत्वावच्छेदेन[142] तद्भूतलनिरूपितविद्यमानत्वाश्रयत्वाभावस्याभावात्, तादृशद्वित्वसामानाधि करण्येन[143] नञर्थस्यान्वये घटद्वयवत्यपि भूतले घटौ न स्त इति स्यादिति वाच्यम्। तादृशद्वित्वत्वावच्छेदेन नञर्थसामानाधिकरण्यस्यान्वयात्[144], घटद्वयवति भूतले च[145] अधिकरणान्तरीयघटद्वित्वे तद्भूतलास्तित्वाभावसामानाधिकरण्य- सत्त्वेऽपि तद्घटद्वयद्वित्वे तदभावेन घटौ न स्त इति प्रयोगस्य बाधि तार्थकत्वात्। एवं घटा न सन्तीत्यत्रापि बोध्यम्। **तेषामि**ति। अनियमपक्षे तु तत्र सत्ताभावो[146] जातिवृत्तिरित्यन्वयबोधे[147] नानुपपत्तिरिति भाव:। समवायेन सम्बन्धसामान्येन वा जातिवृत्तित्वस्याभावो नञा प्रत्याय्य:। आद्ये **जातिसमवेतत्वस्ये**ति[148] द्वितीये **सम्बन्धान्तरेणे**ति एकार्थसमवायादिनेत्यर्थ:। वस्तुतस्तु **जातौ न सत्ते**त्यादौ सत्तापदं सत्तासमवायपरं[149] सप्तम्यर्थश्चानुयोगित्वं

तथाच जात्यनुयोगिकत्वा- भाववान्[150] सत्तासमवाय इत्यन्वयबोधे नानुपपत्तिः न तु गतिरेव नास्तीति तदर्थः। अतएव **गतिश्चिन्तनीये**त्युक्तम्।। **सप्तम्यर्थे**ति। यद्यपि विशेषणस्यैवाभावो बोध्यत इति नियमस्यैव[151] न रक्षणं तथापि प्रथमान्तस्यैव विशेष्यत्वे वचनैक्यनियमोपपत्तिस्तावताप्युपपन्नेत्याशयः[152]। अत्र सप्तम्यर्थान्वयेन जातिवृत्त्यभावस्य प्रतियोगितया सत्तायामन्वयेन जातिवृत्त्यभावीया सत्तेत्यन्वय- बोधः। तथाच द्रव्ये न सत्तेत्यपि स्यात्। तत्र सत्ताया विशिष्टाभावस्य सत्त्वात्। नच सत्तात्वावच्छिन्नप्रतियोगितासम्बन्धः, अनतिरिक्तवृत्तित्वस्या- वच्छेदकत्वस्य तत्रापि सत्त्वात्। अनुयोगितावच्छेदके[153] स्वरूपसम्बन्ध- रूपावच्छेदकत्वमन्तर्भाव्य व्युत्पत्त्यन्तरकल्पने गौरवादित्यस्वरसः **कश्चिदि**-त्यनेन सूचितः। वस्तुतस्तु घटौ न स्त इत्यादितो द्वित्वाद्यवच्छिन्नघटाभाव[154] एव विशेष्यतया प्रतीयते नञः क्रियापदसमभिव्याहारे[155] तस्य प्रतियोगिपदेन समानवचनत्वमपि तन्त्रम्। अतएव घटौ नास्तीति न प्रयोगः। द्विवचनादिकं तु[156] प्रयोगसाधुत्वार्थम्। एवंच भूतले घटौ न स्त इत्यादेर्भूतलाधेयो[157] द्वित्वावच्छिन्न-घटाभावोऽस्तीत्येव[158] वाक्यार्थ इति ध्येयम्।।

३. फलमुखेन नियामकं वक्तुम् अन्योन्याभावबोधस्थल[150] द्रढयति-**यत्र चे**ति। **तत्रान्योन्ये**ति। अभेदेन विशेषणत्वयोग्यस्य विशेष्येऽन्योन्याभावो नञा बोध्यते इत्यर्थः। **अयं घटो नील** इत्यनेनाभेदान्वयो दर्शितः। **अत्र** नञा अन्योन्या-भावबोधने। **समाने**ति। दधि न[160] सुन्दरमित्यादावपि लुप्तविभक्त्यनुसन्धाने-नैव शाब्दधीरिति भावः। चैत्रो न पचतीत्यादौ आख्यातस्य धर्मिपरतायां चैत्रे पाककर्तुः पचति न स्तोकमित्यादौ पाके स्तोकभेदस्य[161] प्रतिपादने समानविभक्तिकत्वाभावादाह[162]**—विरुद्धविभक्तिविरहो**[163] **वे**ति। निर्विभक्ति-कासमस्तनीलादिपदसमभिव्याहृतनञ्पदस्थले विरुद्धविभक्तिविरहेऽप्य-साधुत्वादेव नान्वयबोधः। वस्तुतस्तु उक्त्यैक्यमात्रमेतत् न त्वनेन रूपेण हेतुत्वम्। अनुयोगिप्रतियोग्युपस्थापकनामपदयोः समभिव्याहारे समानविभक्ति-कत्वं तन्त्रम्। तथाच घटो न नील इत्यादौ घटपदार्थान्वितनीलपदार्थान्योन्याभाव-बोधने घटपदसमानविभक्तिकनीलपदसमभिव्याहृतनञ्पदत्वेन, चैत्रो न पचतीत्यादौ धर्मिपराख्यातसमभिव्याहृतनञ्पदत्वेन[164], न स्तोकं पचतीत्यादौ क्रियाविशेषणसमभिव्याहारे द्वितीयान्तस्तोकादिपदसमभिव्याहृतत्वेन विशिष्यैव हेतुत्वं बोध्यम्। अन्यथा न पचतीत्यादौ धर्मिपराख्यातप्रतियोगिपदोत्तरविभक्तेः[166] न स्तोकं पचतीत्यादावनुयोगिक्रियापदोत्तरसुविभक्तेश्चाप्रसिद्धतया प्रतियोगि-पदोत्तरविभक्तिविरुद्धविभक्तिशुन्यानुयोगिपदसमभिव्याहृतनञ्पदत्वेनानुयोगि-पदो-त्तरविभक्तिविरुद्धविभक्तिशून्यप्रतियोगिपदसमभिव्याहृतनञ्पदत्वेन वा

हेतुत्वस्यानुगतस्यासम्भवादसङ्गत्यापत्तेरिति ध्येयम्। **अतएवे**ति। यतएव समानविभक्तिकत्वं तन्त्रमित्यर्थः[167]। **यजतिषु** यागेषु, **ये यजामहं**[168] ये यजामहपदवन्तं[169] मन्त्रम्, **करोति** उच्चारयति[170], **अनुयाजः** यागविशेषः। **एकवाक्यते**ति[171]। अनुयाजभिन्नेषु[172] यजतिषु 'ये यजामह' करणविधाव-थैक्यादेकवाक्यत्वं[173] यजतिषु[174] 'ये यजामह' करणविधौ अनुयाजेषु तत्करण-निषेधे च विधेः[175] अर्थभेदाद्भिन्नवाक्यता स्यादिति भावः। **ये यजामहमित्यादेरि**ति[176] प्रथमानुसन्धानस्य एकवाक्यार्थबोधेनैव[177] पर्यवसिततत्वादिति भावः[178]। **आदि**ना करोतीत्यस्य परिग्रहः[179]। इदं च मणिकारादिलिखनमनुसृत्य व्याख्यातम्[180]। 'नानुयाजेषु करोति' इत्येव[181] वैदिकसम्मतः पाठः[182]। ननु नानुयाजेष्वित्यस्य निषेधविधित्वेऽनुयाजाधि-करणक-तादृशमन्त्रकरणमनिष्टकरणमिति[183] वाक्यार्थे सप्तम्यर्थस्यान्वयात् सप्तम्याः सार्थकत्वं स्यात्, पर्युदासे तु तद्वैयर्थ्यमतस्तदनुरोधात् गौरवादिकमपि न्याय्यमत आह-**विशेषणे**ति। विशेषणविभक्तेः पदसाधुत्वप्रयोजनसत्त्वान्न वैयर्थ्यमिति भावः। नन्वेवं प्रकारीभूतविभक्त्यर्थोपस्थितिं विना कथं नीलो घट इत्यादौ नामार्थयोरन्वयोऽत[184] आह-**नामार्थयोरि**ति।[185] एतत्तु[186] आख्यातवादार्थविवेचने[187] प्रपञ्चितम्[188]। मतान्तरमाह-**लाघवेने**ति[189]। अभेदातिरिक्तसम्बन्धेन नामार्थान्वयबोधत्वापेक्षया नामार्थान्वयबोधत्वस्य लघुत्वादिति भावः। **तथात्वं** प्रकारीभूतविभक्त्यर्थोपस्थितेस्तन्त्रत्वम्[190]। तर्हि नीलो घट इत्यादौ का गतिरत[191] आह-**विशेषणे**ति। शुचि पुष्पमित्यादौ असमासे लुप्तविभक्त्यनुसन्धानं विना साधुत्वमेव नास्तीति यत्र विभक्त्यनु-सन्धानं[192] विनापि साधुत्वं तत्र व्यभिचारमुद्धरति-**नीलोत्पलमि**ति। अत्राप्यनित्यसमासत्वेन[193] विग्रहवाक्यानुसन्धानादेव शाब्दबोध इति यदि[194] ब्रूयात् तदाह-**चित्रगुरि**ति। बहुव्रीहेर्नित्यसमासत्वेन विग्रहवाक्याभावेऽपि चित्रगवोरभेदान्वयबोधोत्तरं चित्रगोस्वामिनि लक्षणायां फलबलेन विभक्त्यनु-सन्धानं कल्प्यमित्यर्थः। तत्र[195] विभक्त्यनुसन्धानं[196] विनापि शाब्दधिय[197] आनुभविकत्वात् नीलो घट इत्यादावभेदस्य संसर्गतयैवानुभवाच्चाह-**मत** इति। विभक्त्यर्थस्याभावबोधने[198] व्युत्पत्तिविरोधो नास्तीति दृष्टान्तमाह-**न राज्ञ इत्यत्रे**ति। **एकवाक्यतानुरोधादि**त्याद्यनुषज्यते[199]। विशेषणविभक्तेर्यद्य-भेदार्थकत्वं[200] तदा[201] अभेदविशेषणत्वेनोपस्थितस्य नामार्थस्य नञर्थान्योन्याभावे विशेषणत्वेनान्वयस्यायोगात्[202] योगेऽपि वा विभक्त्यर्थान्वयत्यागस्यैव दोषत्वादिति भावः। इत्थं च चैत्रो न पचतीत्यादौ तिङो धर्मिपरतायां नञा[203] भेदप्रतीतेर्जननात्[204] पृथक्शक्तिकल्पनमिति[205] ध्येयम्॥

4. एकवाक्यतानुरोधादित्याद्युक्तयुक्तेर्भेदपरतेति[203] स्वयमुक्तम्, **नानुयाजेष्वि**त्यत्र

निषेधपरत्वे तस्य प्राप्तिपूर्वकत्वात् यजतिष्वित्यनेन तस्य प्राप्तिर्वाच्या तथाचैकविषयकविधिनिषेधे[207] विकल्पापत्तेः भेदपरतेति स्मार्तानां युक्तिं दूषयितुमुपन्यस्यति[208]–**यत्त्विति**। **तदितरपरतायाः**[209] विशेषेतरपरतायाः[210]। वैदिकशब्दस्य पक्षसमत्वाल्लौकिकशब्दे[211] व्युत्पत्तिं द्रढयति–**ब्राह्मणेभ्य** इति। **विकल्पानवकाशादि**ति। तथाचात्रापि यजतिष्वित्यादिसामान्य-विधेरनुयाजभिन्नयागपरमित्येकविषयकविधिनिषेधयोरप्रसङ्गादिति[212] भावः। **तत्रापि** कौण्डिन्याय नेत्यत्रापि[213]। **विरुद्धे**ति[214]। समानविभक्तिकत्ववत् समानवचनत्वस्यापि[215] नियामकत्वादिति भावः। इदमेव दृष्टान्तेन[216] द्रढयति–**न खल्वि**त्यादिना। **महतो राज्ञ** इति अभेदान्वयबोधकसमभिव्याहारे[217] नञा अन्योन्याभावस्य बोधनात् भेदान्वयबोधेऽपि[218] समानवचनत्वस्य नियामकत्व-मुक्तं[219] द्वयादिशब्दानां नित्यद्विवचनान्तत्वेन तथा अत्र तु न तथा व्युत्पत्तिरतः–**कथंचिदि**ति। **द्वितीयस्ये**ति। ब्राह्मणेभ्यो दधि दातव्यं कौण्डिन्याय नेत्यत एव कोण्डिन्यभिन्नेभ्यो ब्राह्मणेभ्यो[220] दधि[221] दातव्यमित्यर्थलाभादित्यर्थः[222]। वस्तुतस्तु विभक्त्यर्थे एकत्वद्वित्वादेरविव-क्षितत्वेन[223] भूपास्तृणमित्यादौ एकतृणतुल्यबुद्ध्युदयाद्विरुद्धवचनाभ्यामप्य-भिन्नत्वबोधो[224] भवत्येव, परन्तु न कौण्डिन्यायेत्यादौ[225] विभक्त्यर्थे एकत्वादि-विवक्षायां[226] वीजाभावान्न तथात्वसम्भवः[227] इति[228]। **अतएवे**ति। यतएव विशेषनिषेधे सामान्यविधेस्तदितरपरत्वम्[229] अतएवेत्यर्थः। तत्रापि पर्युदासमाशङ्क्य निषेधति–**न ही**ति। **रात्रौ श्राद्धं न कुर्वीते**त्यस्य रात्रि-भिन्ने श्राद्धं कुर्वीतेत्यर्थः। तथाचामावास्यायामित्यादितो रात्रौ श्राद्धप्रसक्तिः स्यादिति भावः। नन्वेकवाक्यतया रात्रिभिन्नायाममावास्यायां श्राद्धं कुर्वीतेत्यर्थ-कत्वे कुतो रात्रौ प्रसक्तिरत आह–**न खल्वि**ति। क्रियायुक्तवाक्ययोरेक-क्रियापदार्थस्यानन्वयेन तथैकवाक्यत्वासम्भवादिति भावः। **येनेदमि**ति। **इदं** रात्रौ श्राद्धं न कुर्वीतेति वाक्यम्। **तेन** श्राद्धविधायकवाक्येन। **नापीदमि**ति। **इदं** श्राद्धविधायकवाक्यं[230] नानुयाजेष्वित्यादेरप्यानुषङ्गिकक्रियावत्त्वात् **पृथगि**ति। **विकल्पापत्तिरि**ति[231]। रात्रौ श्राद्धस्य रागजप्रसक्त्यभावेन वैधी प्रसक्तिर्वाच्या तदर्थममावास्यायामित्यादिविधेरेव रात्रिपरत्वमपि[232] कल्प्यमित्येकविषयकतया[233] विकल्पः स्यादित्यर्थः। **निषेधानुपपत्तिरि**ति[234]। प्राचां मते वैधस्य रागाधीनस्य वा कर्तव्यताज्ञानस्य निषेधविधिजन्यशाब्दबोधे[235] हेतुत्वादिति भावः। अत्र सोपहासमाह–**साधीयानि**ति। **शाब्दबोधेऽपी**ति। अत्र अभावलौकिकप्रत्यक्षे[236] आहार्यरूपा[237] प्रसक्तिः कारणं कदाचित् सम्भवदपि[238] शाब्दबोधे त्वन्यादृशप्रसक्तेः[239] कारणत्वं न कस्याप्यनुमत-मित्यर्थः। **वैयर्थ्यमि**ति[240]। रात्रौ श्राद्धकरणस्य रागाद्विधितो वा अप्राप्तौ

तन्निषेधप्रतिपादन[241] निष्प्रयोजनकमिति[242] भाव:। यद्यपि न कलञ्जं भक्षयेदित्यादाविव निषेधविधे: प्रत्यवायरूपानिष्टसाधनत्वमेवार्थ: तथापि तत्र भक्षणस्य इष्टसाधनत्वेन तदभावस्य[243] बाधेन[244] बोधयितुमशक्यत्वात् निन्दार्थवादप्रायश्चित्तोपदेशाच्चानिष्टसाधनत्वमेव निषेधविध्यर्थ:[245]। इह तु इष्टसाधनत्वाभावबोधने बाधाभावान्निन्दार्थवादाद्यभावात् प्रत्यवायकल्पनागौरवाच्च इष्टसाधनत्वाभाव एव विध्यर्थ:[246]। इष्टं चामावास्यायामित्यादिविध्युपस्थितं ग्राह्य[247] प्राकरणिकत्वात्। तथाच अमावास्यायामित्यादिविधे: रात्रीतरामावास्यापरत्वे विधानाभावादेव तादृशेष्टसाधनत्वाभावो बोध्यते इति तद्बोधाय[248] रात्रौ[249] श्राद्धं न कुर्वीतेति वाक्य[250] व्यर्थमिति भाव:। **तात्पर्ये**ति। यदि रात्रौ श्राद्धं न निषिध्येत[251] तदा कदाचिदमावास्यायामित्यादिविधे: रात्रीतरामावास्यातात्पर्याननुरोधेन[252] रात्रावपि श्राद्धकरण[253] प्रसज्येत[254]। अतो रात्रौ श्राद्धकरणे निषिद्धेऽमावास्यापदस्य[255] रात्रीतरामावास्यापरत्वनिश्चयान्नैषा प्रसक्ति: एवंचामावास्यायामित्यादिविधेस्तात्पर्यग्राहकतयैव तस्य[256] सार्थकत्वमिति[257] भाव:। अत्र <u>मीमांसका:</u> एकवाक्यत्वं हि[258] द्विविधं विशिष्टैकार्थप्रतिपत्तिजनकत्व[259] तत्तात्पर्यजनकत्वं च। रात्रौ श्राद्धं न कुर्वीतेत्यादे: क्रियान्तरवैयर्थ्येनाद्यस्यासम्भवेऽपि द्वितीयस्य सम्भवे न किञ्चिद्बाधकं यथा 'अग्निहोत्रं जुहोति' 'दध्ना जुहोति'[260] इत्यत्र। तत्र हि 'अग्निहोत्रं जुहोति' इति प्रधानविधिप्रवृत्तौ केन द्रव्येणेति द्रव्याकाङ्क्षायां दध्ना जुहोतीति विधिप्रवृत्ति:। तेन हि प्रधानविधेरेकदेशं जुहोतीत्यनेनानूद्य दधिरूपं द्रव्यं करणत्वेन विधीयते। यज्जुहोति तद्दध्ना इत्येवं बोधिते[261] दधिकरणकोऽग्निहोत्रहोम इष्टसाधनमित्येवंरूपविशिष्टैकार्थपरत्व[262] विधिद्वयस्य निर्वहति। तथामावास्यायामित्यादिप्रधानविधिप्रवृत्तौ कालविशेषाकाङ्क्षायां यत् श्राद्धं कुर्वीत तद्रात्रिभिन्ने इति रात्रौ श्राद्धं न कुर्वीतेत्यनेन पर्युदासलक्षणया बोधिते रात्रिभिन्नामावास्याधिकरणकश्राद्धकरणमिष्टसाधनमित्यर्थपरत्व[263] विधिद्वयस्य[264] निर्वहति। न च मुख्यार्थानुरोधान्निषेधविधित्वमेव[265] युक्तम्। एकप्रकरणाम्नातत्वेन तदाकाङ्क्षाधीनत्वेन[266] चामावास्यादिविशेषणमहिम्ना[267] रात्रिभेदविधित्वे[268] निश्चिते[269] सम्भवार्थमुख्यार्थत्यागस्याप्यदोषत्वात्[270]। अतएव नेक्षेतोऽत्यन्तमादित्यमित्यादेर्व्रतप्रकरणाम्नातत्वेन[271] मुख्यार्थं परित्यज्य लक्षणया ईक्षणविरोधिसंकल्प[262] कुर्यादित्यर्थकत्वं सिद्धान्तितम्। अतएव 'दीक्षितो न ददाति' इत्यादेरपि[273] न निषेधविधित्वं किन्तु दीक्षितस्य दानाभावादिरूपाङ्गविधित्वम्-इत्याहु:।

तदर्थत्वात्[274] निषेधविधिप्रयोजनत्वात्[275]। नन्वेवं विकल्पस्थलमेव दुर्मिलमित्यत[276] आह-**एकविषयतये**ति[277]। **अनन्यगत्ये**ति[278]। अत्र[279] सामान्यविशेष-

भावाभावेन[280] विशेषेतरपरत्वस्यासम्भवादिति भावः। ननु 'न कलञ्जं भक्षयेत्' इत्यादौ नञर्थे विध्यर्थस्य इष्टसाधनत्वादेः प्रतियोगितयान्वयस्य व्युत्पत्तिसिद्ध-त्वात् अत्र तथान्वये ग्रहणविधिना तत्रेष्टसाधनत्वादेर्बोधनाद् विरोध इत्यत आह-**अत्र चे**ति। नेष्टसाधनमित्यादिकमि**त्यादि**ना[281] बलवदनिष्टाननु-बन्धिकृतिसाध्ययोः[282] परिग्रहः[283]। ग्रहणाभाव इष्टसाधनमि[त्यादिकम्] **इत्यादि**ना बलवदनिष्टाननुबन्धी कृतिसाध्यश्चेत्यस्य संग्रहः।[284] नन्वेवं धात्वर्थस्य नञर्थे[285] प्रतियोगित्वेनान्वये[286] नञर्थे च[286] विभक्त्यर्थेष्टसाध नत्वादेरन्वये[288] व्युत्पत्तिविरोधः इत्यत आह-**व्युत्पन्नश्चे**ति। **नञि**ति।नञ्समभिव्याहृतो यो धातुस्तदर्थस्येत्यर्थः।। **अतएव** धात्वर्थस्याभावेऽपि विभक्त्यर्थान्वयस्य व्युत्पत्तिसिद्धत्वादेव। प्राभाकरा इति। तेषां वैदिकलिङः कार्ये शक्तिः। तत्र च प्रकृत्यर्थो विषयतया अन्वेति। तथाच 'स्वर्गकामो यजेत' इत्यत्र स्वर्गकामस्य यागविषयकं कार्यमित्यन्वयधीः। 'न कलञ्जं भक्षयेत्' इत्यत्र कलञ्जभक्षणस्य नञर्थेऽभावेऽभावस्य[289] च लिङर्थे कार्ये निषेधापूर्वरूपे विषयत्वेनान्वये[290] कलञ्जभक्षणाभावविषयकं कार्यमित्यन्वयधीरिति फलबलाद् व्युत्पत्त्यन्तरं कल्प्यमिति भावः। अतएव च

नामूढस्येतरोत्पत्तेः[292] (न्यायसूत्रम् 4-1-6)

नानुपमृद्य प्रादुर्भावात् (न्यायसूत्रम् 4-1-14)

इत्यादेर्नञर्थे विभक्त्यर्थस्यान्वयाद् अमूढस्येतरोत्पत्त्यभावात्[292] अनुपमृद्य[293] प्रादुर्भावाभावादित्यर्थमाहुः[294]। क्वचिद्विभक्त्यर्थप्रतियोगिकाभावस्य[295] धात्वर्थे[296] क्वचिच्च धात्वर्थप्रतियोगिकाभावे विभक्त्यर्थान्वये[297] किं नियामकमत आह-**नियमस्त्व**ति[298]। तात्पर्यादीति **आदिना** प्रकरणादिपरिग्रहः। ननु षोडशिग्रहणस्याङ्गत्वेनाफलकत्वादिष्टसाधनत्वाभावबोधनेऽपि[299] न ग्रहणविधि-विरोधः। एवं ग्रहणाभावस्याप्यङ्गत्वेनाफलकत्वात्[300] तत्रेष्टसाधनत्वबोधने[301] बाध इत्यत आह-**मुख्यफले**ति। फलवत्सन्निधावफलमङ्गमित्यङ्ग- लक्षण[302] तत्र चाफलत्वं[303] मुख्यफलाजनकत्वं न तु सर्वथैव फलशून्यत्वमिति भावः[304]। **उपकारे**ति प्रधानोपकारेत्यर्थः। **अविरुद्धम्** अङ्गत्वेनाविरुद्धम्। ग्रहणा-भावेनैवेष्टसिद्धौ[305] कष्टसाध्ये[306] ग्रहणे कथं प्रवृत्तिरत आह-**ग्रहणविधी**ति। अतिशयितफलाकल्पने अननुष्ठानलक्षणाप्रामाण्यं ग्रहणविधेः स्यादिति भावः। अतिशयितपरमापूर्वं न[307] स्वतः काम्यम् अतः[308] कथं तदिच्छया ग्रहणे प्रवृत्त्या विधेरननुष्ठानलक्षणाप्रामाण्यं[309] न स्यादत आह-**तस्माच्चे**ति। **मुख्यं**[310] **फलं** स्वर्गादिरूपम्।।

५. ननु भूतले न घट इत्यादौ प्रतियोग्यभावयोः प्रतियोग्यनुयोगिभावः भूतलं न घट इत्यादौ चाभावाधिकरणयोराधाराधेयभावः[311] प्रकारतया न[312] भासते तदुपस्थापकषष्ठ्यादेरभावात् न[313] संसर्गतया नामार्थयोर्भेदेन साक्षादन्वयस्याव्युत्पन्नत्वादत[314] आह–**प्रतियोग्यभावयोरि**ति। **निपातातिरिक्ते**ति। फलबलान्निपाताज्जन्यभेदान्वयबोधे[315] विभक्त्यर्थोपस्थितेस्तन्त्रत्वं कल्प्यमिति[216] भावः। एतत्तु[317] एवकारार्थसारमञ्जर्या[318] प्रपञ्चितमस्माभिः[319]। **अतएवे**ति। यतएव निपातार्थान्वयमात्रे न विभक्त्यर्थापेक्षा अतएवेत्यर्थः। इवादीति। चन्द्र इव मुखमित्यादौ इवार्थे सादृश्ये चन्द्रस्य प्रतियोगितया मुखस्य चाधिकरणतया[320] अन्वयः। **आदि**ना एव-वा-तु-चादिपरिग्रहः[321]। ननु नञोऽभावमात्रार्थकत्वे अघटं भूतलमित्यादौ भिन्नाभ्यां रूपाभ्यामेकधर्मिबोधकत्वरूपं सामानाधिकरण्यं न स्यात् एवमघटः पट इत्यादौ अन्वयश्चेत्यत आह–**अघटमि**ति। संसर्गाभावान्योन्याभावार्थकनञ्भेदेनोदाहरणद्वयम्। अघटः पट इत्यत्र[322] सामानाधिकरण्यानुरोधात्[323] नञो लक्षणया[324] अभाववत्परतेति मणिकारेणोक्तम्[325]। तत्र च तत्पुरुषसमासेऽपि[326] अघट इत्यस्यैव सम्भवात्। तेन[327] घटभिन्नस्यैव बोधनात् संसर्गाभाववत्परत्वं[328] नञो न लभ्यत इत्यतो बहुव्रीहिसमासे[329] स्पष्टीकर्तुम् अघटमिति नपुंसकलिङ्गमेव निर्दिष्टम्। तत्र च न विद्यते घटो यत्रेति विग्रहेण संसर्गाभावस्य बोधसम्भवात्[330]। न च चित्रगुपदादावुत्तरपद[331] एव लक्षणाया व्युत्पादितत्वात् प्रकृतेऽप्यघटपदस्यैवाभाववल्लाक्षणिकत्वेऽसङ्गतिरिति[332] वाच्यम्। चित्रगवोरभेदान्वयबोधपुरःसरं[333] चित्रगोसम्बन्धिनि लक्षणायां गोपदार्थस्य[334] साक्षात्सम्बन्धः चित्रपदार्थस्य परम्परासम्बन्धो भासत[335] इति साक्षात्सम्बन्धेन[336] लाघवात् गोपद एव लक्षणेति तद्बीजम्। अत्र च[337] घटाभावयोरन्वयबोधोत्तरं घटाभावसम्बन्धिन उपस्थितौ नञ्पदार्थस्यैव साक्षात्सम्बन्धभानमिति पूर्वपद एव नञि[338] लक्षणायाः सर्वसम्मतत्वात्। एतेनाघटमिति तत्पुरुषसमास[339] एव द्वितीयान्तं पदं पश्येति[240] क्रिया चाध्याहार्या, प्रथमान्तत्वे तु[341]

परवल्लिङ्गं द्वन्द्वतत्पुरुषयोः (पा.सू. 2-4-26)

इत्यनुशासनात् अघटो भूतलम् इति स्यादिति व्याख्यानम् अनादेयं संसर्गाभावार्थकनञि[342] तत्पुरुषस्यासाधुत्वात्[243]।।

६. नामार्थयोर्भेदान्वयबोधे प्रकारीभूतविभक्त्यर्थोपस्थितेस्तन्त्रत्वे[344] निपातातिरिक्तं[245] विशेषणमनिवेशयतां मतमाह–**केचित्त्वि**ति। घटस्याभाव इत्यादौ षष्ठ्यर्थोऽनुयोगित्वम्[346]। तत्र च घटस्य निरूपितत्वेनाभावस्य चाधिकरणत्वे-

नान्वयः[247]। न तु प्रतियोगित्वं षष्ठ्यर्थः[348] घटस्याधेयत्वेनाभावस्य च निरूपकत्वेनान्वय[349] इति। तथा सति[350] घटीयाभावो[351] न घटस्येति स्यात्, घटनिष्ठप्रतियोगित्वस्याभावेऽभावसत्त्वात् निरूपकत्वादिसम्बन्धस्य[352] चाभावप्रतियोगितानवच्छेदकत्वात्[353]। एवंच न घट इत्यादौ प्रतियोगित्वस्य सुबर्थत्वे घटस्य तत्राधेयत्वेनान्वयकल्पने घटस्याभाव इत्यादौ विभक्त्यर्थे निरूपितत्वसम्बन्धेन प्रकृत्यर्थस्यान्वयोऽन्यत्र[354] क्लृप्तो भज्येत। एवं पटस्याभावो न घट इत्यत्र प्रथमायाः षष्ठ्यर्थलाक्षणिकत्वे घटानुयोगित्वाभावः[355] प्रतीयते प्रतियोगित्वस्य प्रथमार्थत्वेन[356] नञर्थान्वयानुपपत्तिश्च[357] इत्यतः **अनुयोगित्वे वे**ति[358]। इदं तु बोध्यम्[359]–भूतले न घट इत्यादौ प्रथमार्थस्यानुयोगित्वस्य नञर्थे अधिकरणत्वेनान्वयः। पटाभावो न घट इत्यादौ तु प्रतियोगित्वेनान्वयः। तत्र च[360] प्रकरणादिकमेव नियामकं षष्ठ्यर्थस्यानुयोगित्वे[361] नञर्थेऽधिकरणत्वेनान्वये[362] षष्ठ्यादेर्विशेषणविभक्तित्वं[363] तन्त्रम्। यत्र तु षष्ठीविशेष्यविभक्तिस्तत्र[364] तदर्थस्यानुयोगित्वस्य[365] नञर्थे प्रतियोगित्वेनैवान्वयः। अतएव अयमभावो न घटस्येत्यादौ अभावे घटानुयोगित्वाभावः एव[366] प्रतीयते न तु घटानुयोगित्ववान्[367] अभाव इति नञुत्तरस्य[368] सुपोऽधिकरणत्वम्[369]। तत्र च लक्षणा[370] इत्युभयकल्पनापेक्षया श्रूयमाणनञोऽभाववल्लक्षणा[371] युक्ता इत्याशयेनाह–**नञो**[372] **वे**ति।

ननु विशेष्याविशेष्यपदयोर्विरुद्धविभक्तिराहित्यं[373] अन्योन्याभावबोधने[374] वा प्राङ्नियामकमुक्तम्[375], तत्र विरुद्धत्वं[376] विरुद्धार्थकत्वम् अन्यथा व्यत्ययस्थले[377] कर्माद्यर्थकप्रथमान्तार्थकस्य[378] शुद्धप्रथमान्तार्थत्वेन[379] नञोऽन्योन्याभावबोधा-पातात्[380]। तथाच[381] प्रतियोगिपदोत्तरस्य सुपः प्रतियोगित्वादौ लाक्षणिकत्वेऽनुयोगिपदस्य शुद्धसुबन्तत्वे[382] च ब्राह्मणस्य धनं न मूर्खस्य इत्यादौ नञर्थे भेदे मूर्खानुयोगित्वस्य बोधे नञर्थस्याधिकरणत्वेनान्वये मूर्खभिन्नस्य ब्राह्मणस्येत्यर्थो लभ्यते इति[383] विरुद्धार्थकत्वमेव[384] विभक्तेरिति प्रागुक्तनियामकासम्भवात् अनियमेन सुबर्थप्रतियोगित्वादेरिव तिङादि-षष्ठ्याद्यर्थस्य[385] कृतिसम्बन्धादेरपि नञर्थेऽन्योन्याभावे[386] साक्षादनन्वये[387] न पचति न राज्ञ इत्यादौ पाकानुकूलकृतिभेदस्य राजसम्बन्धभेदस्य च बोधापत्तिः[388]। एवं[389] नञर्थे[390] संसर्गाभावे भेदान्वयोपपत्त्यर्थमनुपयोगिपदे सप्तम्यपेक्षा, स च नञुत्तरस्य सुपोऽधिकरणत्वे[391] लक्षणयैवोपपन्न इति नञोऽभाववल्लाक्षणिकत्वे तु भेदान्वयप्रसङ्गाभावात्[392] अभिदेनान्वये[393]। च[394] सप्तम्या अप्रयोजकत्वात्[395]। अनुयोगिसमानविभक्तिकार्थस्यापि नञा संसर्गाभावबोधापत्तिरत आह–**विभक्त्यर्थे**ति। विभक्त्यर्थस्यान्योन्याभावबोधेऽनुयोगिसमानविभक्तिकार्थस्य च[396] संसर्गाभावबोधे नञो न सामर्थ्यमित्यर्थः[397]।

तथाच[398] फलबलात् नञ्जन्येऽन्योन्याभावबोधे विभक्तिभिन्नपदजन्या प्रतियोग्युपस्थितिः संसर्गाभावबोधे चानुयोगिसमानविभक्तिकातिरिक्तपदजन्या प्रतियोग्युपस्थितः[399] च[400] कारणं कल्प्यमिति भावः। न चैवं पचतीत्यादौ[401] तिङादेर्धर्मिपरतायां पाककर्त्रादेरन्योन्याभावबोधादन्वयः स्यादिति वाच्यम्, इष्टत्वात्। विभक्त्यर्थस्य[402] शक्त्या निरूढलक्षणया वा[403] विभक्त्युपस्थाप्यस्य कृत्यादेरित्यर्थ इति कश्चित्। न च[404] नामार्थस्य संसर्गाभावबोधे सप्तम्यन्तानुयोगिपदोपस्थापितस्य[405] समभिव्याहृतनञ्पदत्वादिना हेतुत्वेनैवातिप्रसङ्गः[406]। अनुयोगिसमानविभक्तिकार्थस्य संसर्गाभावबोधनाय[407] किमिति नियामकान्तरानुसरणमिष्टम्[408], भवतापि[409] भूतले न[410] घट इत्यादौ घटपदोत्तरसप्तम्याः प्रतियोगित्वादौ लक्षणया भूतले घटप्रतियोगिकसंसर्गाभावबोधस्य[411] वारणासम्भवात्। **कृतिसम्बन्धादे**रिति न पचतीत्यत्र कृतौ न राज्ञ इत्यत्र सम्बन्धस्य[412] नान्योन्याभावबोधनमित्यर्थः।। इति।।

श्रीभवानन्दसिद्धान्तवागीशेन विनिर्मितः।
नञ्वादार्थप्रदीपोऽयं निहन्तुं सुधियां तमः।।[413]

संदर्भसंकेतः

1. P (p. 1010): संसर्गाभावइत्यादि
   Q (12b2): संसर्गाभावेति
   R (1b1) records abenedictionbefore संसर्गाभावः श्रीगणेशाय नमः।।
2. Q (1b1): ०भेदसूचनाय
3. R (1b2): ०भाववत्त्वं
4. R (1b2): कत्वमित्यर्थः for कमित्यर्थः
5. R (1b3) वशात् for बलात्
6. Q (1b3): समवायावच्छिन्न०
   R (16b3): समवायवच्छिन्ना०, Omits च०
7. R (1b3): प्रिति०
8. R (1b4):भानेनैव
9. R (1b4): बोधे for बोध
10. R (1b4) omits त्व०
11. P (p. 1011) omits पटो०
12. P (p. 1012): प्रकारतया
13. R (1b5): तथाविधानात्
14. P (p. 1012) omits हि०
    R (1b6): ० भावस्यैव
15. P (p. 1012): अत्र च for तत्र

16. P (p. 1012): ०त्यन्ताभावध्वंसप्रागभाववत्त्वादिबुद्धित्वादिना
17. P (p. 1012), R (1b8) omit द्वय०
18. P (p. 1012): लाघवेन
19. P (p. 1012) add इति after ० च्छेदकं०
20. R (1b9): समवायाविच्छन्न०
21. R (1b9): निर्वाह इति
22. P (p. 1012), R (1b10): नव्यास्तु
23. P (p. 1012): संसर्गारोपपूर्वकप्रतीतिविषयतावत्त्वं
    R (1b10): संसर्गारोपजैन्यपूर्वकप्रतीतिविषयाभावत्वं
24. R (1b10): ० प्रतियोगिकाभावत्वं
25. P (p. 1013): ०प्रत्यक्षे हेतुत्वे
26. P (p. 1013) adds च after the word.
    R (1b11): व्याप्तिश्च
27. P (p. 1013): संसर्गाद्यवच्छिन्न.
    R (1b11): संसर्गात्वावच्छिन्नप्रतियोगित्वाद्यनिरुक्तेश्च
28. P (p. 1013): संयोग्यन्योभावाद्यतिव्याप्तेश्च
    R (1b12): संयोगान्योन्याभावेऽतिवयाप्तेश्च
29. P (p. 1013): संयोगतया
    R (1b12): संसर्गातया
30. P (p. 1013): चावच्छेदकताया for वा
    R (1b13):चावच्छेदकतया for वा
31. P (p. 1013), R (1b13) omit अवच्छेदकतया.
32. P (p. 1013): तादात्म्यावच्छिन्नाभावत्वं
    R (2a1) omits सम्बन्ध०
33. R (2a2): इत्याकारकानुगत: प्रतीति०
34. P (p. 1014): तथा for तादृश
35. Q (17a4) omits च०
36. R (2a3): नास्तीत्यन्ता०
37. P (p. 1015): ०भावत्वंद्वयमपि
    R (2a5): ०भावत्वंच द्वयं च
38. Q (17a5): प्रांच०
39. P (p. 1016): स्यादित्यत
40. Q (17a6): अन्वयीति
41. R (2a7): प्रतियोगितावच्छेदसम्बन्धेन
42. P (p. 1016): योऽन्वय:
43. R (2a7): तत्तावच्छेदकं
44. P (. 1016), R (2a7) omit the word.
45. Q (17b1): घटप्रकारका०
    R (2a9): ०बोधजनकस्वाभाव्यं
46. P (p. 1017), R (2a10) omit the word.
47. P (p. 1018), R (2a11): ०समभिव्याहारात्
48. R (2a11): तदसमभिव्याहृतत्वेनाज्ञातत्वम् for the entire portion: तदसमभि ˙ ˙ ˙ ज्ञातत्वम्
49. P (p . 1018): प्रयुङ्क्ते
50. P (p. 1018), R (2a12) omit च०
51. P (p. 1018), R (2b1): लोहितस्या०
    Q (17b3): लोहित्यस्या०

52. P (p. 1019): भाव for भातत्वंवह्नित्वे
R (2b2): भातस्य for भातत्वंवह्नित्वे
53. P (p. 1019) omits the word.
54. Q (17b3): संसर्गतया
55. Q (17b4): ०तादृश
56. P (p. 1019), R (2b3): सम्बन्ध for संसर्ग
57. R (2b3): विषयतायांस्तु for विषयःइयांस्तु
58. Q (17b4) omits च.
59. P (p. 1020), R (2b5) omit the wrod.
60. R (2b5): ०तादृशाविशिष्टप्रतियोगितान
61. P (p. 1020): लोहितः स्फटिक
62. P (p. 1020): संसर्गांशे
63. P (p. 1021): प्रतियोगित्वं
64. P (p. 1021): विसकलितमेव
R (2b8): विषकलितमेव
65. P (p. 1021): संसर्गस्तदा
66. Q (18a1): ०स्तदा अवच्छिन्नत्वेऽपि
R (2b10): ०स्तदात्म्यावच्छिन्नत्वेऽपि
67. P (p. 1022): संसर्ग for सम्बन्ध
68. P (p. 1022) omits घटत्वस्य च तदभाने०
R (2b10) omits च.
69. P (p. 1022), R (2b11): कश्चित्
70. R (2b11): लोहितो वह्नि०
71. P (p. 1022), R (2b11)add अपि after the word.
72. Q (18a1): घटत्वस्यावच्छेदकत्व०
73. P (p. 1022) adds अपि before the word.
74. Q (18a3): ०प्रतियोगिताकत्वसम्बन्धेनाभावे
75. P (p. 1023): ०पन्ने धूम
R (3a2): ०पन्नो धूम
76. R (3a2) omits the word.
77. Q (18a5): नीले घटे
78. P (p. 1024): पीतस्यान्योन्याभावस्य
R (3a3): पीतघटस्यान्योन्याभावस्य
79. P (p. 1024): ०भेदेनोदाहरणप्रदर्शनम्
80. Q (18a6) omits the word.
81. P (p. 1030): ०नान्वयबोध
82. P (p. 1030): इदमत्रावधेयम् for इदम् चात्र बोध्यम्
83. R (3a7): पीत
84. R (3a8): अभेदेन सम्बन्धेन for अभेदसम्बन्धेन
85. Q (18a7) omits तच्च.
86. P (p. 1032) adds च after the word.
87. R (3a10): तत्पदेनानवबोधनात्
88. P (p. 1032): पक्ष्यतीत्यादौ
89. P (p. 1033): तिङर्थस्य
90. P (p. 1033): तत्तत्पदो०
R (3b2): तत्तप०

91. P (p. 1033): ०नुयोग्यन्वयबोधे
R (3b2): ०नुयोगिन्यन्वयबोधे
92. R (3b3 omits अपि.
93. P (p. 1034): ०स्थापितस्येति
94. Q (18b6), R (3b6) omit भाव०
95. P (p. 1035): ०स्थाप्य
96. Q (18b7), R (3b8) omit भाव०
97. P (p. 1036) omits the word.
98. P (p. 1036): संग्रहः
99. P (p. 1036) omit अभावोपस्थितिः.
R (3b12) नञ्पदजन्ये प्रथमान्त० for नञ्पदजन्या . . . प्रथमान्त०
100. P (p. 1036): एव बोधव्यः for बोध्यः
101. P (1036): ०म्बन्धेनान्वयः
102. P (p. 1036): षष्ठ्या अर्थः
103. P (p. 1036), R (4a2): स्वत्वस्य षष्ठ्यर्थत्वे
104. P (p. 1036), R (4a2): सम्बन्धेन तत्रान्वय
105. R (4a4): प्रकृत्यर्थत्वेन
106. Q (19a4): वृत्तितानियामक
107. P (p. 1038): षष्ठ्यर्थत्वं
108. P (p. 1038): निरूपकत्वेन सम्बन्धेन
109. R (4a7): ०मेवेति कथमेवेति
110. R (4a9): ०वच्छेदकसम्बन्धत्वे
111. P (p. 1038): बाधकमित्यत
112. P (p. 1038), R (4a10) omit here the sentence: वृत्त्यनियामक . . . .भावः० । Iand C read the sentenceat different places. Vide note nos. 115and 119.
113. R(4a11): ०स्थितिजन्यो
114. Q (19b1): नञ्पदजन्ये घट०
115. R (4a11) adds the very sentence withafew variant readings mentionedat the note no. 112, before this word. The sentence read here runs thus: वृत्तितानियामकसम्बन्धपुरस्कारेणैव सर्वत्राभावप्रतीतिरस्ति एतद्धनस्वामित्वंमैत्रे नास्ति चैत्रस्वत्वमत्र नास्तीत्येवाभावप्रत्ययात्।। न तु निरूपकत्वादिसम्बन्ध प्रतियोगितावच्छेदकीकृत्य क्वचिदभावधीरस्तीति भावः। तादृशशाब्दबोधे।
116. P (p. 1038), R (4b1) omit the portin: नामपदोत्तर . . . वा.
117. Q (19b3) omits न.
118. R (4b2): नञ्पदजन्यनञा ज्ञायते for नञ्पदे न जायते
119. P (p. 1038)adds the sentence mentionedat note no. 112 before the word. The sentence has some differences in reading here: वृत्तितानियामकसम्बन्धपुरस्कारेणैव सर्वत्राभावप्रतीतिरस्ति एतद्धनस्वामित्वं मैत्रे नास्ति चैत्रस्वत्वमत्र नास्तीत्येवाभावप्रत्ययात्।। न तु निरूपकेत्यादिसम्बन्ध प्रतियोगितावच्छेदकीकृत्य क्वचिद्भावधीरस्तीति भावः।
120. R (4b3): नञ्पदजन्य
121. P (p. 1041) adds पद after सप्तमी०
R (4b4): ०नञ्पदजन्या संसर्गा०
122. P (p. 1041) omits तु.
123. P (p. 1041)adds कुतो before the word.
124. Q (19b5): कार्यजननीयेत्येषा
125. P (1041): सप्तम्यर्थस्याभावो
126. R (4b6): चाधारा०

127. P (p. 1041): ०मेवेत्यत for ०मेव तदा
R (4b6): ०मेवैतदत for ०मेव तदा
128. P (p. 1041) omits च०
129. P (p. 1042): ०नुसारे
130. P (p. 1012): मते आह
131. Q (20a1): केचिदिति
132. Q (20a2) , R (4b10): नञ्समभिव्याहारे
133. Q (20a2) omits the word.
134. Q (20a3): नञ्बोध्य
135. P(p. 1043), R (4b14): अभावस्यैकत्वात्
136. Q (20a4): तद्दवित्वबहुत्वयोः
137. P (p. 1043), R (5a1): स्फुटमेवेति
138. Q(20a5): Illegible from तच्च upto तच्चा.
139. Q (20a5): ०तार्थाश्रयत्वे
140. R (5a3): तच्च for स च
141. P (p. 1043): शाब्द for अन्वय
142. P (p. 1043): ०वच्छेदेनै
143. P (p. 1043), omits द्वित्व.
144. R (5a7): ०करण्यान्वयात्
145 P (p.1045) omits the word.
146. P (p.1045), R(5a10): सत्त्वाभावो
147. P (p.1045): ०बोधेन
148. P (p. 1045): ०समवेतत्वेति
149. P (p. 1045): सत्त्वासमवायपरं
150. P (p.1045): जात्यनुयोगित्वा.
R (5a12): ०भाववारणाय
151. Q (20b6): ०स्यैवमपि
152. P (p. 1045), R (5b1): ०पपन्नैवेत्याशयः
153. P (p. 1045): ०वच्छेदक
154. Q (21a2): द्विवत्वावच्छिन्न०
155. Q (21a3): क्रियापदस्य सम.
R (5b5): क्रियापदस्य सति सम.
156. Q (21a3): ०दिकस्तु
157. P (p. 1048): ०लाधेयत्वयोः
158. P (p. 1048) omits घट०
159. P (p. 1048), R (5b8) omit बोध०
160. P (p. 1048) omits न०
161. P (p. 1050): स्तोकभेदस्य
R (5b11): स्तोकस्याभेदस्य
162. R (5b11): ०त्वादाह
163. P (p. 1050): ०विभक्तिराहित्यं
164. Q (21b2): ०व्याहतेन नञ्पदत्वेन
165. R (6a3): ०समभिव्याहृत
166. R (6a3) omits धर्मिपराख्यात; reads पदान्तरे for पदोत्तर०
167. P (p. 1051): तन्त्रमतएवेत्यर्थः
168. Q ((21b5): ययामह०

R (6a7): याजमह०
169. Q (21b5): जयामह for यजामह
170. P (p. 1051): उच्चारयेत्
171. P (p. 1051): एकवाक्यत्वेति
172. Q (21b6): अनुजायभिन्नेषु
173. Q (21b6): जयामह for यजामह
P (p. 1051): जयामहमन्त्रकरण०
174. Q (21b6): जयतिषु
175. P (p. 1051): विधौ
176. Q (21b6): जयामह०
177. Q (22a1): ०सन्धानस्याद्यवाक्यार्थ०
178. R (6a10) omits the entire sentence: ये यजामह · · · · भावः०
179. P (p. 1051): संग्रहः
180. Vide समासवादः in *Tattvacintāmaṇi* vol. IV, Part 2, p 788. The reading there is यजतिषु च ये यजामहे करोति नानुयाजेषु०
181. Q (22a1): इत्येव तु
R (6a11): इत्यत्र तु
182. R (6a11) omits the word.
183. P (p. 1051): ०मनिष्टसाधनमिति
184. P (p. 1051): ०रन्वयइत्यत
185. P (p. 1054) reaods fter this the following portion: ननु यत्र च विशेषणविशेष्ययोरभेदान्वयबोधो व्युत्पन्नस्तत्र भेदो नञा बोध्यते इति नियमात् कथं यजतिषु अनुयाजभेदान्वयः तत्र प्रकारीभूतविभक्त्यर्थोपस्थित्यभावेन विशेषणविशेष्याभेदान्वयासम्भवादित्यत आह–**नामार्थयोरि**ति। अव्ययनिपातातिरिक्तनामार्थयोरि इत्यर्थइत्यपरे।
As it is notavailable in the two other manuscripts of नञ्वाद commentary of Bhavānanda, so the portion so has been left out of the text. Most probably the portion is from some other commentary.
186. P (p. 1055), R (6b1): एतत्तत्त्वं
187. Vide आख्यातवादार्थविवेचन (alias आख्यातवादटिप्पनी, Edited by the present editor for the DRS, Sanskrit, RBU), parano. 2.
188. P (p. 1055) adds after the word.
189. Q (22a3): लाघवेति
190. P (p. 1056): ०स्थितिहेतुत्वं
191. R (6b3): गतिरित्यत
192. R (6b4) omits the portion: विना · · · नुसन्धानं०
193. P (p. 1056): ०समाससत्त्वेन
194. R (6b5) omits the word.
195. Q (22a6): तत्र तत्र
196. R (6b6) omits कल्प्यमि · · · नुसन्धान०
197. R (6b6): शाब्दबुद्धेः
198. P (p. 1056): विभक्त्यर्थाभेदाभावान्वयबोधने
R (6b7) adds नञा before this word.
199. R (6b9): ०दित्यनुषज्यते
200. P (p. 1056), R (6b9) omit the word.
201. Q (22b1): एकदा
202. P (p. 1058), R (6b10): ० न्वयायोगात्
203. P (p. 1058): नञो

204. P (p. 1058), R (6b11): भेदत्वेन प्रतीते.
205. P (p. 1058) omits शक्ति०
206. P (p. 1058): एकवक्यत्वानु०
R (6b12): ०रोधादित्युक्त०
207. R (6b13) omits विषयक०
208. P p. 1059): ०मुत्थापयति
209. Q (22b4): ०परतायां
210. Q (22b4): ०परतायां
R (6b14) omits the word.
211. R (6b14): चाक्षुषामत्वा०, शाब्द for शब्दे
212. Q (22b4): जयतिष्वि० · · · ० रनुजायभिन्न०
P (p. 1059): ०भिन्नयागपरत्वमित्येक.
213. Q (22b5) omits न०
214. R (7a3) omits the word.
215. P (p. 1059): समानवचनस्यापि
216. R (7a3) omits the word.
217. R (7a4)adds एवं after the word.
218. P (p. 1059): बोधनात् भेदा०
219. R (7a5) नियामकत्वोक्तेः
220. P (p. 1059) omits the word.
221. R (7a6) omits the word.
222. P (p. 1059), R (7a7): ०दिति भावः
223. P (p. 1059): विभक्तर्थैकत्व ०· · · ०देर्विवक्षितत्वेन
R (7a7) विभक्त्यर्थे एकद्वित्वादेर्विवक्षितत्वेन
224. P (p. 1059): भूपा एकतृणतुल्या इति for एकतृणतुल्य० मप्यन्वयबोधो
R (7a7): ०तुल्यत्वबुद्ध्यु०, ०मप्यभेदबोधो
225. R (7a8) omits इत्यादौ०
226. P (p. 1059), R (7a8): विभक्त्यर्थैक० · · · ०त्वाविवक्षायां
227. R (7a8): तथात्वमिति सम्भवः
228. P (p. 1058) omits the word.
229. P (p. 1059) सामान्यंतदितरपरम्
2230. P (p. 1066), R (7a13): ०धायकंवाक्यं
231. R (7a13): विकल्पापत्तेरिति
232. R (7b1): रात्रिभिन्नपरत्वमपि न
233. Q (23a6): ०विषयतया
234. Q (23a6), R (7b2) omit इति०
235. P (p. 1067): ०शाब्दबोध
236. P (p. 1067), R (7b3) omit अत्र०
237. P (p. 1067), R (7b4): आहार्यारोपरूपा
238. Q (23b1): सम्भवेपि
R (7b4): सम्भवत्यपि
239. P (p. 1069): तादृश०
240. P (p. 1069) adds शङ्कते before वैयर्थ्यमिति०
241. R (7b5): तन्निषेधनप्रतिपादनं
242. P (p. 1069), R (7b6): निष्प्रयोजनमिति
243. Q (23b3) notes इष्टसाधनत्वाभावस्येत्यर्थः०

244. R (7b7): विरोधे
245. R (7b8): निषेधविधेरर्थः
246. R (7b9): विधेरर्थः
247. R (7b10) omits the word.
248. P (p. 1072): तद्बोधनाय
249. P (p. 1072) omits the word.
250. R (7b12): विधानं
251. P (p. 1072) : निषिध्यते
252. R (7b13): ०तात्पर्यानवबोधने
253. Q (23b5): श्राद्धं
254. R (7b13): प्रसज्यते
255. R (8a1) adds प्रसक्ते before निषिद्धे०
256. R (8a2): एतस्य
257. P (p. 1073): सार्थक्यमिति
258. Q (23b6) omits the word.
259. Q (23b6): विशिष्टार्थ०
260. R (8a4) omits दध्ना जुहोति०
261. R (8a6): बोधितेन
262. P (p. 1073): ०मित्येवंरूपंविशष्टै०
263. R (8a9): ०साधनत्वमित्यर्थ०
264. R (8a9) omits the word.
265. Q (24a4): निषेधत्वं
266. P (p. 1073), R (8a10): तदारभ्याधीनत्वेन
267. P (p. 1073), R (8a10) omit महिम्ना०
268. P (p. 1073): रात्रिभेदपरत्वविधित्वे
R (8a10): रात्रिभेदरूपरद्विधित्वे
269. P (p. 1073): निष्ठित्वे
270. P (p. 1073), R (8a10) omit सम्भवार्थ०
271. P (p. 1073), R (8a11): नेक्षेतोद्यन्त०
Q (24a5): नेक्षितोऽत्यन्त०
272. P (p. 1073): ०विरोधिसङ्कोचं
273. Q (24a5): इत्यादावपि
274. R (8a13): तदर्थकत्वात्
275. P (p. 1073), R (8a13): ०प्रयोजनकत्वात्
276. P (p. 1073), R (8a13): दुर्मिलमित्यत
Q (24a6)at first noted दुर्मिलमत, then र्मिल was scratched outand changed to र्ल्लभ०
Perhaps for simplification.
277. P (p. 1073): एकविषयकतयेति
278. Q (24a6), R (8b1): अनन्यगतिकतयेति० Neither of the two manuscripts of नञ्वाद records this reading. So the text has nnot been changed according to the commentary. Still it maybe the reading in some manuscripts of नञ्वाद०
279. Q (24a6): अत्र
280. Q (24a6): ०भावात्
281. P (p. 1073): आदिभ्या for नेष्टसाधनमित्यादिकमित्यादिना
Q (24b2): नेष्टसाधनमित्यादिकमित्यादिना
R (8b3): ०नेष्टसाधनमित्यादिनान

282. Q (24b2): ०नुबन्धित्वकृतिसाध्यत्व
R (8b4): ०नुबन्धिकृतिसाध्यमित्यस्य
283. R (8b4): संग्रह:
284. P (p. 1073) omits the whole sentence. "A" text collects the meaning of two आदिs by आदिभ्यां mentioned in note no 281.
285. P (p. 1073) reads the word before
286. P (p. 1073): ०नान्वयात्
287. P (p. 1073) omits च०
288. P (p. 1073): विभक्त्यर्थस्यान्वये
Q (24b3) omits रन्वये०
R (8b6): विभक्त्यर्थस्यान्वसाधनत्वादेरन्वये च
289. P (p. 1073) omits अभावे०
290. Q (24b5): ०नान्वय:
291. R (8b11): मृत for मूढ
292. R (8b12): मृत for मूढ
293. Q (24b6), R (8b12): (?)सृत्य for मृद्य
294. Q (24b6) , R (8b12) omit भावा०
295. R (8b12): ०द्विभक्तर्थे प्रति०
296. R (8b13): धात्वर्थेर्थान्वितत्वे
297. Q (25 a1): विभक्त्यर्थस्यान्वये
298. P (p. 1075): नियमतस्त्विति
299. Q (25a1): षोडशी for षोडशि
300. R (9a1): ०फलवत्त्वात्
301. R (9a1): ०साधनबोधने
302. R (9a2) omits फलम०
303. P (p. 1075), R (9a2): ०लक्षणे चाफलत्वं
304. R (9a2) omits the word.
305. R (9a3): ०भावेनेष्टसिद्धौ
306. P (p. 1076): कष्टसाध्य
307. P (p. 1076) omits न०
308. Q (25a4), R (9a5): स्वत:
309. P (p. 1076): विधावननु.
310. Q (25a4): मुख्य
311. P (p. 1076): अभावाधिकरणाधिकरणयोराधाराधेयभाव:
312. P (p. 1076) reads न before प्रकारतया०
313. R (9a7) omits न०
314. Q (25a5): ०त्वात्इत्यत
315. P (p. 1081): ०पातजन्यतदन्वय०
Q (25a5): ०पाताज्जन्यतदन्वय०
316. P (p. 1081): न कल्प्यमिति
317. P (p. 1081): एतच्च
R (9a9) एतत्तत्त्वम्
318. Q (25a6): शब्दालोकसारमञ्जर्यां
319. P (p. 1081): अभिहितम् for प्रपञ्चितम्
320. P (p. 1081) omits च०
321. Q (25a7): वा (?) एवतुचादि

R (9a11) omits एववातु०

322. R (9b1): इत्यादौ

323. Q (25b2): ०करण्यान्वयानु०

324. P (p. 1082), R (9b1) omits the word.

325. P (p 1082): मण्किारोक्तं. Vide *Tattvacintāmaṇi,* vol. VI, Part 2, p. 787: अघटः पट इत्यादौ च प्रसज्यप्रतिषेधार्थे नञि सामानाधिकरण्याद् अभाववल्लक्षणा · · ·।

326. R (9b1): नञ्तत्पुरुष०

327. R (9b2): तेन च

328. P (p. 1082): संसर्गाभावरूपवत्त्वं

R (9b2): संसर्गाभाववापवत्त्वं

329. P (p. 1082): बहुव्रीहिं for बहुव्रीहिसमासं

330. P (p. 1082): संसर्गाभावबोधनात् for संसर्गाभावस्य बोधसम्भवात्

331. P (p. 1082): चित्रगुरित्यादौ उत्तरपद

332. P (p. 1082): प्रकृते च घट०

333. Q (25b4): चित्रगवाभेदा०

R (9b5) omits बोध०

334. Q (25b4) R (9b5): गोशब्दार्थस्य

335. Q (25b4): भाषत

336. P (p. 1082): साक्षात् सम्बन्ध

337. P (p. 1082): तु

R (9b6) omits the word.

338. Q (25b5) omits the word.

R (9b7): न नञि

339. R (9b8): नञ्तत्पुरुष०

340. P (p. 1082): पश्यति for पदंपश्येति

341. P (p. 1082): प्रथमान्तश्चेत् for प्रथमान्तत्वे तु

342. P (p. 1082): नञ् for नञि

343. R (9b10): ०साधुत्वाच्च

344. Q (25b7): ०विभक्तोपस्थि०

345. P (p. 1082): निपातातिरिक्तत्व

346. P (p. 1083), R (9b12): षष्ठ्याद्यर्थो.

347. Q (25b7): निरूपितत्वेन चाभावस्यानधिकरणत्वेनान्वयः

348. P (p. 1083) adds तथा सति after the word.

349. R (9b13): ०नाघटा

350. P (p. 1083) omits तथा सति०

351. P (p. 1083), R (9b13): घटीयाभावेऽपि

352. P (p. 1083), R (9b14): ०त्वादेः सम्बन्धस्य

353. P (p. 1083), R (9b14) omit च०

Q (26a1): ०प्रतियोगित्वाभावात्

R (9b14): ०प्रतियोगित्वावच्छेदकभावाभावात्

354. P (p. 1083): प्रकृत्यर्थान्वयो०

355. P (p. 1083): घटानुयोगिकत्वाभावः

356. P (p. 1083): प्रथमार्थत्वे

357. Q (26a3): नञर्थानुपपत्तिश्च

358. Q (26a3): अनुयोगित्वइवेति for अनुयागित्वे वेति

R (10a3): अनुयोगिके चेति

359. P (p. 1083): बोध्य
360. P (p. 1084) omits the word.
361. P (p. 1084): षष्ठ्याद्यर्थस्यानुयोगित्वस्य
362. R (10a4) omits the entire sentence: पटाभावो न घट · · · नान्वये.
363. R (10a4): ०विभक्तिकत्वं
364. P (p. 1084): षष्ठीविनिमयविभक्ति०
365. P (p. 1084), R (10a5) omit अनुयोगित्वस्य०
366. P (p. 1084), R (10a5) omit the word.
367. P (p. 1084): घटाभावस्यानुयोगिकत्ववान्
368. Q (26a5): नञन्तरस्य
369. Q)26 5), R (10a6): सुपोऽनुसन्धानं
370. Q (26a5): लक्षणा च
371. Q (26a6): ०नञो चाभाव०
R (10a6): ०नञो वाभाव०
372. Q (26a6): नञा
373. P (p. 1085): यत्तु विशेषणविशिष्टपदयो.
374. P (p. 1084), R (10a6): ०बोधे
375. Q (26a6): ०मकत्वमुक्तम्
376. R (10a8) omits the word.
377. P (p. 1085): अव्यय for व्यत्यय
378. P (p. 1085): कर्मत्वाद्य० · · · · ०र्थस्य
R (10a8): ०र्थस्य
379. P (p. 1085), R (10a9): ०न्तार्थेन
380. P (p. 1085): नञो for नञा
381. P (p. 1085) reads here along sentence which is read a little later in "Q" manuscript: यथा ब्राह्मणस्य धनम् न मूर्खस्यइत्यादौ नञर्थे भेदे मूर्खानुयोगित्वस्य बोधे नञर्थस्याधिकरणत्वेनान्वये मूर्खभिन्नस्य ब्राह्मणस्येत्यर्थो लभ्यते तथा
382. R (10a10): for
383. Q (26a7) reads the sentence which is read in "P"alittle former. Vide note no. 381. Emendedaccording to "P" text. The reading in "Q" runs thus: यथा ब्राह्मणस्य धनंमूर्खस्येत्यादौ नञर्थमूर्खानुयोगित्वस्य बोधे नञर्थस्याधिकरणत्वेनान्वये मूर्खभिन्नस्य ब्राह्मणस्येत्यर्थो लभ्यतइति।
R (10a10) omits the sentence herebut reads italongafter. See note no. 398.
384. Q (26b1) omits विरुद्धार्थकत्वमेव०
385. Q (26b1): ०षष्ठ्यर्थस्य
P (p. 1085): ०षष्ठ्याद्यर्थ
R (10a11): तिङापि
386. R (10a11): ०भावेन
387. P (p. 1086) : साक्षादन्वयेन
R (10a11) : साक्षादन्वये
388. P (p. 1086): कृतिसम्बन्धयोर्भेदबोधापत्तिः for पाकानुकूल · · · बोधापत्तिः
Q (26b2): बाधापत्तिः for बोधापत्तिः
R (10b11): पाकानुकूलभेदस्य राजसम्बन्धस्य च बोधापत्तिः for पाकानुकूल बोधापत्ति
389. R (10a12): एचंच
390. Q (26b2): नञर्थ
391. P (p. 1086): अधिकरणत्वेन for अधिकरणत्वे
392. R (10a13): संसर्गा for प्रसङ्गा

393. P (p. 1086), R (10a13): अभेदान्वये
394. P (p. 1086), R (10a13) omit च॰
395. P (p. 1086): अप्रयोजकत्वंइति व्याख्यान्तरअत्यन्तसमीचीनं। The printed text of the commentarybreaks here.
396. Q (26b4) omits च॰
397. Q (26b4):
398. R (10b2) reads a long sentence here which isalready read in "Q" and "R" at different places. Vide note nos. 381and 383. The text reading here is as follows: यथा ब्राह्मणस्य धननं मूर्खस्येत्यादौ नञर्थे मूर्खानुयोगित्वस्य बोधेन नञर्थस्याधिकरणत्वेनान्वये मूर्खभिन्नस्य ब्राह्मणस्येत्यर्थो लभ्यतेइति॰
399. R (10b4) omits संसर्गाभाव · · · योग्युपस्थितिः॰
400. Q (26b5) omits च॰
401. R (10b4): न पचतीत्यादौ
402. Q (26b6) omits the word.
403. R (10b5): च
404. Q (26b6) omits न च॰
405. Q (26b6): सप्तम्यनु॰
R (10b6): ॰योगिपद
406. R (10b7): ॰प्रसङ्गे
407. R (10b7): ॰बोधकरणाय
408. R (10b7): ॰सरणमिति वाच्यं
409. R (10b7): तावतापि
410. Q (26b7) omits न॰
411. R (10b8): घटप्रतियोगिकः संसर्गाभावइति बोधस्य
412. Q (26b7): राजत्वस्य
413. Q (26b7) नञ्वादटिप्पनी समाप्ता for the verse.

List of authorities and quotations in the Text and Commentary

Authorities mentioned in the *Nañvāda*

Quotations in the *Nañvāda*

Authorities and texts mentioned in the *Nañvādaṭippanī*

	Page Nos.
प्राचीनाः	7
प्राभाकराः	16
भवता	19
भवानन्दसिद्धान्तवागीश	19
मणिकार	13, 17
मीमांसक	15
वैदिकसम्मतः पाठः	13
वैयाकरण	10
स्मार्त	14

Quotations in the *Nañvādaṭippanī*

अग्निहोत्रं जुहोति (तैत्तिरीयसंहिता 1-5-9-1)	15
दध्ना जुहोति (मैत्रायणीसंहिता 4-7-7)	15
दीक्षितो न ददाति	15
न कलञ्जं	16
नानुपमृद्य प्रादुर्भावात् (न्यायसूत्रम् 4-1-14)	16
नानुयाजेषु करोति	13
नामूढस्येतरोत्पत्तेः (न्यायसूत्रम् 4-1-6)	16
परवल्लिङ्गं द्वन्द्वतत्पुरुषयोः (पा.सू. 2-4-26)	17
रात्रौ श्राद्धं न	14
स्वर्गकामो यजेत (ताण्ड्यमहाब्राह्मण 16-15-5)	16

Bibliography

Bhāratīya Darśan Kośa (Prācīna-Nyāya, Navya-Nyāya and Vaiśeṣika-Darśana). Vol I. Compiled by Srimohan Bhattacharya and Dinesh Chandra Bhattacharya. Sanskrit College, Kolkata, 1978.

Encyclopedia of Indian Philosophies, vol I. Ed. Karl H. Potter. MLBD, Delhi, reprint, 1974.

Encyclopedia of Indian Philosophies, vol VI. (Indian Philosophical analysis Nyāya-Vaiśeṣika from Gaṅgeśa to Raghunātha Śiromaṇi). Ed. Karl H. Potter and Sibajiban Bhattacharya. MLBD, Delhi, 1993. The volume contains a summary of *Nañvāda* of Raghunātha. The note given there is the following: This summary was initially prepared by Janakivallabha Bhattacharya, with revisions by Potter. The work is edited and translated by Bimal Krishna Matilal in his (RB 5341): *The Navya Nyaya Doctrine of Negation.*

Gautamīya Nyāyadarśana. With the *Bhāṣya* of Vātsyāyana. Ed. Pt. Anantalal Thakur. Indian Council for Philosophical Research, New Delhi, 1997.

Negative Words: Their ways in language. Dr. Pradip Kumar Mazumdar. Sanskrit Pustak Bhandar, Kolkata, 1994.

Nyāyamañjarī (Fifth Āhika), Jayanta Bhaṭṭa. Ed. Prabal Kumar Sen. With Bengali translation and notes. Sanskrit Book Depot, Kolkata, 2008.

Nyāyasiddhāntāmuktāvalī, Viśvanātha Bhaṭṭācārya. With *Bhāṣāparicchedа.* Along with *Vilāsinī* Sanskrit and Hindi commentaries by Jwala Prasad Gaud. Ed Pt. Dhundhiraj Shastry. Chaukhamba Sanskrit Pratisthan, Delhi, 1991.

Nyāyasūtra, Gautama. Vide *Gautamīya Nyāyadarśana.*

Tarkasaṃgraha, Annambhaṭṭa Ed. Gopinath Bhattacharya. Progressive Publishers, Calcutta, 1994

Tattvacintāmaṇi, Gaṅgeśa. Vol. IV, Part 2. Ed. MM Kamakhyanatha Tarkavagisa. Reprint. Oriental Book Centre, Delhi, 1990.